A Visual Basic 6 Programmer's Toolkit

Hank Marquis and Eric A. Smith

Apress™

A Visual Basic 6 Programmer's Toolkit
Hank Marquis and Eric A. Smith

Library of Congress Control Number: 00-133574

ISBN: 1-893115-06-2

Printed and bound in the United States of America
10 9 8 7 6 5 4 3 2 1

Copy Editor: TSI Graphics
Production: TSI Graphics
Indexer: Carla Johnson
Cover Design: Derek Yee Design

Distributed to the book trade worldwide by Springer-Verlag New York, Inc.
175 Fifth Avenue, New York, NY 10010 USA
In the United States, phone 1-800-SPRINGER; orders@springer-ny.com
www.springer-ny.com

For information on translations, please contact Apress directly:
901 Grayson Street, Berkeley, CA 94710-2617
Phone: (510) 549-5930, Fax: (510) 549-5939
www.apress.com, info@apress.com

HANK MARQUIS
This book is dedicated to my wife Nur
and my children Adriana and Rolfe.

ERIC SMITH
To my wife, Jodi

Brief Contents

Detailed Contents

Acknowledgments

MANY PEOPLE HAVE CONTRIBUTED TO THIS BOOK. We would like to thank the people at Apress and all the behind-the-scenes support people for making this project possible.

About the Authors

HANK MARQUIS

HANK MARQUIS is Chief Technical Officer and founder of Celexis, Inc. Hank is well known to the software development community, having written numerous features, articles and opinions in many industry publications. Hank has spoken at several trade shows, including the Visual Basic Insiders Technical Summit, and was the Component Columnist for Microsoft BackOffice/CTO magazine. He is a past chairman of the Component Vendor Consortium (CVC) Quality Committee and a founder of the CVC. Hank is a co-author of the *Visual Basic 6.0 Bible*.

ERIC SMITH

ERIC SMITH is an MCSD and MCSE and has written, edited contributed to ten books covering Visual Basic programming and web technologies. He is an independent consultant and trainer based in the Washington, DC area, and specializes in developing Active Server Pages, SQL Server and Visual Basic. He also maintains several developer web sites, including VB Techniques (http://www.vbtechniques.com) and ASP Techniques (http://www.asptechniques.com). These web sites provide service after the sale, as well as original content and reviews, for his readers. In his spare time, he serves as a volunteer Emergency Medical Technician with the Fairfax County Fire & Rescue Department. Contact him at eric@northcomp.com.

Note: Please visit http://vbtechniques.com
for revised code and information.

Chapter 1

Arrays and Array Manipulation

Virtually every type of application, program, and component uses arrays for data storage—regardless of the programming language used. While Visual Basic lets you easily create arrays, it contains no intrinsic methods for most common tasks for working with arrays. You need to write your own subroutines (or take advantage of those written by someone else) for this. For example, commonly, you'll want to rearrange, or sort, the order of the elements in an array by arranging the elements in ascending order (A-Z, for example) and sometimes in descending order (Z-A).

This chapter provides the code for a class module that you can use for any sort of array handling. This generic class module has methods for sorting, finding, inserting, and removing elements, as well as array arithmetic.

Creating and Using Arrays in Visual Basic

An *array* is composed of a related set of data components, or *elements,* which, with the exception of arrays of variants, must all be of the same data type. Arrays often are the best way for developers to manage information. For example, it's much faster to read one large chunk of data into an array and then process or display that data, than it is to read the data elements one at a time, as they're needed for processing.

You create an array in Visual Basic by using the Dim or ReDim keyword. We recommend always using ReDim, because ReDim creates a *dynamic* array—an array that can be resized during run time to contain a different number of elements. An array created using Dim is called a *static* array. A static array cannot be resized at run time.

The position of an element in an array is referred to as its *index.* Visual Basic provides the Option Base statement for starting your array indexes at position 0 or position 1, but it is better to use the To keyword as in:

```
ReDim Sales(1990 To 2000) As Currency
```

> *NOTE*
> *Visual Basic also accepts negative values for the lower and upper bounds. For example:*

```
Dim anArray( -5 to 5 )
```

> **TIP**
>
> *Another advantage to using ReDim rather than Dim is that you can include the Preserve keyword to keep the existing data in the array when resizing, as shown here:*
>
> ```
> ReDim anArray(1 To 10)
> ReDim Preserve anArray(1 To 11) 'keep first 10 items
> ```

To write a subroutine that receives an array parameter, you declare the parameter with an empty set of parentheses:

```
Sub FooLong (anArray() As Long)
    body of subroutine goes here
End Sub
```

The argument anArray() in the first line above is defined to be an array of type long integer. (The type of the array is simply the type of its data elements.) You cannot pass an array of any other type to the FooLong subroutine; attempting to do so causes a compiler error. One way around this limitation is to create several subroutines, with similar names, that do the same job but operate on arrays of different types. For example:

```
Sub FooLong (anArray() As Long)
    body of subroutine goes here
End Sub

Sub FooString (anArray() As String)
    same code contained in body of FooLong goes here
End Sub

Sub FooCurrency (anArray() As Currency)
    same code contained in bodies of FooLong and FooString
End Sub
```

As you can see, this becomes quite cumbersome! Luckily, Visual Basic provides a better way: the Variant data type. Because the Variant type was invented to enable a variable or argument to accept data of any other type, you can write a single subroutine that accepts an array of any type by using an array of variants. For example:

```
Sub Foo (anArray As Variant)
    body of subroutine goes here
End Sub
```

The parentheses are omitted when declaring an argument of type Variant that you want to use for generic array handling. (After all, the Variant argument can accept data of *any* type, not only array types.) Using anArray() As Variant makes the parameter an array of variants and not a generic array.

You can then call the Foo subroutine in the following manner:

```
ReDim AnArray(1 to 10) As Long
Foo AnArray()
ReDim AnArray(1 to 10) As String
Foo AnArray()
```

In this kind of generic code, you often need to find the type of the entries. Luckily for us, Visual Basic has a function for this: the VarType function. The code in Listing 1-1 shows how to determine the type of array that is contained in the Variant argument. (Of course, you would add code under each Case statement that takes appropriate action for the data type in question.)

```
Public Sub Foo( AnArray As Variant )
Dim vbType As Long
If VarType(AnArray) < vbArray Then Exit Sub
vbType = VarType(LBound(AnArray))
Select Case vbType
    Case vbString
    'code for string elements
    Case vbDate
    'code for Date elements
    Case vbByte
Case vbCurrency
Case vbDouble
Case vbInteger
    Case vbCurrency
Case vbLong
Case vbSingle
    End Select
End Sub
```

Listing 1-1: Using a single subroutine that accepts an array of any data type

Notice we have to be careful: the Variant argument will accept any type of data—whether an array or not. Thus, we must check that the data being passed is actually an array. Thankfully, Visual Basic also has a means to solve this issue as well. We use that method in Listing 1-1. VarType returns a value greater than vbArray if the argument passed to VarType is an array. In this case, the VarType function returns the value of the constant vbArray plus the value of the constant corresponding to the array's type. For example, VarType returns vbArray + vbLong if the argument to VarType is an array of long integers.

The third line of code in Listing 1-1 (shown below) uses this technique to be sure that the argument is an array:

```
If VarType(TheData) < vbArray Then Exit Sub
```

All the example routines presented in this chapter use these techniques. They all specify their parameters as Variants, and they then *check* to make sure that the argument actually contains an array. Where needed, individual subroutines also check the type of data contained in the array to process based on the data type.

> *NOTE*
> *There is one downside to using generic code that takes a variant for array manipulation as we give here: it will run a little slower than code that works with a more basic type. If maximum speed is necessary, then use separate code for each type of array. The gain in maintainability by using code similar to that presented here, however, usually outweighs the (often modest) speed improvements obtained with multiple routines.*

The subroutines presented in this chapter are all based on one-dimensional arrays; that is, arrays that have a single index. Arrays with more than one dimension can be created. In fact, Visual Basic allows up to 60 dimensions. As the human brain normally thinks three dimensionally (height, width, and depth), 60 dimensions might be a bit much to grasp. However, it's not that hard if you think of arrays in each of the cells. For instance, a four-dimensional array is like a cube composed of one-dimensional arrays. A five-dimensional array is a cube composed of two-dimensional arrays, and a six-dimensional array is a cube composed of cubes. After that, the pattern just repeats. We've never needed to use more than three dimensions, but your mileage may vary.

A final note about the code in this chapter. We have left out error handling completely to make the code more readable and, we hope, easier to understand. Instead of generating a run-time error (also called raising an error) if invalid data is passed to these subroutines, these routines simply exit without doing whatever they were intended to accomplish.

The code on disk (versus the code samples in the book) does have complete error handling and raises errors where appropriate.

> *NOTE*
> *You can find the complete source code on the cd under chapter1 in the arrays.cls module. Arrays.cls contains all the code shown in this chapter, as well as the additional code that is referenced in this chapter, but not shown.*

Sorting Arrays

Very often presenting data to people requires sorting. Consider a list of names: If the names on the list are not in alphabetical order, people will have difficulty finding the exact name they are looking for. Numeric data, such as birth dates or social security numbers, are also easier for people to manipulate when they are presented in a sorted fashion. Sorting an array is the most fundamental requirement for most programmers. Sorting requires rearranging the array's elements into some recognizable and definable order—either ascending or descending. Usually, you use ASCII order to sort text. This means lowercase letters follow uppercase letters. You can find an ASCII table in VB's online Help.

There are many methods developed for sorting arrays. Some methods sort from top to bottom, inserting and moving strings or data as needed. Other methods sort an element at a time, shuffling the strings or data repeatedly until they are sorted. Some sorts require lots of memory for a process called *recursion*, in which the sort routine calls itself repeatedly until each element is sorted. Other sorts use other methods of sorting that require less memory, but take longer. There is no perfect method that works best for all situations, and thus there are many styles of sorts. Table 1-1 is a quick overview of the most popular methods of sorting, which are called "sorting algorithms," and how they work.

Table 1-1: Popular Sorting Algorithms

BUBBLE SORT	The Bubble Sort makes a series of passes through the array and exchanges adjacent items if they are in proper sort order. The sort procedure ends when a full pass is made and no exchanges are necessary. It is usually the slowest sort.
SELECTION SORT	A Selection Sort searches an array for the smallest item, and then swaps it with the currently marked lower bound. The lower bound is moved progressively "up" the array until the final element is in proper sort order. The Insertion Sort picks the item right after the current lower bound and finds the correct position for it in the preceding part of the list, moving entries above the insertion up by one position.
SHELL SORT	The Shell Sort is similar to the Insertion Sort, but it tries to sort elements a fixed distance apart, reducing the distance over several iterations. This minimizes the number of elements that need to be moved when an item is inserted, making it faster than a Selection Sort in most implementations.
QUICK SORT	The Quick Sort divides the array into two halves around a center pivot element, and then moves the elements above the pivot to the first half and moves elements that are larger to the second half. The process is applied recursively to each half until the elements are in order.
MERGE SORT	The Merge Sort divides an array into sorted subsections by taking a pair of elements and sorting them. Merge Sort then groups every pair of pairs and merges them into the correct order. The process is repeated until all the elements are in proper sort order.
HEAP SORT	The Heap Sort uses a data structure, called a tree, and divides the array into successive sections. The Heap Sort algorithm inserts each element into the tree and removes them successively, reorganizing the tree as elements are positioned at the end of the list.

Personally, we find the Quick Sort algorithm to be the easiest sort algorithm to implement just about anywhere that a fast and efficient sorting algorithm is required. It's easily customized for different data types (integer, long, double, variant, etc.), as well as being able to sort a Grid or a user-defined type (UDT) with a little magic!

> *NOTE*
> *Although the Quick Sort sort is usually the best general-purpose sort for most large arrays, special care must be taken if the data is likely to be mostly presorted before QuickSort is applied.*

To sort data regardless of type, you can create an implementation that declares parameters of type Variant. To maximize performance, you should declare the parameters with their proper types (i.e., long, integer, string, etc.)

You have just one "gotcha" to keep in mind: the Visual Basic Option Base directive. Option Base controls whether the indexing of array elements begins at 0 or 1. The default is 0. This means that if you create an array such as:

```
Dim AnArray(10)
```

then, by default, your array will have 11 elements numbered 0 through 10. Because the human brain tends to find this scheme unnatural, unexpected errors can creep into your sorting routines and other array-handling code. Therefore, if you are writing general purpose array handling code, it is especially important to use the built-in array bounds functions LBound and UBound to determine the lower and upper bounds of an array.

The code in Listing 1-2 shows a simple Quick Sort implementation. Listing 1-2 is a recursive Quick Sort and has a minimum of code, which is commented to explain the basic concept of the Quick Sort.

```
Private Sub QuickSort(anArray As Variant, _
                      StartEl As Long, StopEl As Long)
    Dim workStart As Long, workStop As Long
    Dim X As Long, Y As Long, I As Long
    workStart = StartEl
    workStop = StopEl
    ' Get the halfway point and assign it to X
    X = anArray((StartEl + StopEl) / 2)
    ' X now holds value of the array item that is
    ' halfway between StartEl and StopEl. The next stop
    ' is to compare the rank of workStart to workStop
    ' to determine when workStart (the lbound value)
    ' equals or exceeds workStop (the ubound value).
    While (workStart <= workStop)
        'while workStart remains less than workStop,
        'compare the value of the array() element
        'at this position against X (set above).
        'In addition, also make sure that workStart
```

```
                 'remains less than the StopEl bound value.
             While (anArray(workStart) < X And _
                     workStart < StopEl)
                 workStart = workStart + 1
             Wend
             ' repeat the same for the array value at
             ' position workStop, also making sure that
             ' workStop remains greater than the StartEl
             ' bound value.
             While (X < anArray(workStop) And _
                     workStop > StartEl)
                 workStop = workStop - 1
             Wend
             Determine the elements to swap based on the
             ' final workStart & workStop relative positions.
             If (workStart <= workStop) Then
                 'a. assign tmp variable Y the value at
                 '   anArray(workStart)
                 'b. swap anArray(workStop) for
                 '   anArray(workStart)
                 'c. reassign the value of tmp to the
                 '   type anArray(workStop)
                 Y = anArray(workStart)
                 anArray(workStart) = anArray(workStop)
                 anArray(workStop) = Y
                 'change the start & stop items
                 workStart = workStart + 1
                 workStop = workStop - 1
             End If
         Wend
         ' if the original StartEl is still less than workStop,
         ' then call the sub again with StartEl & workStop as
         ' the start & stop points
         If (StartEl < workStop) Then _
             QuickSort anArray, StartEl, workStop
         'or if the original StartEl is still less than
         'workStop, then call the sub again with workStart and
         'StopEl as the start & stop points
         If (workStart < StopEl) Then _
             QuickSort anArray, workStart, StopEl
 End Sub
```

Listing 1-2: A recursive Quick Sort

You might notice that at the end of the QuickSort subroutine, QuickSort calls itself again. When a routine calls itself it is referred to as a *recursive* subroutine. Recursive subroutines are found in many advanced programs. In this case, using recursion increases the memory requirements of the application and slows the sorting process itself. Every time a procedure calls another procedure, the current values of all the variables in the procedure must be stored, and then they must be restored when the procedure exits. This is called "pushing" and "popping." The place where the information is stored is a special section of memory allocated to the program called the "program stack." The stack is a temporary workspace where the program stores variables while other procedures are working. Recursive routines have some extra overhead because every time a recursive subroutine is called, the working variables in the subroutine (those not declared Static) are pushed onto the stack. When the code completes, the data on the stack is popped back and execution resumes.

The QuickSort subroutine in Listing 1-2 has two limitations: it sorts in ascending order only, and it requires that you pass start and stop array indexes, which we don't like because you are required to pass starting and stopping indices to the array. In other words, you have to tell the routine where to start and stop sorting.

> NOTE
> *This implementation of Quick Sort performs very poorly if you were passed an array that is already sorted to it. More complex versions of Quick Sort use a more random "pivot" to get around this limitation.*

To add the capability of sorting in descending order and to include default start and stop indexes, we created another subroutine named Sort. This subroutine is simply a wrapper around the QuickSort subroutine, which means that the main part of the code remains the same, but an enumerated type parameter is added to enable us to specify the kind of sort.

The Sort subroutine uses a Variant array, as before, enabling you to sort any type of Visual Basic data. (Of course, for maximum performance, you can always change the declaration and make a copy of this subroutine for each data type. For example, SortL for long integer sort; SortSTR for string sort and so on.)

```
Public Enum DirectionEnum
    cAscending = 1
    cDescending = -1
End Enum
```

Listing 1-3: An enumeration used by the Sort procedure to control the direction of sorting

```
Public Sub Sort(anArray As Variant, _
        Optional StartEl As Long, _
        Optional StopEl As Long, _
        Optional Direction As DirectionEnum = cAscending)
    Dim x As Variant, Y As Variant, i As Long
    If VarType(anArray) < vbArray Then Exit Sub
```

```
' assign to the working variables the values passed to
' the sub as StartEl & StopEl
' if none passed then assign dimensions of array
If StartEl = 0 And StopEl = 0 Then
    StartEl = LBound(anArray)
    StopEl = UBound(anArray)
Else
    ' fix up
    If StopEl > UBound(anArray) Then _
        StopEl = UBound(anArray)
    If StartEl < LBound(anArray) Then _
        StartEl = LBound(anArray)
End If
'let our internal quicksort array to the work
QuickSort anArray, StartEl, StopEl
' if descend then inverse elements
If Direction = cDescending Then
    Y = UBound(anArray)
    For i = LBound(anArray) To Y \ 2
        x = anArray(i)
        anArray(i) = anArray(Y)
        anArray(Y) = x
        Y = Y - 1
    Next
End If
End Sub
```

Listing 1-4: A nonrecursive procedure that calls the recursive Quick Sort, and includes code to reverse the order of the sort

The Sort procedure in Listing 1-4 has an optional parameter, named Direction, that controls the direction of the sort—that is, ascending or descending order. The default order is ascending (because Direction has a default value of cAscending). However, you can pass cDescending to sort the array in descending order. The code that reverses the order of the array is a simple pivot implementation in which array elements in the first half of the array are swapped with those in the second half; that is the first with the last, the second with the second from the end, and so on. This results in an array sorted in the opposite direction.

Now, using the Visual Basic array class supplied on the CD will be much easier, because you do not have to pass start and stop indexes.

```
Dim myArray As New cArray
myArray.Sort anArray
myArray.Sort anArray, , , DirectionEnum.cDescending
```

Working with Sorted Arrays

After your array is sorted, you will probably want to keep it that way. This sounds obvious, but how do you insert an element into a sorted array and not need to sort it again? You can't just add the new element to the end of the array! Also, there are times when array elements must be deleted.

After sorting, locating an element with a specific value is probably one of the most common array activities.

Finding an Element with a Specific Value in a Sorted Array

To find an element in an array, you could simply use a For/Next loop and walk through every array element until you find the one you want. This is easy and works for either a sorted or an unsorted array, but it is slow. We show you how to leverage some of your new sorting skills to quickly find an element in an array that you know has already been sorted.

The binary search algorithm, which follows the "divide and conquer" approach, is implemented in the FindItem function below. This routine assumes that the array passed to it is sorted. FindItem first determines the sort order (ascending or descending) by comparing the values of the first and last elements of the array. If the first element is less than the last element, it is assumed that the array is sorted in ascending order; if the first element is greater than the last element, it is assumed that the array is sorted in descending order.

The binary search algorithm operates by starting in the middle of the array, and then working with each half. We simply ask whether the value we are trying to find is contained (or should be contained) in the first half or the second half. In essence, this enables the size of the array to be halved at each step, which makes the routine run very quickly. For example, if we had a 1,000,000-item array, the stages would go:

```
1,000,000
500,000
250,000
125,000
62,500
33,250
```

and so on.

The code in Listing 1-5 searches a sorted array for an element of a given value and returns the array index of that element. It uses a binary search to optimize the time it takes to locate an element in the array.

```
Public Function FindItem(anArray As Variant, Item As Variant) As Long
    Dim i As Long, p As Long, lb As Long, ub As Long
    If VarType(anArray) < vbArray Then Exit Function
    lb = LBound(anArray)
    ub = UBound(anArray)
    p = ub
    ' assume not in the list
```

```
    FindItem = vbObjectError + 511
    If anArray(lb) < anArray(ub) Then
        While Item < anArray(p)
            p = p \ 2 'move pointer back 1/2 of list
            If p = < lb Then Exit Function
        Wend
    Else
        While Item > anArray(p)
            p = p \ 2 'move pointer ahead 1/2 of list
            If p = 0 Then Exit Function
        Wend
    End If
    For i = p To ub
        If anArray(i) = Item Then
            FindItem = i
            Exit Function
        End If
    Next
End Function
```

Listing 1-5: Searching a sorted array for an element of a given value

NEXT STEPS

FindItem is also very useful to see if an item is actually in the array. If the item is not in the array, FindItem returns a value of vbObjectError + 511, which you can easily test for. Another possibility is to create a function that encapsulates FindItem and that returns True if the item is found, or False if the item is not found.

To focus the search within a given part of the array, consider adding optional parameters to FindItem that accept the indices where to start and where to stop.

After you can quickly sort an array and quickly locate the position of any element within the array, you are now ready to start inserting and deleting array elements.

Inserting an Element into a Sorted Array

When working with arrays, you often need to insert an element into an array while keeping it sorted. The AddItem procedure in Listing 1-6 first adds a new empty element to the end of the array. Then AddItem works through the array until it locates the position where the new item should be inserted. Finally, AddItem moves the elements below the insertion point down and stores the new value in the proper location.

```
Public Sub AddItem(anArray As Variant, Item As Variant)
    Dim i As Long, j As Long, p As Long
    Dim StartEl As Long, StopEl As Long
    If VarType(anArray) < vbArray Then Exit Sub
    ' re-size array
```

```
        ReDim Preserve anArray(LBound(anArray) To _
                              UBound(anArray) + 1)
    ' get start/stop elements
    StartEl = LBound(anArray)
    StopEl = UBound(anArray)
    ' fixup for inverse sorting
    If StartEl > StopEl Then
        StartEl = UBound(anArray)
        StopEl = LBound(anArray)
    End If
    ' verify
    If StartEl < LBound(anArray) Or _
        StopEl > UBound(anArray) Then Exit Sub
    ' find where to insert
    If anArray(StartEl) < anArray(StopEl - 1) Then
        For j = StartEl To StopEl
            If Item < anArray(j) Then Exit For
        Next
    Else
        For j = StartEl To StopEl
            If Item > anArray(j) Then Exit For
        Next
    End If
    ' fix up for end or start of array
    If j > StopEl Then j = StopEl
    ' now move elements
    For i = StopEl To j + 1 Step -1
        anArray(i) = anArray(i - 1)
    Next
    ' insert item
    anArray(j) = Item
End Sub
```

Listing 1-6: Inserts an element into an array, while maintaining the array's sort order

NEXT STEPS

AddItem uses a "brute force" approach to locating the insertion point for the new item. It simply works from one end of the array to the other until it locates the proper position. To determine more quickly the location of the item to insert, consider adding code similar to that found in FindItem.

Deleting an Element from a Sorted Array

Deleting an element from a sorted array is easier than inserting an element into a sorted array. Conceptually, all you need to do is locate the element to remove (FindItem is perfect for this). Then you need to move up all the elements from the element to remove to the end of the array. Finally, the array is resized, which removes the final element of the array. Listing 1-7 is an example of code to delete an element from a sorted array.

```
Public Sub RemoveItem(anArray As Variant, Item As Variant)
    Dim p As Long, i As Long
    Dim StartEl As Long, StopEl As Long
    If VarType(anArray) < vbArray Then Exit Sub
    ' get start/stop elements
    StopEl = UBound(anArray)
    ' find element
    p = FindItem(anArray, Item)
    If p > 0 Then
        ' now move elements
        For i = p To StopEl - 1
            anArray(i) = anArray(i + 1)
        Next
        ' re-size array
        ReDim Preserve anArray(LBound(anArray) To _
            UBound(anArray) - 1)
    End If
End Sub
```

Listing 1-7: Removing an array element while preserving the sort order

NEXT STEPS

You might consider passing optional start and stop indexes to RemoveItem, which enables you to remove a contiguous section of an array. Another possibility is to pass a series of array elements as optional parameters to RemoveItem to remove a noncontiguous selection of elements in one call.

Working with Data in an Array

Now that you can sort an array, find a specific element in an array, and insert and delete array elements in a sorted array, you will want to manipulate the array data itself. To this point, we performed operations that affect the entire array. Now, we work with contiguous subsets, or *ranges,* of the elements in an array. For example, we might want to work with the 43rd to 512th entry in an array. Other common tasks include copying a range of data from one array to another and *persisting* part of the array data, which means storing the data, usually to disk, and then reading it back again later on.

For example, imagine your array contains a list of people's ages. You might want to find how many people are between the ages of 30 and 70, and then find the oldest person within that range. Or, you might need to perform array arithmetic (common in scientific, graphical, and mathematical applications), such as adding a fixed value to a series of elements. Within the array of people's ages, for example, you might want to find everyone between the ages of 59 and 62 on a list and then determine what their ages will be in 3 years as part of a retirement calculation.

Finding Maximum and Minimum Values in an Array Range

Finding the maximum or minimum value in a range in a sorted array is easy, but more complex than you might think it would be for a general array. Probably the best way to implement this code, and the way we plan to show you here, is to preset a variable to the smallest possible value for a given type. This is needed because you have to start somewhere, and if you simply choose the first or last, for example, you may or may not have the smallest possible value. Using the technique of presetting a variable to the smallest possible value for a given type, means you need to write less code and are guaranteed of getting the maximum value back from the array range. (The alternative is to use a temporary variable to hold the current candidate.)

Conceptually, this routine (shown in Listing 1-8) starts with the smallest value the data type contains in the array supports, and then it checks each element in the selected range to determine whether it is larger than the stored value. If the value we are examining is larger than the stored value, the current value under examination becomes the new largest value. As each element in the range is tested, the largest value will overwrite any other large values.

```
Public Function MaxValue(anArray As Variant, _
         Optional StartEl As Long, _
         Optional StopEl As Long) As Variant
   Dim vbType As Long, i As Long, bBig As Variant
   If VarType(anArray) < vbArray Then Exit Function
   ' assign to the working variables the values passed to
   ' the sub as StartEl & StopEl
   ' if none passed then assign dimensions of array
   If StartEl = 0 And StopEl = 0 Then
       StartEl = LBound(anArray)
       StopEl = UBound(anArray)
   Else
       ' fix up
       If StopEl > UBound(anArray) Then _
              StopEl = UBound(anArray)
       If StartEl < LBound(anArray) Then _
              StartEl = LBound(anArray)
   End If
   ' figure out data type
   vbType = VarType(anArray(LBound(anArray)))
   Select Case vbType
   Case vbString
       bBig = Chr$(0)
   Case vbByte
       bBig = 0
   Case vbCurrency
       bBig = -922337203685477.5807@
   Case vbDouble
```

```
        bBig = -4.94065645841247E-324
    Case vbInteger
        bBig = -32768
    Case vbLong
        bBig = -2147483647
    Case vbSingle
        bBig = -1.401298E-45
    Case Else
        Exit Function
    End Select
    ' find max
    For i = StartEl To StopEl
        If anArray(i) > bBig Then bBig = anArray(i)
    Next
    ' assign function & exit
    MaxValue = bBig
End Function
```

Listing 1-8: Finding the maximum value of the elements in an array range

NEXT STEPS

You can also create a complementary procedure to return the minimum value. This is done by changing the starting value of the testing code to be the largest possible value that the data type supports and then examining each element to determine whether it's smaller. See the code on the CD for the sample function that implements MinValue for a range of array elements.

Array Arithmetic

The procedures presented so far make it easy to see how to write a subroutine that performs an arithmetical operation on a range of array elements. Conceptually, you just pass a range of array elements and the value to add, subtract, multiply, divide, or whatever numerical process you want to apply to each element in the range, to the subroutine.

As you can probably tell by now, we like to write a routine to be as generic, high performing, and extensible as possible. We created the Process subroutine in Listing 1-9 to carry out some arithmetical process on a range of array elements. In addition to the array range, Process has Value and Action parameters. Action accepts any value defined in ActionEnum, a public enumeration to which you can add additional constants. Inside the Process procedure is a Select Case statement where different tasks are performed based on the Action's value.

```
Public Enum ActionEnum
        cAdd
        cSubtract
        cMultiply
        cDivide
End Enum
```

```
Private Sub Process(anArray As Variant, Value As Variant,_
        Action As ActionEnum, Optional StartEl As Long = 0, _
        Optional StopEl As Long = 0)
    Dim vbType As Long
    Dim i As Long
    If VarType(anArray) < vbArray Then Exit Sub
        ' if both are the same value, then do the whole array
        If StartEl = StopEl Then
            StartEl = LBound(anArray)
            StopEl = UBound(anArray)
        Else
            ' fix up
            If StopEl > UBound(anArray) Then _
                StopEl = UBound(anArray)
            If StartEl < LBound(anArray) Then _
                StartEl = LBound(anArray)
        End If
        For i = StartEl To StopEl
            Select Case Action
            Case ActionEnum.cAdd
                anArray(i) = anArray(i) + Value
            Case ActionEnum.cDivide
                anArray(i) = anArray(i) / Value
            Case ActionEnum.cMultiply
                anArray(i) = anArray(i) * Value
            Case ActionEnum.cSubtract
                anArray(i) = anArray(i) - Value
            End Select
        Next
End Sub
```

Listing 1-9: An extensible procedure for performing arithmetical operations on a range of array elements

The following code calls the Process subroutine to add the same value to every element in an array range.

```
myArray.Process anArray, 100, cAdd
```

NEXT STEPS

You can add new actions to the ones given in the Enum as long as you also add the code to carry out the action to the Process procedure. Some things you might consider adding are:

1. For string arrays: making strings proper-cased by removing mixed case or enforcing uppercase on first letters, capitalizing, removing extra spaces, etc.

2. Making the array elements convert from one data type to another — for example, making the data type from long to double.

A more complex process is required when you want to work with more than one array at the same time (for example, if you have two arrays: one of stock prices and one of the costs of each stock). To work with both at the same time (for example, to apply the first cost to processing to the first stock price, the second cost to the second stock price, and so on) you could either implement a huge For/Next loop or use array arithmetic, which makes more sense and offers more flexibility.

More on Array Arithmetic

Let's modify our previous example to include arguments for two array ranges. This way, you can apply any portion of one array to any portion of another array. The only potential "gotcha" is that the ranges have to be the same size, so we added code to make sure that the ranges passed are the same size before they are processed. Listing 1-10 shows how to implement this technique using subtraction as the arithmetical operation.

```
Public Sub SubtractArray(TargetArray As Variant, _
        SourceArray As Variant, _
        Optional ByVal RangeStartTarget As Long = 0, _
        Optional ByVal RangeStopTarget As Long = 0, _
        Optional ByVal RangeStartSource As Long = 0, _
        Optional ByVal RangeStopSource As Long = 0)
    Dim i As Long, j As Long
    ' if both are the same value, then do the whole array
    If RangeStartTarget = RangeStopTarget Then
        RangeStartTarget = LBound(TargetArray)
        RangeStopTarget = UBound(TargetArray)
    End If
    ' if both are the same value, then do the whole array
    If RangeStartSource = RangeStopSource Then
        RangeStartSource = LBound(SourceArray)
        RangeStopSource = UBound(SourceArray)
    End If
    ' make sure it fits
    If RangeStopTarget - RangeStartTarget = _
            RangeStopSource - RangeStartSource Then
        ' do it
        j = RangeStartSource
        For i = RangeStartTarget To RangeStopTarget
            TargetArray(i) = _
                TargetArray(i) - SourceArray(j)
            j = j + 1
```

```
        Next
    End If
End Sub
```

Listing 1-10: Subtracting the values in one array's elements from the values in a different array

NEXT STEPS

SubtractArrray was kept simple to illustrate the technique of performing array arithmetic using multiple arrays. Consider using the Process procedure as a template for a new procedure that takes two array ranges to create a generic and extensible procedure to implement many numeric actions.

Copying a Range from One Array to Another

A very common need is to extract a portion of one array and enter it into another array. For example, you might have an array of stock prices within a range of $10.00 to $20.00 that you want to extract.

The sample code in Listing 1-11, called CopyArray, handles this for you. CopyArray copies an entire array unless you specify a range. As with the previous examples, if you specify a range, the ranges must be the same size.

```
Public Sub CopyArray(TargetArray As Variant, _
            SourceArray As Variant, _
            Optional ByVal RangeStartTarget As Long = 0, _
            Optional ByVal RangeStopTarget As Long = 0, _
            Optional ByVal RangeStartSource As Long = 0, _
            Optional ByVal RangeStopSource As Long = 0)
    Dim i As Long, j As Long
    ' if both are the same value, then do the whole array
    If RangeStartTarget = RangeStopTarget Then
        RangeStartTarget = LBound(TargetArray)
        RangeStopTarget = UBound(TargetArray)
    End If
    ' if both are the same value, then do the whole array
    If RangeStartSource = RangeStopSource Then
        RangeStartSource = LBound(SourceArray)
        RangeStopSource = UBound(SourceArray)
    End If
    ' make sure it fits
    If RangeStopTarget - RangeStartTarget = _
                RangeStopSource - RangeStartSource Then
        ' do it
        j = RangeStartSource
        For i = RangeStartTarget To RangeStopTarget
            TargetArray(i) = SourceArray(j)
            j = j + 1
```

```
        Next
    End If
End Sub
```

Listing 1-11: Copying a range of array elements to another array

NEXT STEPS

The same techniques used in CopyArray and SubtractArray can also be used to
clear an array range, fill a range with a default value, or initialize all the
elements of an array with a given value. For example, you might create a Clear
routine to set all elements in a range to a given value, or to use one array's
values as the default values for another array.

Persisting Array Data

Next, we discuss how to make an array persistent. As stated earlier, persisting
data means storing it on, for example, a disk, and then reading it back later.
(See Chapter 7 for more information about persistence.)

There are a number of techniques that rely on knowing secrets about how
Visual Basic stores data internally, and using Windows API calls to move
memory around. We prefer a generic, stable, easy-to-understand procedure. Our
array persistence procedure stores the array elements to a disk file along with
the information required to read the elements back.

SaveArray (Listing 1-12) writes the contents of an array to disk. LoadArray
performs the opposite service; it reads a text file that was created by SaveArray
back into an array.

```
Sub SaveArray(anArray As Variant, lpPathName As String)
    Dim DOSFileHandle  As Long
    Dim i
    If VarType(anArray) < vbArray Then Exit Sub
    DOSFileHandle = FreeFile
    On Error Resume Next
    Kill lpPathName
    Open lpPathName For Binary As DOSFileHandle
    Put DOSFileHandle, , CLng(LBound(anArray))
    Put DOSFileHandle, , CLng(UBound(anArray))
    For i = LBound(anArray) To UBound(anArray)
        Put DOSFileHandle, , anArray(i)
    Next
    Close DOSFileHandle
End Sub
Sub LoadArray(anArray As Variant, lpPathName As String)
    Dim i
    Dim DOSFileHandle As Long
    Dim lTmp As Long
    Dim uTmp As Long
```

```
      If VarType(anArray) < vbArray Then Exit Sub
      DOSFileHandle = FreeFile
      Open lpPathName For Binary As DOSFileHandle
      Get DOSFileHandle, , lTmp
      Get DOSFileHandle, , uTmp
      ReDim anArray(lTmp To uTmp)
      For i = lTmp To uTmp
          Get DOSFileHandle, , anArray(i)
      Next
      Close DOSFileHandle
  End Sub
```

Listing 1-12: Saving an array to disk and then reading it back

The key to the success of both SaveArray and LoadArray is that SaveArray initially stores the array boundaries before storing the array elements. Then, when LoadArray reads the data, it can properly dimension the array. Using these two procedures is very easy. All you need is an array and a file path.

```
myArray.SaveArray anArray, "c:\temp\test.bin"
```

Then, when you want to load the array again, use:

```
myArray.LoadArray anArray, "c:\temp\test.bin"
```

NEXT STEPS

With a little work you can modify SaveArray and LoadArray to read and write a range of values instead of the entire array. You might also consider adding a header to the file created by SaveArray that stores some keyword that LoadArray then checks for when loading the array data. In this way, you could make sure that LoadArray only loads valid files created using SaveArray.

Performance Hints

Declaring arrays to be Variant has several advantages. Variants make array procedures easy to write and easy to use. The Variant array in the SaveArray procedure created earlier illustrates an additional benefit, because the Variant is not an actual data type. Rather, it defines a structure that contains data along with descriptive information identifying the type of data stored. (A Variant is a 16-byte structure, regardless of the size of the data.) Thus, when LoadArray reads the file that was written by SaveArray, the correct data type is set automatically.

As we mentioned briefly earlier, there is a drawback to using Variants. Every use of a Variant requires Visual Basic to perform additional work—Visual Basic has to determine what kind of data is stored, and then has to access the data itself. This takes time. In fact, Variants are slower than virtually all the actual data types. With today's faster computers, this isn't usually a problem. Many, many sins are forgiven with a 400 Mhz or greater processor and a large amount of RAM. However, if you need the absolute highest performance, you can modify the routines presented in this chapter to replace Variants with explicit data types such as a QuickSortLNG procedure that takes a long integer array, a QuickSortSTR procedure that takes a string array, FindItemLNG, FindItemSTR, and so on.

Some people use the Visual Basic VarType keyword to build a Select Case block that calls the properly typed sort or find procedure based on the array passed to it. This enables you to have a very easy-to-use high-level interface that takes any type of array, yet still gain much of the performance benefits of using strictly typed procedures. This type of code tends to be harder to maintain, however, and is often harder to debug than using individual procedures.

Chapter 2

Strings and String Handling

One of the most powerful aspects of Visual Basic—and the envy of developers using most other languages—is the ease with which it lets you work with strings. Visual Basic's built-in string functions, which were further improved in version 6, are the key to an amazing array of capabilities. Strings are the way that much data is represented, and data handling is what most Visual Basic programs are all about, so this chapter is dedicated to the examination, parsing, and changing of the beloved string.

What Is a String?

A *string* is a collection of printable, and sometimes nonprintable, characters. In Visual Basic, a string is given by enclosing the string with leading and trailing double quotation characters (")—like "Hank was here." In many programming languages, such as C, the string contained within the quotation marks is an array of characters that are terminated by a Chr$(0). You have to test where the string ends or remember how large the string is, or you run the risk of a "buffer error." For example, the first entry in the array might be a single byte with the ASCII value for *H*, the second a single byte with the ASCII value for *a*, and so on until the Chr$(0) that marks the end of the string is encountered. For example, the string *Hank was here* would be stored as *Hank was here0*. This is a 14-character array with *H* as the first element, *a* as the second element, and so on, until the *0* was encountered. In fact, what is stored is the value of the character; for example, for H, its ASCII value of 72 is what is stored.

Visual Basic actually uses a more sophisticated method to represent strings called *BSTR format* that puts the number of characters at the beginning of the array, followed by a two-byte encoding for the character (to allow for non-English characters called Unicode), and then it, too, is terminated by a Chr$(0) (ASCII 0). Luckily, the translation from your strings to the internal array for Unicode that VB uses is almost completely transparent to the VB Programmer and you usually only need to worry about it when working with the Windows Application Programming Interface (API) (see below and Chapter 6). Still, such features as the number of characters in the string always being instantly available, helps you understand why Visual Basic string handling is the envy of many a C programmer. (It also helps that you don't have to allocate and de-allocate memory to handle strings; VB does this automatically as well.)

Examining Strings

We have written so many programs that we can't recall how many times we had to examine a string to determine whether it was formatted a certain way. If you program in Visual Basic for any amount of time, you, too, will spend a fair amount of time examining string data.

Much of the string data that we have worked with was form data destined for a database. There are several schools of thought about how to store data, and while we don't want to start a war with our opinions, let us give them anyway.

Some people think data in a database should not be formatted. That is, for example, that a proper name, such as Hank should be stored as hank, and that the program reading and using the data should format the data as needed. We personally don't see anything wrong with storing the data the way you want it, and doing a little checking to make sure that the data is how you want to store it before storing. On the other hand, if you don't format the data before you store it, then, in most cases, you will need to format it when displaying or printing it. So, anyway you look at it, you will be formatting string data!

There are two schools of thought here as well. Some people think you should always format data, without checking to see if the data is already formatted. This sort of goes against our grain, and because we're paranoid (that is, we don't even trust ourselves), we examine the data to see whether it's formatted the way it should be before its stored, and also when we read it back from a database.

SIMPLE STRING-EXAMINATION TASKS

Common string-examination requirements include checking:

- The size of a string
- Whether a string contains a given substring
- Whether a string ends with a null terminator (Chr$(0))
- Whether a string has some form of punctuation

Most of the common string-examination tasks are very easily taken care of using Visual Basic's built-in string functions, such as Len, Instr, and Mid, as well as others. For example, testing the size of a string is as easy as:

```
Dim Size As Long
Size = Len("some string")
```

Likewise, finding a substring with a string is easy, too:

```
Dim Where As Long
Where = InStr("somestring", "string")
```

> **TIP**
> *If you need to find out where a string might occur when working backward (for example when looking at a file name), use the new InStrRev function added to VB6.*

You can use these Visual Basic built-in functions when working with the Windows API (WinAPI), too. (See Chapter 6 for more information about the WinAPI.) Because many WinAPI functions return a string with a null terminator, you can use Instr to determine where Visual Basic considers the end of the string to be—essentially stripping the null terminator from the string as in the following example, which is a declaration for the GetTempFileName WinAPI function:

```
Private Declare Function GetTempFileName Lib "kernel32" _
    Alias "GetTempFileNameA" ( _
    ByVal Path As String, _
    ByVal PrefixString As String, _
    ByVal Unique As Long, _
ByVal TempFileName As String) As Long
```

As described in Chapter 6, GetTempFileName returns a random filename based in part on the system timer. To use GetTempFileName, first create a string of large enough size to hold any return result. In the example shown below, a string of 128 spaces is created.

GetTempFileName puts a temporary filename into the string that was holding the 128 spaces. At the end of the filename, the GetTempFileName places a Chr$(0) character to indicate the end of the filename.

```
Function TempFileName(BnyVal Path As String) As String
    Dim tmp As String
    Dim j As Long
    tmp = Space$(128)
    GetTempFileName Path, "~", 0, tmp
    j = InStr(tmp, Chr$(0))
    If j > 0 Then TempFileName = Left$(tmp, j - 1)
End Function
```

Notice how we use Instr to locate the null terminator. If, and only if, there is a null terminator, we use Left to return just the filename without the null terminator.

TIP

If we had used code similar to this:

```
TempFileName = Left$(tmp, InStr(tmp, Chr$(0)) - 1)
```

then a run-time error would occur if there was no Chr$(0) in the variable named tmp. So, be careful when working with Instr, Left, and other built-in functions for strings; built-in functions can cause your program to crash at the most inopportune times if you are not careful. Always assume the worst, and use code similar to that shown in the TempFileName procedure, testing for a string offset greater than 0 before using.

TIP

Most string functions come in two versions: with and without the trailing $, for example Mid and Mid$. The one with the $ returns a true string whereas the one without returns a string stored in a variant. The ones with a $ are, therefore, faster.

COUNTING SUBSTRINGS

There are other string-handling tasks that require a bit more code than the previous examples did, but they are still easy to do using VB's built-in string functions. For example, suppose you want to count the number of times a certain substring is contained in a string, such as the number of commas in a comma-delimited record string.

The InstrCount function in Listing 2-1 returns the number of occurrences of the substring sSubstring in the sString1 string.

```
Public Function InstrCount(ByVal sString1 As String, _
                           ByVal SSubstring As String) As Long
    Dim j
    Dim c
    j = InStr(sString1, SSubstring)
    While j > 0
        c = c + 1
        j = InStr(j + 1, sString1, SSubstring)
    Wend
    InstrCount = c
End Function
```

Listing 2-1: The code shows how to use Visual Basic's string-handling functions to count the number of occurrences of a character within a string of characters.

The code in Listing 2-1 uses the Instr function to locate the first occurrence of the substring sString1. This gives us the starting value for the counter. Then, while there is still another occurrence, the code increments the counter. Another variable stores the offset of the substring within sString1, and then incrementally "walks" through sString1 checking for the substring. When there are no more occurrences of the substring in the original string, the function exits, returning the number of times the substring was found.

Because the code in Listing 2-1 uses Instr, and because Instr handles any sized strings, the substring you are searching for can be a single character, an individual word, or a much larger unit. This makes InstrCount versatile enough to handle any type of substring hunting.

TESTING FOR A STRING OF LETTERS

Sometimes you don't want string data to contain numbers. When a string does not contain numbers, it probably consists of alphabetic characters only. These kind of strings are called *alpha strings* or *alphabetic strings* and are composed of characters that comprise the alphabet in the current locale, but do not include numbers or punctuation characters. For example, each of the names of the 50 states constituting the United States is an alpha string because the names contain only alphabetic characters; no numbers are included.

Visual Basic does not have a built-in function that checks strings for us with regard to whether or not they are alpha strings. What Visual Basic does offer is the IsNumeric function, which returns True if the variable passed can be evaluated as a number. But this is not what it appears—IsNumeric cannot reliably determine whether a string has only alphabetic characters in it.

IsNumeric can be tricked. Consider the following with a quick trip to the Visual Basic debug window:

```
Print IsNumeric("hank")
```

which returns:

```
False
```

IsNumeric correctly realizes that the string "hank" cannot be treated as a number; thus, you could assume (correctly) that because of this test it is a string. Even changing "hank" to "2hank" won't fool IsNumeric.

You might therefore think that code such as the following snippet would determine whether a string is alpha or numeric:

```
If Not IsNumeric(something$) Then
        ' Alpha!
Else
        'Numeric!
End if
```

However, IsNumeric has some funny ideas about numbers. Let's test some more:

```
Print IsNumeric("1")
True
```

This time IsNumeric correctly indicates that "1" may be considered a number. Let's add a decimal point and see what happens. After all, technically, "1.00" could be a number with a decimal part.

```
Print IsNumeric("1.00")
True
```

IsNumeric thinks "1.00" is a number. That's good and bad. It is a number, so that is good. It's bad, however, because a period is not a numeral! So, IsNumeric doesn't find numerals. Lets continue in this vein (assuming you are running this program in the United States):

```
Print IsNumeric("$1.00")
True
```

Here again, IsNumeric is interpreting the data to deduce that "$1.00" could be considered a number, even though is has the decidedly nonnumeric characters of "$" and "." within it.

While for some purposes this deduction is acceptable, and even desirable, for checking that a string is alpha only, looking to determine whether IsNumeric returns True or False doesn't work reliably.

Luckily, we can simply write a function to do the work. All the function has to do is walk through the string checking each character in turn to make sure there are no nonalphabetic characters. For example, assuming the alphabetical characters are "A" to "Z" and "a" to "z," then the code in Listing 2-2 works:

```
Public Function IsAlpha(sString As String) As Boolean
    Dim i As Long
    For i = 1 To Len(sString)
        Select Case Mid$(sString, i, 1)
            Case "A" To "Z"
                IsAlpha = True
            Case "a" To "z"
                IsAlpha = True
        Case Else
            IsAlpha = False
            Exit Function
        End Select
```

```
      Next
End Function
```

Listing 2-2: This code shows how to use Visual Basic string-handling functions to determine whether a string contains only alphabetic characters.

If the string has any spaces on either end, the code in Listing 2-2 will return False. (Adding a call to Trim$ avoids the False return.)

If all you need to do is to make sure that there are no numerals embedded in the string, the code is even simpler:

```
Public Function IsAlpha(sString As String) As Boolean
    Dim i As Long
    For i = 1 To Len(sString)
        Select Case Mid$(sString, i, 1)
        Case "0" To "9"
            Exit Function
        End Select
    Next
    IsAlpha = True
End Function
```

TESTING FOR A NUMERIC STRING

Sometimes you don't want string data to contain alpha characters. For example, all ZIP codes in the United States are numeric. This is logically the opposite situation to that presented in Listing 5; now we want to determine whether a string contains only numeric characters. This is easily accomplished with a slight variation on the second IsAlpha function. The IsNumber function returns True if, and only if, the string passed contains only the characters "0" to "9", inclusive, as Listing 2-3 illustrates:

```
Public Function IsNumber(sString As String) As Boolean
    Dim i As Long
    For i = 1 To Len(sString)
        Select Case Mid$(sString, i, 1)
        Case "0" To "9"
        'ok continue
        Case Else
            Exit Function
        End Select
    Next
    IsNumber = True
End Function
```

Listing 2-3: The code shows how to use the Visual Basic string-handling functions to determine whether a string contains numeric characters only.

NOTE

Many people use the IsCharAlpha and IsCharAlphaNumeric WinAPI functions to determine whether a string contains alpha or numeric character. These functions do have the advantage of automatically being localized, but you still need to walk through the string character by character— the same problems occur when using them as when using IsNumeric.

Parsing Strings

Probably the single most common aspect of working with strings is the need to extract substrings from larger strings. This is called *parsing* the string.

By way of an example, many database systems, including the ever popular dBASE and compatible xBASE file systems store data in *record strings,* or fixed-length chunks of characters. Within a record string, certain byte offsets represent the starting and ending positions of *fields,* or substrings within the record string. Because the starting and ending positions of each field are known, it's easy to parse a field from the larger record string:

```
Dim Result As String
Result = Mid$(recordstring$, startpos&, endpos&)
```

Part of the challenge of working with strings is that they are usually of variable length. To parse a variable-length string, you can't simply move to some offset within the string and extract the variable-length field you want. Instead, this type of string uses *delimiters* to mark the boundaries of the fields. A delimiter is a predefined character that separates the individual fields in a record, such as the "\" or comma-delimited text files, which store fields separated by commas, as in this example:

```
"marquis,henry,a"
```

The string above contains data, the name of a famous author. "marquis" is the data for field number 1, "henry" for field 2 and "a" for field three. The comma (,) character is used as the delimiter between fields.

Other examples of delimited fields are found in raw hypertext markup language (HTML) code in Visual Basic, Internet Information Server (IIS), and Dynamic HTML (DHTML) projects, and Common Gateway Interface (CGI) programs written in Visual Basic. In all these cases, data is stored as a string with a known delimiter.

NOTE

Delimiters need not be single characters; for example, a carriage return + a linefeed is a common delimiter that is two characters long.

EXTRACTING A VARIABLE LENGTH FIELD

Before Visual Basic 6 added functions for these tasks, you had to write the parsing function yourself. Even though VB6 has a built-in method for splitting a string given a delimiter, the concepts of parsing a string for a given substring (called a *token*) are important to understand; thus, the GetField function in Listing 2-4 shows an implementation of token parsing. These functions are somewhat complex because they handle the delimiters and calculate the offsets. The GetField function shows one implementation of such a parsing function. You tell it what string to parse and where to start. Then it extracts the field bounded by the delimiters from the position you tell it. If you tell it to start at a position larger than where the last delimiter is, it returns the last field anyway. The logic behind GetField is that it locates the delimiters first. Because the first delimiter indicates the end of field 1, the second delimiter indicates the end of field 2, and so on, the code moves through the string, delimiter by delimiter, until the proper delimiter is found.

```
Public Function GetField(ByVal Work As String, _
                         ByVal Delim As String, _
                         ByVal Offset As Long) As String
    Dim s As Long
    Dim lasts As Long
    Dim Pop As Long
    s = InStr(work, delim)
    If s = 0 Then
        GetField = work
    Else
        lasts = 1
        Do While s > 0
            Pop = Pop + 1
            If Pop = offset Then
                GetField = Mid$(work, lasts, s - lasts)
                Exit Do
            End If
            lasts = s + 1
            s = InStr(s + 1, work, delim)
        Loop
        If s = 0 Then GetField = Trim$(Mid$(work, lasts))
    End If
End Function
```

Listing 2-4: The code shows how to use the built-in functions Mid and Instr to extract a given field from a delimited, variable-length string.

Visual Basic 6 added the Split function, which essentially does the job of the GetField function shown in Listing 2-4. Split parses a string at a single delimiter into an array by dividing the string into the fields bounded by the delimiter.

The function shown in Listing 2-5 makes Split a little more user-friendly. The code in Listing 2-5 creates an array to hold the result from the Split function, and then it uses the index of the requested field to get the item. This function requires you to know which field number inside the string is the one you want to extract.

```
Public Function GetField(ByVal Work As String, _
                         ByVal Delim As String, _
                         ByVal Offset As Long) As String
    ' an array to hold items
    Dim items() As String
    ' offset must be from item 1 to n
    If Offset < 1 Then Exit Function
    ' let Split do all the hard work
    items = Split(Work, Delim)
    ' Since Split returns a 0 based array, fixup
    ' offset.
    If (Offset - 1) <= UBound(items) Then
        GetField = items(Offset - 1)
    End If
End Function
```

Listing 2-5: The code shows how to use the Visual Basic Split method to extract a given field from a variable-length string of data that uses a known delimiter.

PARSING AN HTML POST STRING

The above examples show simple string parsing. Another, more complex example is to parse an HTML post string—these are the strings that result from using the POST operation on an HTML form. A POST string looks similar to this:

```
"lastname=marquis&firstname=henry&middle=a"
```

Again, the string contains data. However, this time the string also contains additional data—the field names.

An HTML post string actually uses two sets of delimiters. The equal sign (=) is used to separate a field's name from its data, and the ampersand (&) is used to separate the fields from one another. This sort of string is a bit more complex to parse. For strings such as this one, we need to implement a two-pass system. Listing 2-6 uses the Split method with the ExtractFields function that we created to extract the field names and then the field data to illustrate the technique. ExtractFields creates and returns a reference to a Visual Basic Collection object. A Collection object provides a way to store related information or data in a single object. Think of a collection as a storage location where you can add, delete, or locate specific bits of data; in this example, the Collection object will contain the data separated by tokens. Collections are indexed using a string.

Given the index string, you can retrieve information from the collection. In this example, the Collection uses the field name as the key to get at the field data:

```
Public Function ExtractFields(ByVal Work As String) As Collection
    Dim i As Long
    Dim fields() As String
    Dim data() As String
    Dim result As New Collection
    fields = Split(Work, "&")
    For i = 0 To UBound(fields)
        data = Split(fields(i), "=")
        ' save field name
        result.Add data(1), data(0)
    Next
    Set ExtractFields = result
End Function
```

Listing 2-6: The code shows how to use the Visual Basic Split method to extract a given field from a variable-length string of data that is separated by more than one known delimiter.

The code in Listing 2-6 works by first assuming that the string passed is an HTML post string, that is, fields are delimited using the ampersand character (&) and field data is associated with the field name using the equal sign (=). The first step is to break the input string into a series of field name/data pairs using Split. For example, the first call to Split in Listing 2-6 breaks the raw string into three substrings (assuming the raw string is "lastname=marquis&firstname=henry&middle=a"):

```
"lastname=marquis"
"firstname=henry"
"middle=a"
```

Then, the rest of the code in Listing 2-6 performs a series of splits to break the field name/data pairs down into the name and data components. The HTML post string is parsed and then stored in a Collection object. You may then refer to a field's data using its field name as shown in the code snippet below.

```
Dim myStrings As New cStrings
Dim FormData As New Collection
Set FormData = _
myStrings.ExtractFields("lastname=marquis&firstname=henry&middle=a")
Print "lastname=" & FormData("lastname")
Print "firstname=" & FormData("firstname")
Print "middle=" & FormData("middle")
```

NEXT STEPS WITH EXTRACTING FIELDS

ExtractFields assumes that you already know the field names contained in the original string. Consider improving on ExtractFields so that it also returns the field names, perhaps in an array.

Because you now have the basic code to parse a string into substrings, consider building a generic comma-delimited file-import function. Although comma-delimited files do not use field name/data pairs, they often indicate the field names by reserving the first row of the file for them. (See the code on disk, located under the Chapter2 subdirectory of the CD-ROM for such a routine.)

Changing Strings

After parsing and examining a string, the next most common string-handling function is changing a string. For example, let's assume that you have just made sure that a string actually contains alpha characters, and is, in fact, an alphabetic string. Now, let's assume the string contains a person's name and that you want to enforce proper naming:

```
"henry a marquis"
```

Perhaps the string contains a first name, middle initial, and last name. Now you want to make it a proper name by capitalizing only the first character of the first, middle, and last names, leaving the other letters lowercase, so that it looks like this when complete:

```
"Henry A Marquis"
```

> *NOTE*
>
> *For ease of illustration, we are not adding a period after an initial. However, you could consider adding code to the following sample to insert a period after a one character string to obtain "true" proper naming.*

At first, you might think the answer is to use the Visual Basic LCase and UCase built-in functions. For example, to convert a string to lowercase you could use:

```
sItem = LCase$(sItem)
```

and to convert a string to uppercase you could use:

```
sItem = UCase$(sItem)
```

However, using LCase and UCase involves an awful lot of string manipulations, which, in turn, would make it ugly. Yes, code beauty is a valid consideration for developers when choosing an implementation—it's called "elegance" and all developers should aspire to it.

CAPITALIZING PROPER NAMES

Instead of bulky code to test each character for uppercase or lowercase and then convert as needed, it's much easier (and more elegant) to examine each individual word in the string, and then adjust the case of just the character at the border between words. This can also be done using the character's ASCII value, which lets us use the much quicker numeric processing capabilities of Visual Basic instead of the comparatively slower Visual Basic string-handling capabilities.

The ASCII code for the character "a" is 97 and "z" is 122. The ASCII code for "A" is 65 and "Z" is 90. Thus armed, we can check the start of the word and convert that character to uppercase by simply adding 32 to its ASCII value.

The code shown in MakeProper (Listing 2-7) returns a new string that is obtained by converting the input string to lowercase, and then changing the ASCII value of the very first character, and all other characters that are preceded by a space character (ASCII 32). However, when it finds a space it assumes that the space represents the start of a word so that it will not work when there are multiple spaces inside the string. It also assumes that the character after a space is a letter so it can convert the character to uppercase by adding 32 to the character's ASCII value.

```
Public Function MakeProper(ByVal sString1 As String) As String
    Dim i
    Dim j
    sString1 = LCase$(sString1)
    If Len(sString1) > 0 Then
        For i = 0 To Len(sString1) - 1
            If j = 32 Or j = 0 Then
                j = Asc(Mid$(sString1, i + 1, 1))
                Mid$(sString1, i + 1, 1) = Chr$(j - 32)
            End If
            j = Asc(Mid$(sString1, i + 1, 1))
        Next
        MakeProper = sString1
    End If
End Function
```

Listing 2-7: The code illustrates enforcing proper case on a string.

REMOVING SUBSTRINGS

Once you can locate any substring quickly and easily using code similar to that shown previously, you may need to remove all occurrences of that substring from the larger string. Commonly, this is done when creating index keywords, passwords, and the like. For example, to create an index on the phrase "now is the time," you might want to store "nowisthetime"—in other words, the string without the spaces in it.

This is also easily accomplished using Visual Basic's built-in string-handling functions, as shown in Listing 2-8. The Remove procedure shown in Listing 2-8 cycles through a string looking for a substring that passes the original string in by reference so that changes are made to the original string. If the substring is found, the original string is compacted by removing the substring.

```
Public Sub Remove(sString1 As String, ByVal sString2 As String)
    Dim j
    j = InStr(sString1, sString2)
    While j > 0
        sString1 = Left$(sString1, j - 1) &_
                        Mid$(sString1, j + Len(sString2))
        j = InStr(sString1, sString2)
    Wend
End Sub
```

Listing 2-8: The code illustrates compacting a string by removing substrings.

The Remove procedure is a generic string compacter. A more typical implementation might be similar to that shown in Listing 2-9, in the StripBlanks function. StripBlanks works like the Visual Basic Trim function, except that StripBlanks removes nulls and tabs, as well as embedded spaces.

```
Public Function StripBlanks(ByVal sString1 As String) As String
    Remove sString1, Chr$(0)
    Remove sString1, Chr$(9)
    Remove sString1, Chr$(15)
    Remove sString1, Chr$(32)
    StripBlanks = sString1
End Function
```

Listing 2-9: The code illustrates using the Remove procedure to remove nulls, tabs, and spaces from a string.

CIPHERING

No chapter on playing with strings is complete without a little bit on ciphering. Ciphering is the process of changing a string into something that is not recognizable. The goal is to store or communicate information without an unwanted party being able to view the data.

Visual Basic has the XOr operator, which performs an exclusive Or operation. The nice things about XOr are that:

- If you XOr twice with the same number you return to where you started: (A XOr B) XOr B = A
- Given any two of the three parts of an equation, you can determine the third. For an example of the second point, try the following in the Visual Basic Immediate window:

```
100 XOr 5
97
Print 97 XOr 100
5
Print 100 XOr 97
5
```

As you can see, using XOr results in the ability to create a number derived from two other numbers. Given the result and at least one of the factors, you can determine the missing factor. This is ideal for ciphering because we can use the ASCII value of the data as one factor, and some other secret value as the other factor. We XOr them together. The result is the ciphered string.

To decipher, use the first point we mentioned. XOring twice returns you to where you started. Thus, to return to the original message, just XOr one more time with the same password. The output is the original string! This is the beauty of using XOr.

A typical implementation is to store a ciphered password by looping through the original password, XOring each character in the password with a character in a predefined data string, and storing the result. If the data string is larger than the password string, most implementations wrap around the password and start over with the first character of the password.

However, this use of the password directly is prone to a problem—patterns in the result. A good analyst will spot the patterns caused by the small password getting wrapped around as its characters are used over and over again against a relatively larger block of data. While this scheme is good for some implementation, it is pretty easy to figure out the original password.

So, we modified this very common "string trick." This implementation is easy to do, and much tougher to crack because instead of using the password directly, in the Cipher procedure shown in Listing 2-10, we use the password to initialize the Visual Basic random-number generator. Then, we use the Rnd function to return the next random number in the random sequence based on the password.

NOTE

The cipher function shown here is for example purposes only and is not intended as a secure method for storing or communicating vital data. Should you choose to use this code for storing or communicating data, you do so at your own risk.

Note that XOr (and this Cipher function) can be easily broken with enough computer power. However, this routine will stop a casual probe. You need to understand quite a bit about cryptography to break this code. (If you were an amateur cryptographer or have access to a fast enough computer, you could easily break this code because the built-in random-number generator in Visual Basic has a finite number of seeds, and the routine used to generate the numbers from the seed isn't "cryptographically secure.").

The code in Listing 2-10 first calls the Visual Basic Rnd function with a negative value to initialize the random number generator. Then Rnd is used again to return "random numbers" to avoid obvious patterns in the data. Rnd is used to select a character from A to Z, which is then used to cipher a character in the source string.

```
Public Function Cipher(ByVal Password As String, _
                       ByVal txt As String) As String
    Dim i As Long
    Dim j As Long
    Dim x As String
    Dim m_TextEncrypted As String
    m_TextEncrypted = txt
    ' randomize using password
    For i = 1 To Len(Password)
        j = j + Asc(Mid$(Password, i, 1))
    Next
    ' so we can duplicate this
    Rnd -j ' negative value inits to this point
    ' XOr using random A-Z char
    For i = 1 To Len(m_TextEncrypted)
        ' get a random A-Z character
        x = Int((vbKeyZ - vbKeyA + 1) * Rnd + vbKeyA)
        ' doit toit
        Mid$(m_TextEncrypted, i, 1) = _
        Chr$(Asc(Mid$(m_TextEncrypted, i, 1)) XOr x)
    Next
    ' assign & exit
    Cipher = m_TextEncrypted
End Function
```

Listing 2-10: The code implements an exclusive or ing cipher implementation.

CREATING MARQUEES

Finally, Listing 2-11 is a festive application based on string manipulation. These are "tickers" or "marquees." They "scroll" a string by wrapping the string around on itself. These make interesting additions to form captions, and can also be used in programs that need to get someone's attention! MarqueeLeft and MarqueeRight create an interesting visual effect, especially when used in a timer event to update a form caption.

```
Public Function MarqueeLeft(sString1 As String) As String
    Dim tmp As String
    MarqueeLeft = Mid$(sString1, 2) + Left$(sString1, 1)
End Function
Public Function MarqueeRight(sString1 As String) As String
    Dim tmp As String
        MarqueeRight = Right$(sString1, 1) + Left$(sString1, _
            Len(sString1) - 1)
End Function
```

Listing 2-11: The code illustrates creating marquees using simple Visual Basic string-handling functions.

Chapter 3

Fun with Numbers, Numeric Processing, and Logic

Processing numeric data is fundamental to programming. Although you might not know it, most of the tough questions about numeric processing have already been answered! If you don't know the answers then perhaps you can figure them out—given enough time. But why waste time? High-bytes, low-words, most significant bits...and more all await you. Read on!

Binary Analysis of Numbers

At the lowest level, all programming is about *bits, bytes,* and *words.* A *bit* is the lowest level of data storage, a single on or off state, representing a 1 or a 0. A *byte* is a collection of eight bits and can, therefore, represent any number from 0 to 255 because computers use base 2 arithmetic. People most often use a 2 as the subscript to indicate binary numbers. For example, in binary, 111_2 is the equivalent of a 1 in the four's place, a 1 in the two's place and a 1 in the one's place, and so it is the number 7. Bits are counted starting at 0. Therefore the rightmost bit is called *bit number 0* or the *zero'th* bit. (It is also called the *least significant bit.*)

A *word* is composed of two bytes—a so-called high-byte and a low-byte—and is used to represent, for example, integers. A word contains 16 bits and can be thought of as representing an *unsigned* integer between 0 and 65535 or, with a little work to deal with the question of how to represent negative numbers (see below), an ordinary Visual Basic (VB) integer between –32,768 and +32,767. Groups of words can be combined together as well. Two words are combined, for example, to represent a *Dword* in the Windows API (Application Programming Interface) and again, with some work to take account for negative numbers, a *long integer* (sometimes shortened to *long*) in Visual Basic. A long integer is thus composed of a high-word and a low-word, and contains 32 bits.

While the byte type is strictly positive (unsigned), integers and longs must be both positive and negative. There are, therefore, extra complications as to just how the bits will represent numbers for both the integer and long types, which complications do not occur for bytes. In particular, for both the integer and long types, you can't use base 2 arithmetic to represent the negative numbers.

Table 3-1 lists the primary Visual Basic data types and how they are composed.

Table 3-1: Visual Basic Data Types		
Long Integer	Double Word	32-bits (positive and negative)
Integer	Word	16-bits (positive and negative)
Byte	Byte	8-bits (positive only)

> **NOTE**
> *You might be wondering why we didn't include the Boolean data type in the list. We didn't because in Visual Basic, a Boolean value is really stored as an Integer that Visual Basic forces (coerces is the buzzword) to be a 0 (False) or –1 (True) whenever you use a Boolean value.*

Now, you are probably wondering why you should care about all this. Here are some reasons:

- When you use masking to determine whether the Alt or Ctrl key was pressed in the KeyUp/KeyDown event procedure, you are actually working on the bit level to tease out whether a specific bit is on or off.
- When using the Windows API, you are often required to extract things such as the low-order byte from a word or the low-order word from a Dword.

Negative Numbers

Visual Basic uses what is called two's-complement notation to handle negative numbers. This notation reserves the rightmost (most significant) bit for the sign, which is 1 for a negative number and 0 for a positive number. Unfortunately, the rest of the representation isn't quite that simple (for reasons that are only interesting to chip designers). VB, like most computer languages, also does some tricks on the bit level to get the representation of a negative number. Here's how it works.

To turn a positive number into its negative:

1. Represent the number in binary using all but the leftmost (most significant) bit (i.e., leave bit number 15 out).
2. Turn any bits that are on in this representation off and vice versa. (This is the same as applying the Not operator on the bit level).
3. Set the leftmost (most significant) bit to 1.
4. Add 1 to the result.

For example, to determine what the integer –1 is on the bit level, follow these steps:

1. Take the bit pattern for 1, which is lots of zeros and a 1 at the end, but leave off the most significant (leftmost) bit:

   $000\ 0000\ 0000\ 0001_2$

2. Change all the zeros to 1 and the single 1 to a zero:

   $111\ 1111\ 1111\ 1110_2$

3. Set the leftmost bit to be 1:

   $1111\ 1111\ 1111\ 1110_2$

4. Now add 1 to the result:

   $1111\ 1111\ 1111\ 1111_2$

So, –1 is actually represented as a fully packed word with all the bits on!

> **NOTE**
>
> *Now you can see why VB uses –1 for True and 0 for false. Not(0) is –1 because the NOT operator sets all 0 bits to 1 bits!*

Binary Digits in Visual Basic Numbers

Now that we've got you hooked, let us point out that Visual Basic has no intrinsic methods for extracting bits, bytes, or words from a variable of any data type. You need to program them yourself!

You can get at the binary digits of a byte or of a positive integer or of a positive long by simply dividing the byte, integer, or long by successive powers of 2 and determining whether there is a remainder. For example, if you divide a positive integer or long by 2 and get a remainder, that is, the positive integer or long is odd, then the last binary digit is a 1. Now take the result of dividing the original number by 2 and divide by 2 again: If there is another remainder, the second binary digit is also a 1. Continue the dividing process until there is nothing left to divide by 2. For example:

$7/2 = 3$ remainder 1
$3/2 = 1$ remainder 1

Because 1 can't be divided by 2 anymore, $7 = 111_2$.

Listing 3-1 contains code for a function to convert a positive long into its binary representation as a string (see below for code that handles the problem of negative numbers).

```
Private Function ConvertToBinary(lngNumber As Long) As String
    Dim sBinaryForm As String
    Dim Digit As Long If lngNumber < 0 Then Exit Function
    Do
        Digit = lngNumber Mod 2
        If Digit = 0 Then
            sBinaryForm = "0" & sBinaryForm
```

```
      Else
          sBinaryForm = "1" & sBinaryForm
      End If
      lngNumber = lngNumber \ 2
  Loop Until lngNumber = 0
  ConvertToBinary = sBinaryForm
End Function
```

Listing 3-1: A routine to convert a positive integer to binary

For signed numbers, however, you need to do a lot more work. You'll see a way to convert negative integers to their bit equivalent later in this chapter.

USING THE *AND* OPERATOR TO GET AT THE BITS

Although dividing by successive powers of 2 certainly works, the best way to get at the bits packed inside a positive integer or long is to use a little bit of math combined with the And operator. The idea is that when you use the AND operator with two numbers, VB returns only those bits that are on in both numbers. For example, because $7 = 0111_2$ in binary and $13 = 1101_2$ in binary:

$$13 \text{ And } 7 = 1101_2 \text{ AND } 0111_2 = 0101_2 = 5 \text{ in binary}$$

because only second and zero'th bit of both numbers are on simultaneously. This means that if you AND a number with a power of 2 and check what you get, you can determine if that bit is on:

```
If X and (2^b) = 2^b …'then b-1'th bit is on
```

(Remember bits are counted from 0.)

The OR operator, on the other hand, turns a bit on if either one of the two bits is on, so: $13 \text{ OR } 7 = 1111_2 = 15$ in binary. This means using the OR operator with a power of 2 guarantees that a certain bit is on. Finally, as we mentioned earlier, the NOT operator turns on bits off and vice versa.

THE KEYDOWN EVENT PROCEDURE

About the simplest use of the AND operator is when you need to get at the lowest four bits of the Shift parameter in a KeyDown event procedure. By using the AND operator with the number 7 (which equals 111_2 in binary), you can determine which of the lowest three bits of the Shift parameter that contains the needed information is on. Listing 3-2 illustrates this:

```
Private Sub Text1_KeyDown(KeyCode As Integer, _
          Shift As Integer)
    Select Case (Shift And 7) 'isolate lower 3 bits
        Case 0
              Print "Neither Ctrl nor Alt nor Shift key pressed"
```

```
              Case vbShiftMask '=1
                  Print "Only Shift key pressed"
              Case vbCtrlMask '=2
                  Print "Only Ctrl key pressed"
              Case vbShiftMask + vbCtrlMask '=3
                  Print "Shift + Ctrl keys pressed"
              Case vbAltMask '=4
                  Print "Only Alt key pressed"
              Case 5 ' or vbAltMask + vb ShiftMask
                  Print "Alt + Shift keys pressed"
              Case 6
                  Print "Alt + Ctrl keys pressed"
              Case 7
                  Print "Alt, Shift, and Ctrl keys pressed"
        End Select
End Sub
```

Listing 3-2: Using AND in the Key events to isolate the bits

Hexadecimal Hocus Pocus

Hexadecimal, or *hex* as it's called, is very convenient when working with binary
arithmetic. Hex numbers use base 16 instead of base 10. The convention is to
use the digits 0 to 9 for the first 10 *hexadecimal digits,* and A to F for the next 6
(10 through 15). Thus, a hex number may look like FF_{16} (which represents
15x16 + 15, or 255 in base 10) or $1A_{16}$ (which is 1 16 + 10×1 = 26_{10}). A single
hexadecimal digit represents four binary digits; F, for example, equals 1111_2 and
$F0_{16}$ equals 11110000_2. Visual Basic allows you to specify a hex number by
prefixing the string with the reserved symbols &H. Thus, &H1A means the
integer equivalent of the hex number $1A_{16}$ (1×16 + 10 = 26).

It's easy to get the hex equivalent of a base 10 number; the Visual Basic
Hex() function does this for you. But Visual Basic has no built-in function to go
the opposite way. There are various techniques for converting from Hex to
decimal and back again, but our favorite way uses a Visual Basic idiosyncrasy.
What we would like to do is to simply say:

```
Hex2Num = CLng("&H" & num$)
```

But there are complications for negative numbers and if the person uses the
&H. Still, CLng is smart enough to do the correct conversion, thereby illustrating
the flexibility (some would say chaos) that Visual Basic has brought to developers.

```
Public Function Hex2Decimal(num$) As Long
    Select Case Left(num$, 1)
        Case "-"
            If Mid(num$, 2, 2) = "&H" Then
```

```
                    Hex2Decimal = -CLng(Mid$(num$, 2))
              Else
                    Hex2Decimal = -CLng("&H" & num$)
              End If
         Case Else
              If Left(num$, 2) = "&H" Then
                    Hex2Decimal = CLng(num$)
              Else
                    Hex2Decimal = CLng("&H" & num$)
              End If
         End Select
End Function
```

Listing 3-3: A technique to convert a hexadecimal number contained in a string into a long integer

Another method is to simply run through each hexadecimal digit starting from the right end and then build up the number by adding the appropriate multiple of the right power of 16. Listing 3-4 shows the code that does this provided there's no minus sign and that the "&H" isn't used in front of the string. (We leave it to you to add the code for those two cases.)

The trick to the code in Listing 3-4 is that the position of the digit in the H string is used to tell us what to multiply the power of 16 by (the 1 is in the first position in H, the 2 in the second, and so on).

```
Public Function Hex2Num2(num$) As Long
    Dim N As Long
    Dim nm$
    Dim I As Long
    Const H = "123456789ABCDEF"
    nm$ = UCase$(num$)
    For i = 1 To Len(nm$)
        N = N + InStr(H, Mid$(nm$, Len(nm$) - i + 1, 1)) * _
            16 ^ (i - 1)
    Next
    Hex2Num2 = N
End Function
```

Listing 3-4: Another routine to convert a positive Hex representation to a number

> *NOTE*
>
> *Using the Hexadecimal representation for numbers is often the simplest way to get at packed numbers, numbers whose binary representation has all ones, such as $11111111_2 = 255$. Each hexadecimal "digit" represents four bits, thus, for example, &HFF is $11111111_2 = 255 =$ one packed byte. There is, however, one complication: VB thinks of &HFFFF as being the byte representation of –1 for the reasons described above. If you want VB to understand it as a positive long equal to 65535, use &HFFFF&, which tells VB to make a long out of it, thereby giving you 65535!*

More on Bit Flags

The Shift parameter in the KeyDown example packs its information in the individual bits of the integer. These individual bits are usually called *bit flags, but* sometimes are called *state flags* . Bit flags let you pack a lot of information in a single integer. For example, an integer variable has the capability of storing 16 bit flags because the binary representation uses 16 bits to represent the numbers from –32768 to +32767. In other words, each bit could be set on or off to represent the True/False state of a particular flag.

> *NOTE*
>
> *You might think that the Boolean data type is just the ticket for packing information. But it's not, because a Visual Basic Boolean is stored as an integer (for example, True is represented as a –1) and because Boolean data types use 16 bits to represent a flag, not 1 bit. Thus, VB uses 16 bits to store what really requires 1 bit—thereby wasting 15 bits of space. If you work with databases, binary files, or other file types with limited space, you want to store as many flags as possible in the available bits.*

Here's an example. The GetAsyncKeyState API function returns the up/down status of a keyboard key stored in a 16-bit integer. Here's the declare statement:

```
Public Declare Function GetAsyncKeyState Lib "user32" _
Alias "GetAsyncKeyState" (ByVal vKey As Long) As Integer
```

Sounds simple enough, until you learn more about this API function and discover that if the most significant bit of the return value from GetAsyncKeyState is 1, then the key is currently down, if it is 0 then the key is not down. So, how do learn whether a given bit is on (1) or off (0)? In the case of GetAsyncKeyState, we can use a shortcut, because in the two's complement notation described earlier, the most significant bit is on if and only if the integer is negative. Thus, we need only test whether the integer returned by GetAsyncKeyState is negative as the code in Listing 3-5 does.

```
Public Function KeyIsDown(ByVal vKeyCode As Integer) _
    As Boolean
    Dim nTemp As Integer
    nTemp = GetAsyncKeyState(vKeyCode)
    KeyIsDown = (nTempvKeyCode < 0)
End Function
```

Listing 3-5: One technique for determining whether the high bit of an integer is set by checking whether the integer is negative

The KeyIsDown function implements this trick, but while this algorithm is quick, it is not scalable and cannot check any bit in an integer other than the most significant bit. What we really want is the capability to both check whether any bit is on or off and to turn any bit in a number on or off. To do this, we need to write some code. Unfortunately, we can't just use the AND operator on the number because of the complications caused by the two's complement notation. Instead, we need to convert the integer to a positive (unsigned) long and *then* use the AND operator with the appropriate power of two. The formula to convert an integer to an unsigned long is a bit tricky (although one could simply program the steps for two's complement notation in reverse). It uses &HFFFF& in a long whose bit pattern is 1111111111111111_2; the AND operator gives you an on bit only if both representations are 1.

```
lngVersion = intShort And &HFFFF&
```

Here's the formula for going from a 16-bit long to the signed integer version:

```
intVersion = (lngVersion And &H7FFF&) - _
                        (lngVersion And &H8000&)
```

Here's a function that checks whether a specific bit in both positive and negative numbers is on:

```
Function IsBitOn(ByVal n As Integer, _
                        ByVal bit As Integer) As Boolean
    Dim lngTemp As Long
    If Bit < 0 or Bit > 15 then Exit Function
    lngTemp = n And &HFFFF&
    IsBitOn = (lngTemp And 2 ^ bit)
End Function
```

Because using the OR operator gives you an on bit when ever you have any one of the two bits on, the following is function turns a specific bit on and then returns an integer with that bit changed:

```
Function TurnBitOn(ByVal n As Integer, _
                         ByVal bit As Integer) As Integer
' remember bits start at 0
    Dim lngTemp As Long
    If bit < 0 Or bit > 15 Then Exit Function
    lngTemp = n And &HFFFF&
    lngTemp = (lngTemp Or 2 ^ bit)
    TurnBitOn = (lngTemp And &H7FFF&) - _
                         (lngTemp And &H8000&)
End Function
```

If you use this function by trying:

```
TurnBitOn(32767, 15)
```

in the immediate window, you'll see again that a packed word really is –1 to
Visual Basic.

Bytes from Words

Just like extracting words from longs, you can extract bytes from words. Again,
if the word is represented as an integer, that integer may be positive or negative
and extra work is needed to account for the complexities of the two's
complement notation described earlier. For example, first use the above trick to
first convert an integer to an unsigned long and then use this to create both the
HighByte and LowByte functions shown in Listing 3-6:

```
Public Function HighByte(wByte As Integer) As Long
    'return the HIGH byte (bits 8 to 15) from a long
    Dim lngVersion As Long
    lngVersion = wByte And &HFFFF&
    HighByte = lngVersion \ (2 ^ 8)'chop out high byte
    HighByte = HighByte *(2^8)  'right shift 8 bits
End Function
Public Function LowByte(wByte As Integer) As Long
        'Returns the LOW order byte (bits 0-7) from a given
        'word
    Dim lngVersion As Long
    lngVersion = wByte And &HFFFF&
    LowByte = lngVersion And &HFF&
End Function
```

Listing 3-6: Two functions that illustrate the extraction of bytes from a word

Using these techniques, you can pack your own data. For example, suppose
you need to combine two byte values into a long integer? The MakeLong

function does just this. It implements the reverse of the extraction process as Listing 3-7 illustrates.

```
Public Function MakeLong(HighB As Byte, LowB As Byte) _
       As Long
       '--Makes a long integer from two bytes
       MakeLong& = (HighB * 256) + LowB
End Function
```

Listing 3-7: How to pack two bytes in a long integer

> *NOTE*
> *Why are we are using two byte values and making them into a long integer instead of an integer? The answer again is that Visual Basic integers are signed and only hold values from –32768 to +32767. We chose to make this function return a long integer because passing a value higher than 127 in the HighB argument would overflow a Visual Basic integer.*

Words from Longs

Many API functions either return a long or use pass-by-reference to change the value of a long parameter—but the needed information is then most often stored in the low words in the long, providing 65536 possible values. For example, a Windows API call such as the GetCursorPos function uses a parameter that is a type consisting of two long integers. When you call GetCursorPos, Windows fills the two long integers inside the type with a number between 0 and 65536 that represents the position of the mouse cursor with respect to an absolute form of the screen coordinates (and not just the form's coordinates as with the mouse move event). This lets you determine, for example, whether the mouse pointer is in a window that does not belong to your application.

So, how do we obtain the information from a long such as that are used in GetCursorPos? If you want the low-order word, simply use the AND operator with &HFFFF&!

Here's the declare and the record type you need, which can be put in a BAS module:

```
Public Declare Function GetCursorPos Lib "user32" Alias _
"GetCursorPos" (lpPoint As POINTAPI) As Long
Public Type POINTAPI
               x As Long
               y As Long
End Type
```

Now, pass a variable of type POINTAPI to the API function and store the result in a long variable, which tells you whether the call was successful (nonzero on success, 0 on failure), as shown in Listing 3-8:

```
Dim pt as POINTAPI
Dim Result As Long, YCoord As Long
'set pt as desired not necessary for most uses
If GetCursorPos(pt)<> 0 Then
    YCoord = (pt.y) And &HFFFF&
End If
```

Listing 3-8: Using the AND operator to determine the lower word in a long

Binary-Coded Decimal

Binary-coded decimal (BCD) is an encoding system in which numeric data is converted to a string. You are probably thinking that the Visual Basic CStr() function already converts to a string, but BCD works differently because it keeps all the resulting strings the *same length*.

```
Dim lSumNum As Long
lSumNum = 1234567890
```

Converting lSumNum to a string using CStr(), results in a string that is 10 characters long. However, if lSumNum was then set to a value of 1, then CStr() would create a one-character string.

BCD strings enable storage of any positive value from 0 to 4,294,967,295 in a *fixed* string space. When working with databases and files, having a variable length field is hard to manage. Being able to store numeric data in a fixed space has tremendous value.

> *NOTE*
>
> *Before invention of the Currency type, BCD was also used as a way to do arithmetic without roundoff errors.*

Ironically, earlier versions of BASIC from Microsoft, such as GW-BASIC, QuickBasic, and the BASIC Professional Development System, came with a series of functions for converting numbers to fixed strings and back again such as MKL and CVL. MKL created a 4-byte string from a long integer; CVL converted a 4 -byte string to a long integer.

We were disappointed with Visual Basic 1.0 because it did not include the MKL and CVL (and other) functions for working with BCD values. We don't know why Microsoft decided these functions weren't needed anymore, because we still often need these functions. So, we had to create our own functions for working with BCD numbers.

The concept is pretty straightforward; each character represents an increasing power of 256. A BCD string is composed of ASCII characters, and ASCII characters have values from 0 to 255. Thus, one character can be considered to hold a value from 0 to 255. Add another character, and now you can have values from 0 to 255 plus 0 to 255 $\times$ 255—or 65535. Thus, two characters can hold a value up to 2^{16}. Add another character, and another, for a total of four characters, and you now have the capability to hold values up to 2^{32}.

The MKL function in Listing 3-9 does this job for you. MKL uses the principles presented earlier in extracting values from numbers to determine the quantity of 1s (256^0), 256s (256^1), 65536s (256^2), and 16777216s (256^3). It then combines these values into their character forms and concatenates the string. The result? A four-character string for any positive value input. In Listing 3-9, MKL converts a long integer to a four-character BCD string and CVL converts a four-character BCD string to a long integer.

```
Public Function MKL(ByVal lNum As Long) As String
    Dim s2, s3, s4
    s4 = lNum \ 16777216
    If s4 > 0 Then lNum = lNum - (16777216 * s4)
    s3 = lNum \ 65536
    If s3 > 0 Then lNum = lNum - CLng(65536 * s3)
    s2 = lNum \ 256
    If s2 > 0 Then lNum = lNum - CLng(256& * s2)
    MKL = Chr$(lNum) + Chr$(s2) + Chr$(s3) + Chr$(s4)
End Function
Public Function CVL(ByVal sBCD As String) As Long
    CVL = Asc(Mid$(sBCD, 1, 1)) + _
                    (CLng(Asc(Mid$(sBCD, 2, 1))) * 256) + _
                    (Asc(Mid$(sBCD, 3, 1)) * 65536) + _
                    (Asc(Mid$(sBCD, 4, 1)) * 16777216)
End Function
```

Listing 3-9: Converting to and from binary-coded decimal format

If you use MKL to create strings, then you need the CVL to convert back to a long integer. CVL performs the reverse function of MKL, expanding the binary-coded characters into a single number. Use MKL and CVL anywhere you need or want to convert a positive number to a fixed length string. BCD is also invaluable when working with files opened in binary mode. Programs such as those that handle dBASE files store numeric data using the same algorithm.

Next Steps for Working with BCD Strings

Create a MKI function that converts an integer value into a 2-byte string. Then create a corresponding CVI function to convert a 2-byte string to an integer.

Consider how to handle negative values. Microsoft chose to implement the integer data type in Visual Basic in 16 bits with a value range from –32768 to +32767 instead of 0 to 65535. Hint: You need to include logic to convert a negative value (e.g., –32768 to –1) into its true value (e.g., 0 to 32768).

Metrics

If your software is used anywhere in the world outside of the United States, you will want to convert data to the metric system. Windows controls the format of display data, but not the data itself. Visual Basic has no internal functions for converting from English units, such as feet and pounds, to metric units. Once again, we are back to coding. This time, there isn't much logic involved, just arithmetic for converting. For example, if you know that there are .3937 inches in a centimeter, it's easy to write a function such as that shown in Listing 3-10:

```
Public Function Inch2Cm(ByVal Inches As Double) As Double
    Inch2Cm = Inches / 0.3937
End Function
Public Function Cm2Inch(ByVal Cm As Double) As Double
    Cm2Inch = Cm * 0.3937
End Function
```

Listing 3-10: A simple formula for converting from inches to centimeters and vice versa

As Listing 3-11 illustrates, the other functions are implemented the same way:

```
Public Function Feet2Met(Feet As Double) As Double
    Feet2Met = (Feet * 12) / 39.37
End Function
Public Function Met2Feet(Meters As Double) As Double
    Met2Feet = (Meters * 39.37) / 12
End Function
Public Function Met2Yds(Meters As Double) As Double
    Met2Yds = (Meters * 39.37) / 36
End Function
Public Function Yds2Met(Yards As Double) As Double
    Yds2Met = (Yards * 36) / 39.37
End Function
Public Function Cent2Fahr(lDegreesC As Single) As Single
    Cent2Fahr = (lDegreesC * (9 / 5)) + 32
' centigrade result to fahrenheit
End Function
Public Function Fahr2Cent(lDegreesF As Single) As Single
    Fahr2Cent = (lDegreesF - 32) * (5 / 9)
' Fahrenheit to centigrade
End Function
```

Listing 3-11: Simple formulas for converting various measurements from English to metric formats and vice versa

Spelling Out Numbers

One function that is very commonly needed in programs that display information to a user is the capability of spelling out a number as a text string as on a check. The process is a bit cumbersome, but not conceptually much more difficult than what you have seen before. For example, the number 1961 would become "one thousand nine hundred sixty one." This function can't yet handle cents. Listing 3-12 shows the coding to convert a number to text.

```
Public Function Spell(nNumber As Currency) As String
    Dim tmp As String
    Dim work As String
    Dim i As Integer
    Dim c As Integer
    Dim N1(10) As String
    Dim n2(10) As String
    Dim N3(10) As String
    N1(0) = vbNullString
    N1(1) = "one"
    N1(2) = "two"
    N1(3) = "three"
    N1(4) = "four"
    N1(5) = "five"
    N1(6) = "six"
    N1(7) = "seven"
    N1(8) = "eight"
    N1(9) = "nine"
    n2(0) = "ten"
    n2(1) = "eleven"
    n2(2) = "twelve"
    n2(3) = "thirteen"
    n2(4) = "fourteen"
    n2(5) = "fifteen"
    n2(6) = "sixteen"
    n2(7) = "seventeen"
    n2(8) = "eighteen"
    n2(9) = "nineteen"
    n2(10) = "ten"
    N3(0) = vbNullString
    N3(1) = "ten"
    N3(2) = "twenty"
    N3(3) = "thirty"
    N3(4) = "fourty"
    N3(5) = "fifty"
    N3(6) = "sixty"
    N3(7) = "seventy"
    N3(8) = "eighty"
    N3(9) = "ninety"
    N3(10) = "one hundred"
    work = Format$(nNumber, "############")
    tmp = vbNullString
    For i = 1 To Len(work)
```

```
c = Val(Mid$(work, i, 1))
Select Case Len(work) - i + 1
Case -1
Case 0
Case 1   'ones
    If tmp <> vbNullString Then
        tmp = tmp + " " + N1(c)
    Else
        tmp = N1(c)
    End If
Case 2   'tens
    If c = 1 Then
        i = i + 1
        c = Val(Mid$(work, i, 1))
        If tmp <> vbNullString Then
            tmp = tmp + " " + n2(c)
        Else
            tmp = n2(c)
        End If
    Else
        If tmp <> vbNullString Then
            tmp = tmp + " " + N3(c)
        Else
            tmp = N3(c)
        End If
    End If
Case 3   'hundres
    If N1(c) <> vbNullString Then
        If tmp <> vbNullString Then
            tmp = tmp + " " + N1(c) + " hundred"
        Else
            tmp = N1(c) + " hundred"
        End If
    End If
Case 4   'thousands
    If tmp <> vbNullString Then
        tmp = tmp + " " + N1(c) + " thousand"
    Else
        tmp = N1(c) + " thousand"
    End If
Case 5   'ten-thousands
    If c = 1 Then
        i = i + 1
        c = Val(Mid$(work, i, 1))
        tmp = tmp + " " + n2(c) + " thousand"
    Else
```

```
                    If tmp <> vbNullString Then
                        tmp = tmp + " " + N3(c) '+ " thousand"
                    Else
                        tmp = N3(c)
                    End If
                    'tmp = tmp + " " + N3(c)
                End If
                'tmp = N3(c)
            Case 6  'hundred-thousands
                If N1(c) <> vbNullString Then
                    If tmp <> vbNullString Then
                        tmp = tmp + " " + N1(c) + " hundred "
                    Else
                        tmp = N1(c) + " hundred"
                    End If
                End If
            Case 7  'millions
                If tmp <> vbNullString Then
                    tmp = tmp + " " + N1(c) + " million"
                Else
                    tmp = N1(c) + " million"
                End If
            Case 8  'ten millions
                If c = 1 Then
                    i = i + 1
                    c = Val(Mid$(work, i, 1))
                    tmp = tmp + " " + n2(c) + " million"
                Else
                    If tmp <> vbNullString Then
                        tmp = tmp + " " + N3(c) '+ " thousand"
                    Else
                        tmp = N3(c)
                    End If
                    'tmp = tmp + " " + N3(c)
                End If
            Case 9  'hundred millions
                If N1(c) <> vbNullString Then
                    If tmp <> vbNullString Then
                        tmp = tmp + " " + N1(c) + " hundred "
                    Else
                        tmp = N1(c) + " hundred"
                    End If
                End If
            Case 10 'billion
                If tmp <> vbNullString Then
                    tmp = tmp + " " + N1(c) + " billion"
```

```
            Else
                tmp = N1(c) + " billion"
            End If
        Case 11 'ten billion
            If c = 1 Then
                i = i + 1
                c = Val(Mid$(work, i, 1))
                tmp = tmp + " " + n2(c) + " billion"
            Else
                If tmp <> vbNullString Then
                    tmp = tmp + " " + N3(c) '+ " thousand"
                Else
                    tmp = N3(c)
                End If
                'tmp = tmp + " " + N3(c)
            End If
        Case 12 'hundred billions
            If N1(c) <> vbNullString Then
                If tmp <> vbNullString Then
                    tmp = tmp + " " + N1(c) + " hundred "
                Else
                    tmp = N1(c) + " hundred"
                End If
            End If
        End Select
    Next
    While InStr(tmp, "  ") > 0
        tmp = Left$(tmp, InStr(tmp, "  ") - 1) + _
                    Mid$(tmp$, InStr(tmp, "  ") + 1)
    Wend
    If nNumber < 0 Then
        Spell = "Minus " & tmp
    Else
        Spell = LTrim$(RTrim$(tmp))
    End If
End Function
```

Listing 3-12: A function that converts numbers to text

A variation of this function is SpellDollar (Listing 3-13), which handles numbers with decimal trails, for example: $1961.02. SpellDollar uses Spell to do all the hard work, but includes the handling of the cents as well as the whole dollars. SpellDollar produces a result such as "one thousand nine hundred sixty one Dollars and two cents."

```
Public Function SpellDollar(nNumber As Currency) As String
    Dim fpart As String
    Dim spart As String, splural As String
    Dim tmp As String
    tmp = Format$(nNumber, "############.00")
    If Right$(tmp, 1) = "." Then tmp = tmp + "00"
    fpart = Left$(tmp, InStr(tmp, ".") - 1)
    fpart = Spell(CCur(fpart))
    spart = Mid$(tmp, InStr(tmp, ".") + 1)
    spart = Spell(CCur(spart))
    If spart = vbNullString Then spart = "no"
    If Right(tmp, 2) = "01" Then
        splural = " cent"
    Else
        splural = " cents"
    End If
    SpellDollar = fpart + " Dollars and " + _
                spart + splural
End Function
```

Listing 3-13: A function that converts dollar and cents value strings to their text equivalent

Chapter 4

Working with Dates and Times

Almost every program we have ever written had to implement some form of date manipulation or display. Unfortunately, Visual Basic does not handle dates consistently. Furthermore, getting just the date information you want is often frustrating because of the multitude of possible date formats. In this chapter, you learn to implement standard, reliable date and time functions.

Dates and Times

If a standard system of working with dates existed, it would be easy to implement date and time arithmetic. Unfortunately, date formats vary a great deal. For example, the following all convey the same information to a reader in the United States:

> 2/6/61
> 02/06/61
> Feb. 6, 1961
> February 6th, 1961

Worse yet, French, German, and other readers may be confused by 2/6/61 because in those countries it is typical for the month and day order to be day and month, which is the reverse of the order used in the United States. European readers, for example, are likely to interpret the date as June 2nd instead of February 6th. This potential confusion applies to programmers as well, because Windows allows users to define a date format based on a user's country or personal preference. Finally, even though many countries other than the United States use a different date ordering for year, month, and day, US and European countries at least use the same Gregorian calendar. In Japan, however, Windows may be setup for Emperor Calendar, a system in which the year is based on the number of years that the current Emperor has been on the throne.

Sounds awful doesn't it? Now let's mix in Visual Basic. Visual Basic has quite a number of built-in date-formatting functions. Unfortunately, their operation is often inconsistent. For example, consider the Date and Date$ functions. Both of these functions return the current date—the first as a variant, the second in string format. A quick trip to the Visual Basic debug window shows an interesting quirk. Start Visual Basic, then show the debug window. Try displaying the return values of the Date and Date$ functions. Enter the command to display the function result, and then press Enter to see a screen similar to this:

```
? date
3/21/99
? date$
03-21-1999
```

Notice how the Date function returns information formatted differently than the Date$ function. In fact, Date$ always returns the date using a MM-DD-YYYY format. The Date function, on the other hand, formats the date using the current windows date preferences. In our humble opinion, this is a bug because it violates the Visual Basic paradigm that both the variant and the string implementations of a function should perform the same job. For example, the Str and Str$ functions do the same job, one returning a variant and one returning a string. They both return their value with a leading space as well. The differences between the return values of the Date and Date$ functions have been responsible for some spectacular bugs.

The intent of this introduction is not to depress you, but rather to energize you! Or at least to help you understand the importance of this chapter.

Date Arithmetic

Date arithmetic consists of calculating future or past dates based on another date. Visual Basic has a number of date arithmetic functions, including DateAdd, DateSerial and DatePart.

The Visual Basic DateAdd function, for example, lets you add or remove any number of days, months, or years to or from a date. It is a key function for implementing many common date-based operations.

Before we delve too deeply into date arithmetic, we need to look at a few issues that many developers forget to consider.

Leap Years

Leap years are the bane of most poorly thought out algorithms that handle dates.

Detecting a leap year is fairly easy: If the year is divisible evenly by 4, then it's a leap year. For example, 1996 was a leap year. How do I know? By going to Visual Basic's debug window and dividing 1996 by 4:

```
? 1996 / 4
499
```

The year 1996 divided by 4 has no remainder, so 1996 is a leap year.

There is just one other rule to be aware of. If a year is divisible by 100, it is not a leap year, unless it is evenly divisible by 400. Thus, 1900 was not a leap year, but 2000 is. Listing 4-1 is an algorithm that implements these rules.

```
Public Function LeapYear(sDate As String) As Boolean
    If (Year(sDate) Mod 400) = 0 Then
        LeapYear = True
        Exit Function
    End If
    If (Year(sDate) Mod 100) = 0 Then
        Exit Function
    End If
    LeapYear = (Year(sDate) Mod 4) = 0
End Function
```

Listing 4-1: Determining whether the year in a date is a leap year

If LeapYear returns True, then the month of February for that year will have 29 days instead of 28. Now that you can determine whether a year is leap year, you can start figuring out other interesting pieces of information.

Calculating Days

Some information, such as determining the number of days in a month, cannot be retrieved using built-in functions. The DaysInMonth function in Listing 4-2 returns the number of days in any month in the current year. Similarly, DaysInYear returns the number of days in a year, which is 365 or 366 if it's a leap year.

```
Public Function DaysInMonth(ByVal iMonth As Integer) _
    As Integer
        Dim iYear As Long
        iYear = Year(Date$)
        Select Case iMonth
        Case 2
            DaysInMonth = 28
            If DaysInYear(Date$) = 366 Then DaysInMonth = 29
        Case 1, 3, 5, 7, 8, 10, 12
            DaysInMonth = 31
        Case 4, 6, 9, 11
            DaysInMonth = 30
        End Select
End Function
Public Function DaysInYear(ByVal vDate As Date) As Integer
    If (Year(vDate) Mod 400) = 0 Then
        DaysInYear = 366
        Exit Function
    End If
    If (Year(vDate) Mod 100) = 0 Then
```

```
        DaysInYear = 365
        Exit Function
    End If
    If (Year(vDate) Mod 4) = 0 Then
            DaysInYear = 366
    Else
            DaysInYear = 365
    End If
End Function
```

Listing 4-2: Determining the number of days in a month or a year

It's important to know what day of the year any given date is in order to determine such things as the number of days left in a year, or the number of days already passed in a year, or any other interval-based calculation. You can use Visual Basic DatePart function to obtain the current day of the year, as the DayOfYear function in Listing 4-3 illustrates.

```
Public Function DayOfYear(ByVal vDate As Date) As Integer
    DayOfYear = DatePart("y", vDate)
End Function
Public Function DaysLeftInYear(ByVal vDate As Date) _
    As Integer
    DaysLeftInYear = DaysInYear(vDate) - DayOfYear(vDate)
End Function
```

Listing 4-3: Determining current day number and how many days remain in the year

NEXT STEPS

Consider implementing a days in week function, that tells how many days are left to work in a week. Or write a function that determines the number of workdays in a month, the number of days until some holiday, or the number of days until the first of the month.

Formatting Dates

Now that you know how to determine the date information that you need, the next step is to format dates and display them the way you want.

Visual Basic has a very powerful function called Format that can format dates any way you wish. However, Format is not 100 percent safe because Format uses system information to determine the order of days, months, and years. Microsoft calls Format *locale aware*. Locale aware means that the code that composes Format (or any locale-aware function) reads a user's Regional Settings as configured via the Windows Control Panel and performs operations based on the regional preferences.

Conversely, a *locale-independent* date system does not consider the configuration of Visual Basic or Windows. Instead, it requires a fixed format for dates. This is very important for date arithmetic. Just consider the earlier discussion of the order of day and month. If a stored string has the value 2/6/61, how do you know what it means? In Germany, it means the second day of the sixth month; in the United States it means the sixth day of the second month. If you base your calculations on strings returned by the Format function, you could end up operating on days when you think you are operating on months, or, worse yet, mixing days and months in your equations.

Before we solve this locale-aware problem, let's look at date formatting using the Format function, even if it isn't portable. Strange as it may sound based on our earlier comments, the Format function is the key to implementing portable date arithmetic and presentation.

The Format function takes two arguments: the date to format and a formatting string. To control how the function returns the date, you use the characters m, d, and y alone or in combination, along with any literal characters you want in the formatting string.

Table 4-1: Character Combinations Allowed in the Formatting String

CHARACTER COMBINATION	MEANING
"d"	day of month, without leading pad if single digit; e.g., "7"
"dd"	day of month, with leading pad if single digit; e.g., "07"
"ddd"	day of month, spelled out, in short form; e.g., "Sun"
"dddd"	day of month, spelled out, in long form; e.g., "Sunday"
"mmm"	month, abbreviated short form; e.g., "Jan"
"mmmm"	month, full name; e.g., "January"
"yy"	year, two digits; e.g., "99"
"yyyy"	year, four digits; e.g., "1999"

Some examples of calling Format using the formatting strings are listed in Table 4-2:

EXAMPLE FUNCTION CALL	EXAMPLE RETURN DATE

Table 4-2: How to Format the Same Date in Different Ways

Format (Now, "m/d/yy")	3/21/99
Format (Now, "dddd, mmmm dd, yyyy")	Sunday, March 21, 1999
Format (Now, "d-mmm")	21-Mar
Format (Now, "mmmm-yy")	March-99

Listing 4-4 illustrates a simple method for implementing a set of date-formatting functions.

```
Public Function MonthNameShort(dDate As Date) As String
    MonthNameShort = Format$(dDate, "mmm")
```

```
End Function
Public Function MonthNameLong(dDate As Date) As String
    MonthNameLong = Format$(dDate, "mmmm")
End Function
Public Function DayNameLong(dDate As Date) As String
    DayNameLong = Format$(dDate, "dddd")
End Function
Public Function DayNameShort(dDate As Date) As String
    DayNameShort = Format$(dDate, "ddd")
End Function
```

Listing 4-4: Simple functions that format dates using the Format function

The logic of Listing 4-4 holds true for formatting days, years, or any combination of dates. By creating your own wrappers for the Format function, and taking advantage of the Visual Basic DateSerial function (described below), you can create and implement an entire locale-independent date system.

So, how do we implement a locale-independent system? Well, one technique is to force all dates into a "YYYYMMDD" format, and use that format consistently. In other words, all functions that take a date expect the date to be in the format of "YYYYMMDD." All functions that return a date return a date string in the format of "YYYYMMDD."

The Date2Str function converts any date, for any locale, to a string with the format YYYYMMDD. Str2Date, which is a wrapper for the DateSerial function, performs the opposite function: it converts a date string in the format YYYYMMDD to a locale-specific date. DateSerial takes a year, month, and day and converts them into a locale-aware date. Listing 4-5 illustrates these functions.

```
Public Function Date2Str(ByVal d As Date) As String
    Date2Str = Format(d, "yyyymmdd")
End Function
Public Function Str2Date(ByVal s As String) As Date
    Str2Date = DateSerial(Left(s, 4), Mid(s, 5, 2), _
                Mid(s, 7, 2))
End Function
```

Listing 4-5: Functions that convert a date to a locale-independent string and converts that string back to a locale-aware date

NEXT STEPS

Consider expanding Date2Str and Str2Date to include time in hours, minutes and seconds. Hint: You need to use TimeSerial as well as DateSerial.

Julian Dates

Julian dates are long integer values that may be used instead of Visual Basic date variables and functions. Julian dates automatically handle leap years, century changes and all the issues that we have to make sure to implement when we use the Visual Basic date type. However, if you choose to use Julian dates instead of the date data type, you will have to accept a limitation in the range of supported dates. Julian dates are supported in the range of January 1, 1583 to December 31, 9999. The Visual Basic date range for date data types is from January 1, 100 to December 31, 9999.

We don't delve into the reasoning of the algorithm used to determine Julian dates. We believe that this implementation is taken from a 17th century monk who spent most of his life figuring this out. Instead, we present to you Julian dates—use them when you want to create 100 percent date data type free, 100 percent local-independent date arithmetic.

In Listing 4-6, ToJulian converts a string in the format YYYYMMDD to a long integer Julian date and FromJulian converts a Julian date value from a long integer to a string in the format of YYYYMMDD.

```
Public Function ToJulian(Arg1$) As Long
'YYYYMMDD to Julian
    Dim DateToChange$, dia&, yr&, a&, b&, mnth&
    DateToChange$ = Arg1$
    If Val(DateToChange$) < 15830101 Or _
            Val(DateToChange$) > 99991231 Then Error 5
    mnth& = Val(Mid$(DateToChange$, 5, 2))
    dia& = Val(Mid$(DateToChange$, 7, 2))
    yr& = Val(Left$(DateToChange$, 4))
    a& = (mnth& - 14) \ 12
    b& = dia& - 32075 + (1461 * (yr& + 4800 + a&) \ 4)
    b& = b& + (367 * (mnth& - 2 - a& * 12) \ 12)
    b& = b& - (3 * ((yr& + 4900 + a&) \ 100) \ 4)
    ToJulian = b&
End Function
Public Function FromJulian(Arg1 As Long) As String 'Julian to YYYYMMDD
    Dim a&, b&, yr&, c1&, mnth&, result$,
    Dim JulianDate&, dy, d$, da$
    JulianDate& = Arg1
    If JulianDate& < 2299239 Or _
        JulianDate& > 5373484 Then Error 5
    a& = JulianDate& + 68569
    b& = 4 * a& \ 146097
    a& = a& - (146097 * b& + 3) \ 4
    yr& = 4000 * (a& + 1) \ 1461001
    c1& = yr&
    a& = a& - (1461 * c1& \ 4) + 31
    mnth& = 80 * a& \ 2447
    c1& = mnth&
    dy = a& - (2447 * c1& \ 80)
    a& = mnth& \ 11
    mnth& = mnth& + 2 - (12 * a&)
```

```
        yr& = 100 * (b& - 49) + yr& + a&
        result$ = LTrim$(Str$(yr&))
        d$ = LTrim$(Str$(mnth&))
        If mnth& < 10 Then d$ = "0" & d$
        result$ = result$ & d$
        da$ = LTrim$(Str$(dy))
        If dy < 10 Then d$ = "0" & da$ Else d$ = da$
        FromJulian = CStr(result$ & d$)
End Function
```

Listing 4-6: Two functions for working with Julian dates

Doing date arithmetic with a Julian date is easy; simply add the number of days you want to the Julian date, as shown in Listing 4-7.

```
Private Sub Form_Load()
    Dim jd As Long      'julian date
    Dim ds As String 'date string

    Show
    ds = Format(Now, "YYYYMMDD")
    jd = ToJulian(ds)
    ' today
    Print "Date", "Julian"
    Print ds, ToJulian(ds)

    ' move to next week
    Print FromJulian(jd + 7), ToJulian(FromJulian(jd + 7))
    ' move to yesterday
    Print FromJulian(jd - 1), ToJulian(FromJulian(jd - 1))
End Sub
```

Listing 4-7: A simple implementation that calculates a date a week from another date without using a Visual Basic date variable or date function

Next Steps

Consider implementing a function to display the result of Julian arithmetic in some format other than YYYYMMDD.

Working with Time

You can work with time values as well as date values. Just as you saw with dates, it's very common to want to parse time into its constituent elements, for example, the number of hours, minutes, and seconds represented by some time value.

The function ParseTime, in Listing 4-8, converts the number of days, hours, minutes, and seconds you specify into a 32-bit long integer value containing the equivalent number of seconds. It can also reverse the process, converting the number of seconds into the equivalent number of days, hours, minutes, and seconds. The direction of conversion depends on the value of the mode argument.

```
Public Sub ParseTime(TotalSecs As Long, Days As Long,_
    Hours As Long, Mins As Long, Secs As Long, _
    mode As Boolean)
        Dim worktime As Long
        If mode = True Then ' from seconds to days, hours, min
            worktime = TotalSecs
            Days = worktime \ 86400
            worktime = worktime - (Days * 86400)
            Hours = worktime \ 3600
            worktime = worktime - (CLng(Hours) * 3600)
            Mins = worktime \ 60
            worktime = worktime - (CLng(Mins) * 60)
            Secs = worktime
        Else    ' from days, hours, mins to total seconds
            TotalSecs = Days * 86400
            TotalSecs = TotalSecs + (Hours * 3600)
            TotalSecs = TotalSecs + (Mins * 60)
            TotalSecs = TotalSecs + Secs
        End If
End Sub
```

Listing 4-8: Parsing a time into its constituent parts (days, hours, minutes, and seconds) and vice versa

Time arithmetic is similar to date arithmetic. Using ParseTime, you can implement time arithmetic by directly modifying seconds, hours, or minutes.

Another common task is to convert some time value into a human-readable string. The FormatTime function shown in Listing 4-9 converts a number of seconds into a formatted string, such as "14 Days, 6 Hours, 56 Minutes, 7 Seconds."

```
Private Function FormatTime(ByVal lSeconds As Long) _
As String
        Dim Days As Long
        Dim Hours As Long
        Dim Minutes As Long
        Dim Seconds As Long
        Dim tmp As String
        ParseTime lSeconds, Days, Hours, Minutes, _
                    Seconds, True
        If Days > 0 Then tmp = Days & " " & _
                IIf(Days > 1, "Days", "Day")
```

```
        If Hours > 0 Then  tmp = tmp & _
            IIf(Len(tmp) > 0, ", ", "") & Hours & " " _
                   & IIf(Hours > 1, "Hours", "Hour")
        If Minutes > 0 Then tmp = tmp & _
            IIf(Len(tmp) > 0, ", ", "") & Minutes & " " _
            & IIf(Minutes > 1, "Minutes", "Minute")
        If Seconds > 0 Then tmp = tmp & _
            IIf(Len(tmp) > 0, ", ", "") & Seconds & " " _
            & IIf(Seconds > 1, "Seconds", "Second")
    FormatTime = tmp
End Function
```

Listing 4-9: Implementation that formats seconds into a human-readable string

Summary

Visual Basic has many processing and formatting functions that enable your programs to manipulate dates and times. Dates and times are used in almost all programs, and in many cases, your programs can have hidden bugs because of the locale-aware features of Visual Basic. To avoid problems follow these guidelines:

1. When working with dates be sure to account for leap years. A leap year is any year that when divided by 4 has no remainder.
2. Take into account locale-aware date functions such as Date and DateSerial. The return value of many of Visual Basic's variant functions is modified based on the locale settings of Windows or through user-defined preferences.
3. Also, account for the difference between Date and Date$—a source of innumerable problems in many programs that use dates. Remember that Date is locale aware, and the format that it returns is based on system configuration. Date$ always returns a value formatted according to the US standard of MMDDYYYY.
4. You can implement a locale-insensitive date scheme in your program to help avoid problems with dates in your programs. Using Julian dates is one method of avoiding many of the common problems found in date arithmetic.

Chapter 5

Data Structures: Versatile Vehicles for Data Storage

As you already know, your programs often use one of the standard variable types, such as currency, to represent single fields. However, sometimes you need more complex types of variables to represent more complex data. For example, you might want to store 10 pieces of information for each of your customers. Wouldn't it be nice if you could store each customer's data in a single variable, enabling you to work with that data as a single unit? How to represent complex data in this fashion requires understanding data structures.

Data Structures in Visual Basic

Visual Basic (VB) supports, directly and indirectly, a wide variety of data structures. Some of them are created using specific VB keywords, while combining several built-in data structures creates others. The data structures available to you are arrays, user-defined types, enumerated types, classes, and key-item pairs associated with Collections and the new Dictionary object.

Arrays

In Chapter 1, you encountered the most commonly used data structure—the array. The array is the next step up after a single, scalar variable. It is used when you need a more complex variable. (A *scalar variable* is simply one that contains a single value.) Visual Basic enables you to create an array with elements of any simple, built-in data type. Fortunately, you can also define the elements to be any of the complex data structures covered in the following sections.

User-Defined Types

Although you could use an array to store multiple values, you'd have to assign particular indexes to particular parts of the data so that the data was locatable. For example, you might decide that the element at index 2 holds a customer's street address. Indexing parts of the data isn't exactly intuitive. To store multiple values in a single data structure in an intuitive fashion, Visual Basic provides the *user-defined type*.

Instead of going through the extra step of managing the indices, you can create a data structure to contain all the pieces of data you want to store. For example, a customer's record in a database might contain these fields:

- Customer ID
- Name
- Address
- City
- State
- ZIP

To create a user-defined type that holds the data from these fields, place the following code in the declarations section of a Visual Basic code module:

```
Type Customer
    CustomerID As Long
    Name As String
    Address As String
    City As String
    State As String
    ZIP As String
End Type
```

Each piece of data, or *member,* is listed on a separate line within the Type/End Type statement. The name of the user-defined type can be any valid variable name within Visual Basic. Each field can be of any valid built-in type, object type, or even another user-define type, as shown here:

```
Type ZIPCode
    FrontHalf As Long
    BackHalf As Long
End Type

Type Customer
    CustomerID As Long
    Name As String
    Address As String
    City As String
    State As String
    ZIP As ZIPCode
End Type
```

In this example, we would first define the ZIPCode type, which is then used in the Customer type.

TIP
You must define a type before you can use it in another user-defined type.

To access the members of a user-defined type variable, you use dot notation, just as is done with objects. For example, you might have code like this:

```
Dim test As Customer
test.Name = "Eric Smith"
test.Address = "123 Main St."
test.City = "Springfield"
test.State = "VA"
test.ZIP.FrontHalf = 22150
test.ZIP.BackHalf = 1182
```

Note the use of two dots to fill each half of the ZIP member. Using the dot notation to drill down into this data structure can go on for as many levels as you need. Alternatively, you can save a bit of keyboard typing by using the With statement, as shown in this revised example:

```
Dim test As Customer
With test
    .Name = "Eric Smith"
    .Address = "123 Main St."
    .City = "Springfield"
    .State = "VA"
    With .ZIP
        .FrontHalf = 22150
        .BackHalf = 1182
    End With
End With
```

There are some restrictions to user-defined types. First, although you can add them to a form or class, they have to be declared as private. If you want to have a user-defined type available throughout your application, it must be public in a standard code module. Second, you can't copy a variable of a user-defined type via a single statement because there is no collection of the members as there is, for example, for an Active Data Objects (ADO) recordset. (See Chapter 15 for more information about ADO.)

Enumerated Types

Large applications inevitably have a set of constants that is used for a variety of purposes. For example, there may be some numerical constants to indicate the state of windows or numerical constants to represent the type of credit card a person used. The VB Const keyword lets you create lots of constants, but they're not categorized in any way. A special kind of user-defined type, the *enumerated type,* enables you to put constants in logical groupings.

Let's assume that you want to create a set of constants that reflect the status of a form. You can easily do this by declaring an enumerated type named FormStatus, as shown here:

```
Enum FormStatus
    AddMode = 1
    EditMode = 2
    ViewMode = 3
End Enum
```

You would then declare a variable of the FormStatus type by using this line of code:

```
Dim enmStatus As FormStatus
```

An assignment statement would look like one of these three lines:

```
enmStatus = AddMode
enmStatus = EditMode
enmStatus = ViewMode
```

> **TIP**
> *The IntelliSense feature of the Visual Basic programming environment provides a bonus when you use enumerated types. Whenever you enter an assignment statement or procedure that requires one constant in an enumerated type, the available constants automatically appear, and you can just pick the required constant from the list. As long as you've used a good naming convention, this feature is especially helpful when there are a lot of constants and your memory fails you.*

You can also use enumerated type variables within other type declaration statements, just as you might use another type within a type declaration. Enumerated types can be declared in standard code modules or within classes. They can be either public or private in both locations. If you are declaring an enumerated type as part of another object, you must specify the parent object in order to get to the enumerated value.

The one bad thing about enumerated types is that you can't use them for string constants. This is disappointing, because we normally have a lot more string constants than numerical ones.

Classes

Another major data structure available in Visual Basic is a class. You can think of a *class* as a user-defined type that can (and usually does) include code. A class can have all of these elements in it:

- Private member variables that hold data
- Accessor properties to retrieve the data from the private member variables

- Modifier (sometimes called mutator) properties to make changes to the data in the private member variables
- Private and public subroutines and functions that provide other features
- Private and public events to pass information to other objects

Here is a sample class, which looks like the Customer user-defined type we created earlier:

```
Option Explicit
Private m_lngCustomerID As Long
Private m_strCustomerName As String
Private m_strAddress As String
Private m_strCity As String
Private m_strState As String
Private m_strZIP As String

Public Property Let CustomerID(ByVal vData As Long)
    m_lngCustomerID = vData
End Property

Public Property Get CustomerID() As Long
    CustomerID = m_lngCustomerID
End Property

Public Property Let CustomerName(ByVal vData As String)
    m_strCustomerName = vData
End Property

Public Property Get CustomerName() As String
    CustomerName = m_strCustomerName
End Property

Public Property Let Address(ByVal vData As String)
    m_strAddress = vData
End Property

Public Property Get Address() As String
    Address = m_strAddress
End Property

Public Property Let City(ByVal vData As String)
    m_strCity = vData
End Property

Public Property Get City() As String
```

```
    City = m_strCity
End Property

Public Property Let State(ByVal vData As String)
    m_strState = vData
End Property

Public Property Get State() As String
    State = m_strState
End Property

Public Property Let ZIP(ByVal vData As String)
    m_strZIP = vData
End Property

Public Property Get ZIP() As String
    ZIP = m_strZIP
End Property
```

The first few lines declare private variables to hold the class' data. These variables protect the data from other objects and code from modifying the data directly. Any changes are handled through the Public Property Let statements that follow. For each variable, there is a corresponding Property Let and Property Get statement. The Property Let statement is used to change the member variable, and the Property Get statement retrieves the value. In this class, the Property Let statements simply pass through the changes without any validation. However, you could combine some of the validation code from Chapter 10 with this code. In the following example, the class enforces the ZIP code being exactly 5 or 10 characters. The 10 character version accounts for the ZIP+4 format, which has five digits, a dash, and four more digits.

```
Public Property Let ZIP(ByVal vData As String)
    If Len(vData) <> 5 And Len(vData) <> 10 Then
        Err.Raise vbObjectError + 1, _
            "Customer Class", _
            "ZIP Code must be in NNNNN or NNNNN-NNNN format."
    Else
        m_strZIP = vData
    End If
End Property
```

Instead of just taking the new data and putting it in the private member variable, this routine first verifies that the data is the correct length. If the data is not the right length, this routine raises an error that can be trapped by the calling code. Here is an example of how to use this code:

```
Private Sub Form_Load()
    On Error GoTo EH
    Dim objCustomer As New Customer
    objCustomer.ZIP = "452132"
EH:
    If Err.Number <> 0 Then
        MsgBox "Error occurred: " & Err.Description
    End If
End Sub
```

In this case, we first set up an error handler to catch any errors from the object. We then instantiate a new Customer object by using the Dim statement with the New keyword. Next, we attempt to store an invalid ZIP code in the object. Running this code raises an error message by the object in the Property Let statement you created earlier. The error number is added to the vbObjectError constant, which lets you create error numbers that are out of VB's built-in error number ranges. If you want to make this number accessible through the object, you can add this line to the declarations section of the class:

```
Private m_lngValidationError As Long
```

Add this code to the class file, as well:

```
Private Sub Class_Initialize()
    m_lngValidationError = vbObjectError + 1
End Sub
Public Property Get ValidationError() As Long
    ValidationError = m_lngValidationError
End Property
```

This code creates a separate member variable for the error number, and then creates a Property Get accessor method to return the value. (Unfortunately, you can't define a constant as vbObjectError + 1.) There is no Property Let statement because changes are not allowed to the number. In addition, the member variable must be populated when the class is instantiated, which can be done in the Class_Initialize event.

You can now change the ZIP code's modifier to return the m_lngValidationError variable, instead of the actual constant. The final change is in the test code you are using. The error-handler section of the code now looks like the following:

```
EH:
    If Err.Number = objCustomer.ValidationError Then
        MsgBox "The following validation error occurred: " _
            & Err.Description
    End If
```

> *NOTE*
> *We could have created a global constant for this value stored in the ValidationError property; however, that breaks the idea of encapsulation. In this case, encapsulation means that the object is self-contained and doesn't need any other constants defined for it. Encapsulation is a key reason to use classes because with encapsulation, you never let the user of your code see the private data. Instead, you provide mutator methods that can, for example, do validation checking. Enforcing encapsulation is extra work, but it does make the code easier to read and there is no guessing about which error numbers are being used.*

Key-Item Pairs

Sometimes your application needs to create and later access pairs of strings. The Dictionary object, which is included with the Microsoft Scripting Library that is installed with Internet Explorer, is designed for quick access to such key-item pairs. To use the Dictionary object, you have to reference the Microsoft Scripting Library in your project.

> *NOTE*
> *In other languages, such as Perl, Dictionaries are known as associative arrays.*

The Dictionary object enables you to add an entry that has two parts:

1. Key—an alphanumeric string that identifies the entry. This could be a database primary key or other unique identifier.
2. Item—the string associated with the key.

The important thing is that the key must be unique within the Dictionary. If you attempt to add a second entry with the same key, you'll get this error message:

457: This key is already associated with an element of this collection.

For best results, use a value known to be unique, such as an AutoNumber/sequence value or a unique identifier field value from Structured Query Language (SQL) Server. The main advantage of a Dictionary over a Collection is that you can get at the key associated with an item or even an array of all the keys. For example, here's a modified version of the parsing example from Chapter 2 that lets you get at the various field names via code:

```
Dim Stuff As Dictionary, I as Integer
Set Stuff = ExtractFields2("lastname=marquis&firstname=henry&middle=a")
For I = LBound(Stuff.Keys) To UBound(Stuff.Keys)
    'work with Stuff.Keys(I)=field name
Next
```

Here's the modified version of the ExtractFields example from Chapter 2:

```
Public Function ExtractFields2(ByVal Work As String) As Dictionary
    Dim i As Long
    Dim fields() As String
    Dim data() As String
    Dim result As New Dictionary
    fields = Split(Work, "&")
    For i = 0 To UBound(fields)
        data = Split(fields(i), "=")
        ' save field name
        result.Add data(0), data(1)
    Next
    Set ExtractFields2 = result
End Function
```

Here's a quick ADO-based example that loads a Dictionary object with data from a database table in the Northwind Traders sample database that comes with Visual Basic:

```
Sub Main()
    Dim dcnDB As New ADODB.Connection
    Dim rsData As New ADODB.Recordset
    Dim objDict As New Scripting.Dictionary

    dcnDB.ConnectionString = "Provider=Microsoft.Jet.OLEDB.3.51;" _
        & "Persist Security Info=False;" _
        & "Data Source=C:\Visual Studio\VB98\NWind.mdb"
    dcnDB.Open
    rsData.Open "SELECT CustomerID, " _
        & "CompanyName FROM Customers", dcnDB, adOpenStatic, adLockReadOnly
    Do Until rsData.EOF
        objDict.Add rsData("CustomerID"), rsData("CompanyName")
        rsData.MoveNext
    Loop
    rsData.Close
    dcnDB.Close
End Sub
```

The Add method of the Dictionary object enables you to add a new key and value pair to the Dictionary. After looping through all the records, the Dictionary object has all the customer IDs and company names available for later use.

This code looks pretty straightforward; however, the Add method seems to have a bug in it. After adding the first record from the standard table (key value 'ALFKI'), the next record is key value 'ANATR'. While these two values are obviously different, VB generates an error message indicating that the values are the same. Thinking that it might have something to do with this particular key, we moved to the next record to see if it would be added. The key value, in this case, was 'ANTON', and it wouldn't add either.

Seems like a bit of a problem, doesn't it? The Dictionary object doesn't seem to be working the way it is advertised to work. We did find a workaround to this problem, however. When you are performing the Add method, change the code to the following:

```
objDict.Add "Item" & rsData("CustomerID"), rsData("CompanyName")
```

Modifying this code enables you to add all the records without any further errors!

Even after you have resolved the Dictionary object problem, this question remains: How well does this object work? To find out, we're going to use the GetTickCount WinAPI function to check before and after a retrieval in both the Dictionary object and the recordset (using FindFirst) to determine which is faster. To try this out, add this code after the Loop keyword:

```
Option Explicit
Private Declare Function GetTickCount Lib "kernel32" () As Long

Sub Main()
    Dim dcnDB As New ADODB.Connection
    Dim rsData As New ADODB.Recordset
    Dim objDict As New Scripting.Dictionary
    Dim lngStartCount As Long
    Dim lngEndCount As Long

    dcnDB.ConnectionString = "Provider=Microsoft.Jet.OLEDB.3.51;" _
        & "Persist Security Info=False;" _
            & "Data Source=C:\Program Files\" _
                & "Microsoft Visual Studio\VB98\NWind.mdb"
    dcnDB.Open

    rsData.Open "SELECT CustomerID, " _
        & "CompanyName FROM Customers", dcnDB, adOpenStatic, adLockReadOnly

    Do Until rsData.EOF
            objDict.Add "ITEM" & rsData("CustomerID"), rsData("CompanyName")
        rsData.MoveNext
    Loop

    lngStartCount = GetTickCount()
    Debug.Print objDict("ItemALFKI")
    lngEndCount = GetTickCount()

    MsgBox "Dictionary search: " & lngEndCount - lngStartCount & " ms"

    lngStartCount = GetTickCount()
```

```
    rsData.MoveFirst
    rsData.Find "CustomerID = 'LILAS'"
    Debug.Print rsData("CompanyName")
    lngEndCount = GetTickCount()

    MsgBox "Recordset search: " & lngEndCount - lngStartCount & " ms"

    rsData.Close
    dcnDB.Close
End Sub
And got no error

    lngStartCount = GetTickCount()
    Debug.Print objDict("ItemALFKI")
    lngEndCount = GetTickCount()

    MsgBox "Dictionary search: " & lngEndCount - lngStartCount & " ms"

    lngStartCount = GetTickCount()
    rsData.MoveFirst
    rsData.Find "CustomerID = 'LILAS'"
    Debug.Print rsData("CompanyName")
    lngEndCount = GetTickCount()

    MsgBox "Recordset search: " & lngEndCount - lngStartCount & " ms"

    rsData.Close
    dcnDB.Close
```

The GetTickCount WinAPI function is declared as follows:

```
Public Declare Function GetTickCount Lib "kernel32" () As Long
```

Be sure to declare the lngStartCount and lngEndCount variables at the top of the page. When you run this code, both the Dictionary object and the recordset are queried for a record in the middle of the customer table. You'll get message boxes indicating how many milliseconds elapsed for the searches. What you should see is that searching a recordset is quite fast. On a Pentium II 400MHz with 256MB RAM, we saw a time of 20 milliseconds to search the 100 records. The Dictionary object ran quicker; however, there are three drawbacks to using it:

1. You have to load it from the database recordset that you've already created.
2. You may have to handle the error we found earlier by adding key values.
3. You only get one field for your data, CompanyName. The recordset has all the fields available.

In short, the Dictionary object isn't a great solution because of the problems we've uncovered. It's much easier to just use the recordset object, which can be disconnected from the database.

Hashing

While most databases can quickly retrieve information based on criteria you specify, it's often helpful to keep a local cache of frequently used data. However, having to search through an entire set of data to find the record you're looking for is time consuming and will, on average, require to you search half the records each time you need data.

Instead of this, we can use a process called *hashing*. First, we create a data structure called a hash table. A *hash table* uses a formula to convert a piece of text to a number. That number is then keyed to an array that has a list of all the items that match that hash value. Each one of the hash values is called a *bucket*. You can have any number of buckets, but if you have too few buckets, you will search too many elements to find the one you're looking for. Too many buckets means that you're wasting storage space.

There are two methods commonly used for hashing:

- *Open hashing* provides a list of buckets that are linked to the elements matching the bucket's hash value. This method gives you an unlimited number of spaces for text elements.
- *Closed hashing* stores all the elements in an array. If you collide with another string that is already in the bucket when hashing your text, you move ahead in the array until you find an open space. This method provides a limited number of spaces for elements and you have to deal with rehashing if elements are removed or you fill the array.

We're going to create a scheme for open hashing using the sample Biblio database located in your Visual Basic installation directory, but you can adapt the code here to create your own closed hashing scheme. The Titles table has over 8000 rows, which is a good sample size to learn how quickly the hash table can find data.

Creating the Data Structures Needed for Hashing

The first data structure we need is an object to hold a hashed record. This object will be small and will only hold the primary key for the record, which will minimize the amount of space that is required to hold all the elements in memory in the hash table. This object will also have a reference to the next object in the same bucket, which will let us create a *linked list*. The first element, or *head* of the list, points to the next element. You can then traverse the list by moving through each of the objects until you hit an empty reference (Nothing in VB).

The object, which we'll call TitleNode, is fairly simple (cutting down the memory requirements) and is shown here:

```
Option Explicit

Private m_strISBN As String
Private m_strTitle As String
Private m_objNextNode As TitleNode

Public Property Set NextNode(ByVal vData As TitleNode)
    Set m_objNextNode = vData
End Property

Public Property Get NextNode() As TitleNode
    Set NextNode = m_objNextNode
End Property

Public Property Let ISBN(ByVal vData As String)
    m_strISBN = vData
End Property

Public Property Get ISBN() As String
    ISBN = m_strISBN
End Property

Public Property Let Title(ByVal vData As String)
    m_strTitle = vData
End Property

Public Property Get Title() As String
    Title = m_strTitle
End Property
```

The other data structure we need is the hash table. In this case, the hash table is simply an array to hold each of the buckets. The trick is to determine how many buckets are needed. The hash value is created by adding the ASCII values of the book title together, and then using the Mod function to get the remainder when the total is divided by the number of buckets. For example, assume that the ASCII total of a title is 520 and we had decided to create 400 buckets. The hash value for this title is 120.

Using the sample value of 400 buckets means that there will be an average of 21 elements per bucket. To find a particular element, the code:

1. Determines the hash value of the title.
2. Looks at the first object in the array with that hash value.
3. If the object doesn't match, goes to the object stored in NextNode. Repeats until the element is found or there are no more elements for that bucket.

On average, you will have to look at half of the elements in each bucket. So to find an element in a 400-bucket array, requires 12 operations: 1 to get the hash value, and 11 to find the element in the bucket. Considering that you're looking through more than 8000 records, that's not bad. You can increase the number of buckets to 8000, for example, thereby reducing the number of operations needed to find the element to 2. However, you will then require that much more storage space. In our case, we're using an array of objects. The only space we need is for the object reference in the array, which will only be used if we have an element in the bucket.

For this next example, we'll use 501 buckets so that we see some buckets with more than one element in them. The declaration you need in your code (either a module or a form) is this:

```
Private m_arrHashTable(0 To 500) As TitleNode
Const BUCKETS = 501
```

Hashing the Data

The next step is to actually load the table with the database data. The code to do this is shown in the following CreateHashTable subroutine:

```
Sub CreateHashTable()
    Dim dcnDB As New ADODB.Connection
    Dim rsData As ADODB.Recordset
    Dim objNewNode As TitleNode
    Dim objTraverse As TitleNode
    Dim intHashValue As Integer

    dcnDB.ConnectionString = _"Provider=Microsoft.Jet.OLEDB.3.51;" _
        & "Persist Security Info=False;" _
            & "Data Source=C:\Program Files\" _
                & "Microsoft Visual Studio\VB98\NWind.mdb"
    dcnDB.Open
    Set rsData = dcnDB.Execute("SELECT Title, ISBN FROM Titles")
    Do While Not rsData.EOF
        intHashValue = GetHashValue(rsData("Title"))
        Set objNewNode = New TitleNode
        objNewNode.ISBN = rsData("ISBN")
        objNewNode.Title = rsData("Title")
        If m_arrHashTable(intHashValue) Is Nothing Then
            Set m_arrHashTable(intHashValue) = objNewNode
        Else
            Set objTraverse = m_arrHashTable(intHashValue)
            Do Until objTraverse.NextNode Is Nothing
                Set objTraverse = objTraverse.NextNode
            Loop
            Set objTraverse.NextNode = objNewNode
```

```
        End If
        rsData.MoveNext
    Loop
    rsData.Close
    dcnDB.Close

End Sub
```

We first make a connection to the Biblio database (be sure to change the path to your local copy if you don't use the default install for Visual Basic) and retrieve the ISBN and Title fields from the Titles table. For each record, we create a new TitleNode and populate the values for the object. We then determine the hash value of the title using the GetHashValue function.

```
Function GetHashValue(strInput As String) As Integer
    Dim i As Integer
    Dim lngSum As Long

    For i = 1 To Len(strInput)
        lngSum = lngSum + Asc(Mid(strInput, i, 1))
    Next i
    GetHashValue = lngSum Mod BUCKETS

End Function
```

The GetHashValue function could have been included in the TitleNode object, but that would take extra memory. If you have memory to spare, you could easily put this function in the object.

Based on the hash value, we check the hash table. If the array cell is empty, we store the new node in that cell. If the array cell isn't empty, we traverse the list until we find an empty NextNode, which means we found the end of the list. The new node is stored there, and we move on to the next record.

Because there are so many records, this routine does take a little while to run. However, you only have to do it once, when the application starts. At that point, the relevant fields are stored in memory and you can drop your database connection.

To see how the table did for distributing the records evenly, you can add this simple subroutine to count the buckets:

```
Sub CountBuckets()
    Dim i As Integer
    Dim iNodes As Integer
    Dim intMax As Integer
    Dim intMin As Integer

    intMax = 0
```

```
        intMin = 10000
        Dim objTraverse As TitleNode

    For i = O To BUCKETS - 1
        iNodes = 0
        Set objTraverse = m_arrHashTable(i)
        Do Until objTraverse Is Nothing
            Set objTraverse = objTraverse.NextNode
            iNodes = iNodes + 1
        Loop
        Debug.Print "Bucket #" & i & ": " & iNodes & " nodes"
        If iNodes < intMin Then
            intMin = iNodes
        End If

        If iNodes > intMax Then
            intMax = iNodes
        End If

    Next i
    Debug.Print "Minimum # of nodes: " & intMin
    Debug.Print "Maximum # of nodes: " & intMax
End Sub
```

You'll get a listing of how the titles were distributed among the 501 buckets in the table. When we ran this routine, we received a minimum number of 4 and a maximum of 29. The average was 21, which is just what we wanted. You can generate all the statistics you want on the buckets using routines similar to CountBuckets. However, let's learn to search the hash table.

Searching the Hash Table

Now that the table is built, it's time to put it to use. We're going to prompt for a title and then look for it in the hash table. We'll keep count of how many operations we need to find the title. Here is the code to find a particular title:

```
Function FindTitle(strTitle As String) As String
    Dim intHashValue As Integer
    Dim objTraverse As TitleNode
    Dim intOperations As Integer

    intOperations = 1
    intHashValue = GetHashValue(strTitle)
    Set objTraverse = m_arrHashTable(intHashValue)
    If objTraverse Is Nothing Then
        MsgBox "Title not found."
    Else
```

```
        Do Until strTitle = objTraverse.Title Or _
            objTraverse.NextNode Is Nothing
            Set objTraverse = objTraverse.NextNode
            intOperations = intOperations + 1
        Loop

        If strTitle = objTraverse.Title Then
            MsgBox "Title's ISBN is " & objTraverse.ISBN
        Else
            MsgBox "Title not found."
        End If
    End If
    MsgBox "Total operations: " & intOperations

End Function
```

To call the FindTitle function, you can use this line of code:

```
MsgBox FindTitle(InputBox("Enter title"))
```

The trick is to enter the title exactly. A short title we found was
Inside Smalltalk. When running this through the routine, it had to perform 15
operations to find the title. That's pretty good considering there are over 8000
records in the hash table. The only bad thing is that it can't match partial titles
because of the way the hash key is created. In addition, the hash key doesn't
consider that the user might enter lowercase or uppercase letters. A good
improvement would be to modify the hash key creation routine to look like
the following:

```
Function GetHashValue(strInput As String) As Integer
    Dim i As Integer
    Dim lngSum As Long

    For i = 1 To Len(strInput)
        lngSum = lngSum + Asc(UCase(Mid(strInput, i, 1)))
    Next i
    GetHashValue = lngSum Mod BUCKETS

End Function
```

Adding the UCase function will cause the routine to add the uppercase letter
values. You can then compare the uppercased titles in the FindTitle routine, as
shown here:

```
Function FindTitle(strTitle As String) As String
    Dim intHashValue As Integer
```

```
        Dim objTraverse As TitleNode
        Dim intOperations As Integer

        intOperations = 1
        intHashValue = GetHashValue(strTitle)
        Set objTraverse = m_arrHashTable(intHashValue)
        If objTraverse Is Nothing Then
            MsgBox "Title not found."
        Else
            Do Until UCase(strTitle) = UCase(objTraverse.Title) Or _
                objTraverse.NextNode Is Nothing
                Set objTraverse = objTraverse.NextNode
                intOperations = intOperations + 1
            Loop

            If UCase(strTitle) = UCase(objTraverse.Title) Then
                MsgBox "Title's ISBN is " & objTraverse.ISBN
            Else
                MsgBox "Title not found."
            End If
        End If
        MsgBox "Total operations: " & intOperations

End Function
FindTitle InputBox("Enter title")
```

Testing the Hashing Solution

Now that the hash table is built and we can retrieve data from it, let's see how
retrieval from the hash table stacks up against just looking in the recordset
using a Find command. To make life easier, we'll create the database
connection and recordset in Sub Main and pass it to the CreateHashTable
routine. That way we eliminate duplicate code in the test. Modify the Sub Main
and CreateHashTable routines as follows to test the code:

```
Private Declare Function GetTickCount Lib "kernel32" () As Long

Sub Main()
    Dim dcnDB As New ADODB.Connection
    Dim rsData As New ADODB.Recordset
    Dim lngStartCount As Long
    Dim lngEndCount As Long
    Dim strTitle As String

    dcnDB.ConnectionString = _"Provider=Microsoft.Jet.OLEDB.3.51;" _
        & "Persist Security Info=False;" _
            & "Data Source=C:\Program Files\" _
```

```
                & "Microsoft Visual Studio\VB98\NWind.mdb"
    dcnDB.Open
    rsData.Open "SELECT Title, ISBN FROM Titles", _
        dcnDB, adOpenStatic, adLockReadOnly

    lngStartCount = GetTickCount()
    CreateHashTable rsData
    lngEndCount = GetTickCount()
    Debug.Print "*** Time to create Hash table: " _
        & lngEndCount - lngStartCount & " ms"

    'CountBuckets

    strTitle = InputBox("Enter title")

    lngStartCount = GetTickCount()
    FindTitle strTitle
    lngEndCount = GetTickCount()
    Debug.Print "*** Time to find item in hash table: " _
        & lngEndCount - lngStartCount & " ms"

    lngStartCount = GetTickCount()
    rsData.MoveFirst
    rsData.Find "Title = '" & strTitle & "'"
    Debug.Print rsData("ISBN")
    lngEndCount = GetTickCount()
    Debug.Print "*** Time to find item in recordset: " _
        & lngEndCount - lngStartCount & " ms"

    rsData.Close
    dcnDB.Close

End Sub

Sub CreateHashTable(rsData As ADODB.Recordset)
    Dim objNewNode As TitleNode
    Dim objTraverse As TitleNode
    Dim intHashValue As Integer

    Do While Not rsData.EOF
        intHashValue = GetHashValue(rsData("Title"))
        Set objNewNode = New TitleNode
        objNewNode.ISBN = rsData("ISBN")
        objNewNode.Title = rsData("Title")
        If m_arrHashTable(intHashValue) Is Nothing Then
            Set m_arrHashTable(intHashValue) = objNewNode
        Else
```

```
            Set objTraverse = m_arrHashTable(intHashValue)
            Do Until objTraverse.NextNode Is Nothing
                Set objTraverse = objTraverse.NextNode
            Loop
            Set objTraverse.NextNode = objNewNode
        End If
        rsData.MoveNext
    Loop

End Sub
```

In addition, change the MsgBox calls in the code (except for those in Sub Main) to Debug.Print statements instead. If you don't, the GetTickCount routine will count the time while the message box is being displayed; this will cause the number to be inaccurate.

We ran this code on a Pentium II 400MHz with 256MB of RAM on Windows 98, and looked for 'Mastering Turbo Debugger,' which is in the middle of the database table. Here's what our results were:

```
*** Time to create Hash table: 4320 ms
*** Time to find item in hash table: 7 ms
*** Time to find item in recordset: 251 ms
```

Based on where the element is in the recordset, the time to find it will change. For instance, the book *Zen of Code Optimization/Book and Disk* is near the end of the table. The results for that search were:

```
*** Time to create Hash table: 4320 ms
*** Time to find item in hash table: 3 ms
*** Time to find item in recordset: 524 ms
```

While these results look excellent, there are several downsides to the hash table:

- It only works for complete searches. For instance, we had to enter the title words exactly for the hash value to come up correctly.
- There is a significant amount of time required to build the table. The Titles table had about 8000 records and it took about 4000 seconds to build the hash table.
- We only get one value back from the hash table search: the ISBN number. If we wanted additional fields, we'd have to change the TitleNode object to accommodate them.
- Any changes to the underlying table means that the hash table will need to be, at least partially, rebuilt. Depending on how you know changes are being made, you may have to rebuild the entire table.

If you work within the restrictions, the hash table can be a helpful tool for fast searches of relatively static data.

Chapter 6

Windows Files, Directories, and Drives

File locations, drive space, finding files, determining whether files exist—these are very common chores. Windows has powerful file-, directory-, and drive-manipulation capabilities that can make your life much easier...if you know how to use them.

Files, Directories, and Drives

Windows applications need to be stored on some form of media, and your applications will need to read and write information to and from some form of media as well. Visual Basic has many options for reading and writing files, but many of these assume that you already know the location of the file. For example, you must pass a path and file name to the Visual Basic Open statement to open a disk file. Now, suppose that you want to open a data file in the Windows directory?

In Windows 95 and 98, the default Windows directory is named Windows. However, when installing Windows, you can give this directory any name you want. In Windows NT, the default Windows directory is named WINNT; it, too, can have any name. It should be obvious that you cannot assume that the Windows system directory will be named C:\Windows\System, which raises this question: How does one reliably determine the name of the Windows system directory? Another point to consider is this: Suppose the default system drive is not the C drive. How can you determine the drive letter of the system drive? Or how can you find out how many drives are installed, and what type they are?

These and other similar questions are not answered directly by Visual Basic, but rather indirectly through the Windows Application Programming Interface (WinAPI). (You can use the new Microsoft Scripting library, which can be downloaded from Microsoft's Web site and is part of Windows 2000, but this is not as flexible as using the API.) This chapter shows you how to use the WinAPI to tap into this "secret" information about the PC that you'll need to retrieve in many of your programs.

> *NOTE*
> The WinAPI is well documented through a number of sources, including the
> Microsoft Platform SDK and Dan Appleman's Visual Basic Programmers Guide to
> the Win32 API. You can find VB declarations for many API functions in the API
> Declarations viewer that comes with Visual Basic.

Windows Application Programming Interface

Windows programs, and the Windows operating system itself, are built on a
series of Dynamic Link Libraries (DLLs) and, in some cases, executable
programs (EXEs) that contain common system functions—a sort of standardized
infrastructure. These system functions enable Windows to start, load programs,
and run applications, among other tasks. The DLLs and EXEs that compose the
infrastructure of Windows *expose* a set of functions that can be called both by
the system and applications. These exposed functions make up the WinAPI.

The WinAPI provides access to system resources such as disk drives,
keyboards, video, sound, and other computer hardware. The WinAPI also
provides a rich source of detailed information about the configuration of the
hardware. While the WinAPI is not built into Visual Basic, you can access the
WinAPI from Visual Basic using the Declare statement.

To access the WinAPI, you *declare* the WinAPI function and the DLL that
contains the function in the Declarations Section of a module (such as class or
form). Once declared, you can use the WinAPI function almost like a standard
Visual Basic function, with three important exceptions:

1. Many WinAPI functions take a string argument that must be preset to
   the size of the string it will return. Failure to presize this string can
   result in a system crash. (In fact, any failure to use the WinAPI properly
   can lead to a system crash.)
2. Many WinAPI functions that return a string do so with a trailing null
   character appended to the end of the string. This null character, and
   any subsequent characters, must be removed before the string is used
   in your program.
3. In most cases, you should wrap the required WinAPI function into your
   own Visual Basic function or class member to be sure that all string
   setup, argument parsing, and return-result handling is implemented in a
   standard fashion. Strive to implement stable, reusable wrappers to your
   WinAPI functions that mimic Visual Basic in implementation and style,
   so that they will be easy for you and others to use. You'll find another
   plus to this technique: Wrappers enable you to use Visual Basic's
   higher-level built-in functions and data types (such as Date), which
   make working with the lower-level WinAPI functions easier.

Using the WinAPI takes a little getting used to, but once you have discovered
the power just under the hood of Visual Basic, you will never go back! Now, let's
get some information that is not readily available from Visual Basic.

Files

Visual Basic has built-in functions that let you manipulate files. However, there are several common tasks for which Visual Basic does not provide, and there are other tasks that are more reliably implemented using the WinAPI. One excellent example of how the Windows API can provide functionality not found directly in Visual Basic is determining whether a file exists.

File Existence

It is very common to want to determine whether a file already exists. The Visual Basic Dir function can be used to check for a file. However, we have found it unreliable. We have also found that a lot of code has to be written to handle all the errors and conditions that the multipurpose Dir function can generate.

For example, consider the following code:

```
Dim a$
Print Dir$(a$)  ' print a file even though a$ is empty
```

An empty string makes Dir$ return the first file it "finds." Worse, passing a string with invalid characters throws an error.

```
Print Dir$("1:\\\junk.junk")    ' throws error 53
```

A much simpler technique, which is foolproof and error free, is to use a WinAPI call designed specifically to check for file existence! Well, perhaps not solely for checking whether a file exists, but it is designed for this purpose. We are referring to the OpenFile WinAPI. Who would expect a WinAPI named OpenFile to also check for a file's existence? Well, this is where a good WinAPI reference comes in. The OpenFile function is designed to check for the presence of a file before attempting to open a file. Here is the declaration for the WinAPI OpenFile, exported from Kernel32.exe by the Windows operating system function:

```
Private Declare Function OpenFile Lib "kernel32" ( _
    ByVal FileName As String, _
    OpenBuff As OFSTRUCT, _
    ByVal Style As Long) As Long
```

OpenFile takes three arguments: a filename (with path) to open or determine the existence of a file; a user-defined type that will be loaded with information about the file; and a constant expression indicating what action to take. OpenFile then performs the action indicated by the Style argument on the file indicated by the FileName argument, and returns the results in the structure specified by the OpenBuff argument.

You can open files and create files using OpenFile; however, that is also easily done using Visual Basic. We find that this is most useful in checking for file existence. Here's how to use the OpenFile function to determine a file's existence. First, you need to create a user-defined type as follows:

```
Private Type OFSTRUCT
    Bytes As Byte
    FixedDisk As Byte
    ErrCode As Integer
    Reserved1 As Integer
    Reserved2 As Integer
    PathName(260) As Byte
End Type
```

Then, you use the OpenFile function as shown in Listing 6-1, using the OF_EXIST Style.

```
Public Function FileExist(ByVal FileName As String) _
As Boolean

    Dim typOfStruct As OFSTRUCT
    Const OF_EXIST = 16384

    If Len(FileName) > 0 Then
        OpenFile FileName, typOfStruct, OF_EXIST
        FileExist = typOfStruct.ErrCode <> 2
    End If

End Function
```

Listing 6-1: OpenFile reliably determines whether a file exists

FileExist always works, even in the face of filenames that would make the Visual Basic Dir function throw an error. The way FileExist works is simple: It asks the OpenFile WinAPI to check for a file's existence without opening the file. The OpenFile function sets the ErrCode member of the OFSTRUCT user-defined type to a value of 2 if the file is present.

Finding a File

Closely related to checking for a file's existence is learning where a particular file is stored. The SearchPath function searches for a specified filename, and returns the full path to the file, if the filename is found. However, SearchPath is not foolproof because it searches only certain directories:

1. First, the directory from which the application is running is searched; then
2. the current (default) directory is searched; then
3. the Windows system directory is searched; then
4. the Windows directory is searched; and, finally,
5. the directories in the PATH environment variable are searched.

Here is the declaration for the SearchPath function, as exported by the Windows operating system from Kernel32.exe. This declaration is used to tell Visual Basic about the function, where to locate it, and what arguments it takes.

```
Private Declare Function SearchPath Lib "kernel32" _
    Alias "SearchPathA" ( _
    ByVal Path As String, _
    ByVal FileName As String, _
    ByVal Extension As String, _
    ByVal BufferLength As Long, _
    ByVal Buffer As String, _
    ByVal FilePart As String) As Long
```

The sample function in Listing 6-2 takes just a filename, for example, autoexec.bat or win.ini. Then, if it finds a file with that name in one of the places enumerated above, it returns the full path of the file; for example, c:\autoexec.bat or c:\windows\win.ini.

```
Public Function FindFile(ByVal FileName As String) _
As String

    Dim Buffer As String
    Dim j
    Dim FilePart As String
    Dim Path As String
    Dim Extension As String

    Buffer = Space$(260)
    SearchPath Path, FileName, Extension, _
    Len(Buffer), Buffer, FilePart

    j = InStr(Buffer, Chr$(0))
    If j > 0 Then FindFile = Left$(Buffer, j - 1)

End Function
```

Listing 6-2: FindFile searches for and returns the full path of a file

Getting a Unique Temporary Filename

How many times have you needed to create a temporary work file for one of your programs? If you are like us, probably all the time. The problem is how do you create a known temporary file without possibly overwriting another file? Once again, WinAPI has the answer. This time it's in the form of the GetTempFileName function.

```
Private Declare Function GetTempFileName Lib "kernel32" _
    Alias "GetTempFileNameA" ( _
    ByVal Path As String, _
    ByVal PrefixString As String, _
    ByVal Unique As Long, _
    ByVal TempFileName As String) As Long
```

GetTempFileName returns a unique filename based in part on the system timer, with an extension of .tmp. There are three arguments to GetTempFileName that control how it works. First, the Path argument. GetTempFileName returns the unique filename appended to the path specified in the Path argument. For example, if you pass C:\Temp to GetTempFileName, it might return C:\Temp\5045.tmp. Second, the PrefixString argument. You cannot avoid getting a filename back because that is the purpose of GetTempFileName; however, you can control to some degree the format of the name GetTempFileName returns. If you pass a string in PrefixString, the first three characters in that string are prepended to the start of the unique filename. Finally, the Unique argument. When Unique is zero, GetTempFileName ensures that the name returned does not already exist in the directory indicated by the Path argument. In this way, you avoid overwriting a temporary file that you've previously created. If you don't care whether filenames were previously used, then you can set the Unique argument to a nonzero value. This is handy when you create a lot of temporary files and do not delete them when you are done with them. When Unique is nonzero, it sets the numeric portion of the filename, but it does not verify that the resulting filename is unique. Taken together, you can create a unique filename generator as shown in Listing 6-3:

```
Function TempFileName(Path As String) As String

    Dim tmp As String
    Dim j As Long

    tmp = Space$(128)
    GetTempFileName Path, "~", 0, tmp

    j = InStr(tmp, Chr$(0))
    If j > 0 Then TempFileName = Left$(tmp, j - 1)
End Function
```

Listing 6-3: TempFileName returns a unique filename

The TempFileName function returns a filename with a tilde (~) prepended. Because the Unique parameter to the GetTempFileName WinAPI function is zero, it also creates an empty file with the new unique temporary filename in the path indicated by the Path argument.

> ### NOTE
> *Do not pass a path with a closing forward slash because GetTempFileName provides one automatically.*

NEXT STEPS

Combine TempFileName with the equivalent directory function to return a temporary file in the temporary directory. (Hint, see the section in this chapter on Windows directories.)

Changing a File's Date and Time Stamp

Windows stores the date and time a file was last changed along with the directory information for the file. Visual Basic has no built-in method for changing this date and time stamp, but you can read and write it via the WinAPI.

First, you need to understand a bit about how Windows thinks about time. The Windows system time includes both the date and the time. More importantly, Windows runs on Greenwich Mean Time. Windows adjusts the time it displays based on your time zone preferences settings. Why is this important? Because the WinAPI functions that let you read and write a file's date and time stamp use raw time information that is not adjusted for your time zone preferences.

The WinAPI functions you will need are GetFileTime and SetFileTime.

```
Private Declare Function GetFileTime Lib "kernel32" _
(ByVal hFile As Long, lpCreationTime As FileTime, _
lpLastAccessTime As FileTime, _
lpLastWriteTime As FileTime) As Long
Private Declare Function SetFileTime Lib "kernel32" _
(ByVal hFile As Long, lpCreationTime As FileTime, _
lpLastAccessTime As FileTime, _
lpLastWriteTime As FileTime) As Long
```

The trick to using these functions is to realize that you must open the file before you can access the file's time information. Windows NT and Windows 2000 require you to have Read access rights for GetFileTime and Write access rights for SetFileTime. The following code uses the WinAPI open and close methods (lOpen and lClose) because beginning with Visual Basic 5.0, Microsoft removed an important backward compatibility feature from Visual Basic: the Open and Close statements do not return file handles that can be used with WinAPI calls.

The API open and close functions are named _lOpen and _lClose, which are declared as follows:

```
Private Declare Function apiOpen Lib "kernel32" _
Alias "_lopen" (ByVal lpPathName As String, _
ByVal iReadWrite As Long) As Long

Private Declare Function apiClose Lib "kernel32" _
Alias "_lclose" (ByVal hFile As Long) As Long
```

Because _lOpen and _lClose are not valid Visual Basic names—they start with a subscore (the "_" character)—we use the Visual Basic Alias keyword to select a name compatible with Visual Basic. In the above declarations, apiOpen and apiClose are the call names for _lOpen and _lClose.

The FileTime structure contains two long variables that together form a 64-bit number that contains the number of 100 nanosecond intervals since January 1st, 1601.

```
Type FileTime
        dwLowDateTime As Long
        dwHighDateTime As Long
End Type
```

This is an awkward value for people to use, so Windows also defines a SystemTime structure that describes the date and time in a way that is easy for people to understand. Windows also has functions called FileTimeToSystemTime and SystemTimeToFileTime that convert between FileTime dates and SystemTime dates. The SystemTime structure, FileTimeToSystemTime and SystemTimeToFileTime functions, are shown below:

```
Type SystemTime
        Year As Integer
        Month As Integer
        DayOfWeek As Integer
        Day As Integer
        Hour As Integer
        Minute As Integer
        Second As Integer
        Milliseconds As Integer
End Type

Private Declare Function FileTimeToSystemTime _
Lib "kernel32" (lpFileTime As FileTime, _
lpSystemTime As SystemTime) As Long

Private Declare Function SystemTimeToFileTime _
```

```
Lib "kernel32" (lpSystemTime As SystemTime, _
lpFileTime As FileTime) As Long
```

The process is to open the file, read the file time information, convert the resulting FileTime value to a SystemTime structure, and then parse it to a Date variable.

> *NOTE*
> *The Date data type includes both date and time information.*

```
Public Function GetFileDate(ByVal FileName As String) _
As Date

    On Error Resume Next

    Dim hFile As Long
    Dim TYP_SystemTime As SystemTime
    Dim TYP_CreationTime As FileTime
    Dim TYP_LastAccessTime As FileTime
    Dim TYP_LastWriteTime As FileTime

    Const OF_READWRITE = &H2

    hFile = apiOpen(FileName, OF_READWRITE)
    GetFileTime hFile, TYP_CreationTime, _
            TYP_LastAccessTime, TYP_LastWriteTime

    FileTimeToSystemTime TYP_LastWriteTime, _
        TYP_SystemTime

    GetFileDate = DateSerial(TYP_SystemTime.Year, _
        TYP_SystemTime.Month, _
        TYP_SystemTime.Day) & " " & _
        TimeSerial(TYP_SystemTime.Hour, _
                TYP_SystemTime.Minute, _
                TYP_SystemTime.Second)
    apiClose hFile
End Function
```

Listing 6-4: Function to return the date and time stamp of a file

GetFileDate works by first creating the user-defined types that the WinAPI function calls require. Then the file in question is opened, and it's date and time stamp is read using GetFileTime. FileTimeToSystemTime then converts the result of GetFileTime into a usable time format. Finally, the Visual Basic DateSerial and TimeSerial methods convert the raw time information into a standard Visual Basic Date format.

The next step is to set the file's date and time stamp. The SetFileDate code in Listing 6-5 does just that. It works much like GetFileDate, except in reverse.

```
Public Function SetFileDate(ByVal Filename As String, FileDate As Date)
    On Error Resume Next
    Dim TYP_SystemTime As SystemTime
    Dim TYP_FileTime As FileTime
    Dim TYP_CreationTime As FileTime
    Dim TYP_LastAccessTime As FileTime
    Dim hFile As Long
    Const OF_READWRITE = &H2
    TYP_SystemTime.Year = Year(FileDate)
    TYP_SystemTime.Month = Month(FileDate)
    TYP_SystemTime.Day = Day(FileDate)
    TYP_SystemTime.Hour = Hour(FileDate)
    TYP_SystemTime.Minute = Minute(FileDate)
    TYP_SystemTime.Second = Second(FileDate)

    hFile = lOpen(Filename, OF_READWRITE)
    SystemTimeToFileTime TYP_SystemTime, TYP_FileTime
    SetFileTime hFile, TYP_FileTime, TYP_FileTime, _
        TYP_FileTime
    apiClose hFile
End Function
```

Listing 6-5: SetFileDate sets the date and time stamp of a file

SetFileDate works by creating the FileTime variables that the SetFileTime function requires. The date and time information is assigned to the members of a SystemTime structure. The SystemTimeToFileTime WinAPI function converts the information from a human-readable time format to the required FileTime format, which is what is actually stored in the file structure information on disk. The file in question is opened, and the date and time stamp is written using SetFileTime.

NEXT STEPS

Consider adding code to make up for the shift in time zones; in other words, determine the system's time zone setting and offset the results of GetFileDate accordingly. Here's a hint: look in your API documentation for a function called FileTimeToLocalFileTime.

Retrieving a Short Filename

Windows supports long file and directory names such as z:\my documents\some filename.doc. Windows also maintains a compatible "old-style" filename as well. The z:\my documents\some filename.doc might become c:\mydocu~1\somefi~1.doc. Some older programs cannot work with long filenames, others create short filenames, called aliases. There are many occasions when you will want to determine the short filename (alias) for a long filename.

The GetShortPathNameWinAPI function does this for you automatically.

```
Declare Function GetShortPathName Lib "kernel32" Alias _
        "GetShortPathNameA" (ByVal LongPath As String, _
        ByVal ShortPath As String, _
        ByVal LongPathSize As Long) As Long
```

To retrieve the alias to a long filename, write a wrapper around GetShortPathName, as shown in Listing 6-6:

```
Public Function ShortFilename(ByVal Filename As String)_
        As String
    Dim ShortPath As String
    Dim Size As Long
    ShortPath = Space$(220)
    Size = GetShortPathName(Filename, ShortPath, _
            Len(ShortPath))
    ShortFilename = Left$(ShortPath, Size)
End Function
```

Listing 6-6: ShortFilename returns the short filename alias of a long filename

ShortFilename works by first calling the GetShortPathName WinAPI function. The alias, with a null (Chr$(0)) terminator, is returned in ShortPath. To trim the ShortPath string to proper size, the filename size (returned by GetShortPathName) is used.

NEXT STEPS

Create a function to convert a path, with or without a filename, to its alias. Try to create a function for converting from short filenames to long filenames. (Hint: use the FindFirstFile WinAPI function.)

Recycling Instead of Deleting

Users are somewhat spoiled because when they delete a file, they expect to be able to restore it from the Recycle Bin. Unfortunately, the Visual Basic Kill method permanently deletes a file, and does not move it to the Recycle Bin.

The WinAPI function SHFileOperation lets you move files to the Recycle Bin, with optional prompting for confirmation.

```
Private Declare Function SHFileOperation Lib _
    "shell32.dll" Alias _
    "SHFileOperationA" (FileOperation As SHFILEOPSTRUCT) _
    As Long
```

SHFileOperation can perform several operations based on the contents of the SHFILEOPSTRUCT user-defined type, which is defined as follows:

```
Private Type SHFILEOPSTRUCT
        hwnd As Long
        wFunc As Long
        pFrom As String
        pTo As String
        fFlags As Integer
        fAnyOperationsAborted As Long
        hNameMappings As Long
        lpszProgressTitle As String
End Type
```

The Recycle function in Listing 6-7 can move files to the Recycle Bin. The function accepts wildcards to delete multiple files, but only copies files to the Recycle Bin when they are called individually with a complete path and filename.

```
Public Function Recycle(FileName As String) As Boolean
    Dim FileOperation As SHFILEOPSTRUCT
    Const FO_DELETE = &H3
    Const FOF_ALLOWUNDO = &H40
    FileOperation.wFunc = FO_DELETE   'delete a file
    FileOperation.pFrom = FileName    ' file to delete
    FileOperation.Flags = FOF_ALLOWUNDO
    Recycle = SHFileOperation(FileOperation) = 0
End Function
```

Listing 6-7: Recycle either deletes a file or moves it to the Recycle Bin

Recycle works by setting up SHFileOperation to delete files. SHFileOperation uses a user-defined type named SHFILEOPSTRUCT. Recycle sets the filename of the file or files to delete to the pFrom member of the SHFILEOPSTRUCT variable. The function then sets the flags to control the deletion, telling SHFileOperation to confirm the deletion and show a progress bar.

The end result is that instead of deleting files permanently, they are moved to the Recycle Bin, enabling users to recover them.

NEXT STEPS

The SHFileOperation function only recycles files that are specified individually. Try combining the Visual Basic Dir function with the Recycle function to create a function that can recycle multiple files specified by wildcards.

Windows Directories

All versions of Windows have at least three special directories in which Windows stores its own program and data files. These directories can have any name, although Windows 95 and 98 names them by default:

1. \Windows
2. \Windows\System
3. \Windows\Temp

Often, you will want to store information in the Windows directory, or you will need to create a temporary file. As you'll soon see, it's easy to determine the name of these directories by using the WinAPI.

Windows System Directory

The Windows System directory holds files used by all Windows applications, including Windows itself. These files include fonts, DLLs, and controls.

> *NOTE*
> *Windows may write protect the System directory. You should use the Windows directory unless you really need to store something in the System directory..*

To determine the path name of the Windows System directory, the WinAPI has a function called GetSystemDirectory. GetSystemDirectory returns a string containing the Windows System path, for example, c:\windows\system or c:\winnt\system32. The function is declared as follows:

```
Declare Function GetSystemDirectory Lib "kernel32" _
Alias "GetSystemDirectoryA" (ByVal lpBuffer As String, _
ByVal nSize As Long) As Long
```

After the WinAPI function is declared, you can write code to use it from your Visual Basic code, as shown in Listing 6-8:

```
' this const goes in the declaration section
' of the  module
Private Const MAX_PATH = 260
Public Function GetSystemDir() As String
    Dim tmp As String
    Dim result As Long
    tmp = Space$(MAX_PATH)
```

```
    result = GetSystemDirectory(tmp, MAX_PATH)
    If result > 0 then _
        GetSystemDir = Left$(tmp, result)
End Function
```

Listing 6-8: GetSystemDirectory returns the path of the Windows System directory

The GetSystemDir function in Listing 6-8 requires a little explanation. First, the GetSystemDirectory WinAPI function takes two arguments: a string (to return the path in) and a long integer (to indicate the length of the string). This is an excellent example of how to use a WinAPI function. You need to define all the variables and presize them in advance, as shown in GetSystemDir.

Unlike many Visual Basic functions, the GetSystemDirectory WinAPI function does not return a string as its result (in fact, WinAPI functions never return strings). Instead, it returns a numeric value indicating the length of the string placed into the tmp argument. If the result of GetSystemDirectory is greater than zero, then the function succeeded and the tmp string variable contains the path.

The last step in using GetSystemDirectory is to strip off the excess spaces and to return just the length of the path.

It seems like a lot of work to use the WinAPI, but the results are well worth the extra effort.

Windows Directory

The Windows directory is where you are supposed to store your private applications files, such as INI files, Help files, and license files. Unlike the Windows System directory, even a shared version of Windows will have its Windows directory write enabled. Just like the Windows System directory, the WinAPI has a function to return the path name of the Windows directory, for example, c:\windows or c:\winnt. This WinAPI function is GetWindowsDirectory:

```
Declare Function GetWindowsDirectory Lib "kernel32" _
    Alias "GetWindowsDirectoryA"(ByVal lpBuffer As String, _
    ByVal nSize As Long) As Long
```

The function in Listing 6-9, named GetWindowsDir, is a wrapper around the GetWindowsDirectory function that returns the path of the Windows directory.

```
' this const goes in the declaration section of the module
Private Const MAX_PATH = 260
Public Function GetWindowsDir() As String
    Dim tmp As String
    Dim result As Long
    tmp = Space$(MAX_PATH)
    result = GetWindowsDirectory (tmp, MAX_PATH)
```

```
    If result > 0 then _
        GetWindowsDir = Left$(tmp, result)
End Function
```

Listing 6-9: GetWindowsDir returns the path of the Windows directory

The GetWindowsDir function works in virtually the same way as the
GetSystemDir function presented earlier.

Temporary File Directory

Windows also provides a place to create temporary files. Temporary files are
those files that your program creates but does not require on subsequent
starts. The GetTempPath WinAPI function returns the path name of the
temporary directory.

```
Private Declare Function GetTempPath Lib "kernel32" _
Alias "GetTempPathA" (ByVal nBufferLength As Long, _
    ByVal lpBuffer As String) As Long
```

GetTempPath uses a particular logic to locating the temporary directory.
First, if Windows has an environment variable named TMP, the path in that
variable is returned. Second, if a TMP environment variable is not found,
GetTempPath checks for an environment variable named TEMP, and returns its
value. Finally, if there are no entries named TMP or TEMP, GetTempPath returns
the currently active directory as set by using ChDir or ChDrive.

The GetTempPath WinAPI function is as easy to use as the previous
directory information WinAPI functions. The function in Listing 6-10,
GetTempDir, uses the GetTempPath WinAPI function to return the path name of
the directory where you can store temporary files.

```
' this const goes in the declaration section of the module
Private Const MAX_PATH = 260
Public Function GetTempDir() As String
    Dim tmp As String
    Dim result As Long
    tmp = Space$(MAX_PATH)
    result = GetTempPath(MAX_PATH, tmp)
    If result > 0 then _
        GetTempDir = Left$(tmp, result)
End Function
```

Listing 6-10: GetTempPath returns the path name of the temporary directory

Again, GetTempDir works in virtually the same way as the GetWindowsDir (Listing 6-9) and GetSystemDir (Listing 6-8) functions presented earlier. However, the order of the arguments for GetTempDir are reversed from those previous WinAPI functions.

> **WARNING!**
>
> *Do not store files that you need in the temporary directory (including any that your program needs to start up). The temporary directory is only for working files and other nonpersistent data used by the current instance of an application.*

Windows Disk Drives

At some point you might need to know how many disk drives there are in a system, what their letters are, how much free space they have, and so on. Windows makes all this low-level information available to you through the WinAPI.

All you need is a list of the appropriate WinAPI functions and some simple formulas, and you, too, can know all about your systems drives. You can easily determine the number of drives installed, a particular drive's type (such as fixed or CD-ROM), the amount of free (and used) disk space on a particular drive, a drive's name and serial number, and whether a drive's file system supports long filenames.

Determining the Number of Drives

A PC may have up to 26 drives, which are numbered from 0 to 25 and usually referenced by a drive letter character from A to Z. Most of the time in Visual Basic you refer to a drive by its drive letter. Some WinAPI functions, however, use the drive number instead. So, before we can get busy with our drives, we need to translate a drive letter to a drive number.

The WinAPI function GetLogicalDrives returns a long integer indicating which drives are installed.

```
Declare Function GetLogicalDrives Lib "kernel32" ()_
As Long
```

Unfortunately, the result of GetLogicalDrives is bit coded, so you can't simply use the value itself. Instead, you have to think of the long integer result of GetLogicalDrives as a series of flags. Each of the possible 26 drives (drive 0 to drive 25) has a corresponding bit position in the long integer. Then, if a drive is present, its corresponding bit position in the result of GetLogicalDrives is a 1. If a drive is not present, its corresponding bit position is a zero. Bit 0 represents drive A, bit 1 is drive B, bit 2 is drive C, and so on.

So, all we need is a function that reads the value of the bits. Listing 6-11 is such a function. It enables us to determine two things: first, if any particular drive letter exists; and second, how many drives are installed.

```
Public Function NumDrives () As Long
    Dim BitMask As Long
    Dim j As Long, i As Long

    BitMask = GetLogicalDrives()
    For i = 0 To 25
        If BitMask And 2 ^ i Then
            j = j + 1
        End If
    Next
    NumDrives = j
End Function
```

Listing 6-11: NumDrives counts the number of drives installed on a system

NumDrives works by calling the GetLogicalDrives WinAPI function, and then examining each bit from 0 to 25 to determine whether the bit is 1 or 0. If a bit is a 1, then a counter is incremented. The total counter value is returned as the result of the function.

In your code, you would use the function like this:

```
MsgBox "You have " & NumDrives & " drives installed."
```

The code in Listing 6-12 demonstrates the other use of GetLogicalDrives—to learn whether a particular drive is present.

```
Public Function DriveExists(ByVal DriveLetter As String)_
As Boolean
    Dim DriveNumber As Integer
    DriveNumber = Asc(Ucase$(DriveLetter)) - 65
    If GetLogicalDrives And 2 ^ DriveNumber Then
        DriveExists = True
    End If
End Function
```

Listing 6-12: DriveExists determines whether a particular drive is installed

DriveExists takes a single argument containing the drive letter to find, and it converts that letter into a drive number. The drive letter, for example, A, is converted to an ASCII value from which 65 is subtracted, which results in a 0-based drive number. Drive A = 0, drive B = 1, and so on. This 0-based drive number is then used with the Windows API call to indicate the drive being referred to. Then DriveExists calls the GetLogicalDrives WinAPI function and checks whether the return result has a 1 or 0 in that drive number's bit position. If the drive is installed, DriveExists returns True; otherwise, it returns False. To call DriveExists, use code similar to this:

```
If DriveExists("B") Then …
```

Detecting Drive Type

The GetDriveType WinAPI function can be used to determine the type of drive that a drive letter represents. The function is declared as follows:

```
Private Declare Function GetDriveType Lib "kernel32" _
Alias "GetDriveTypeA"(ByVal nDrive As String) As Long
```

GetDriveType returns a value from two to six, as indicated in the following code constants:

```
Public Const DRIVE_REMOVABLE = 2
Public Const DRIVE_FIXED = 3
Public Const DRIVE_REMOTE = 4
Public Const DRIVE_CDROM = 5
Public Const DRIVE_RAMDISK = 6
```

> NOTE
> *You must pass the drive's full path, for example, A:\ or C:\, to the GetDriveType function.*

All you need is a quick little function to call GetDriveType, check its result, and return a value. The DriveType function in Listing 6-13 does just that:

```
Public Function DriveType(ByVal DriveLetter As String)_
    As String
        Select Case GetDriveType(Left$(DriveLetter, 1) + ":\")
        Case DRIVE_REMOVABLE
            DriveType = "Removable"
        Case DRIVE_FIXED
            DriveType = "Fixed "
        Case DRIVE_REMOTE
            DriveType = "Network"
        Case DRIVE_CDROM
            DriveType = "CD"
        Case DRIVE_RAMDISK
            DriveType = "RAM "
```

```
        Case Else
            DriveType = "unknown"
        End Select
End Function
```

*Listing 6-13: DriveType returns a string indicating the type of drive a drive
letter represents*

DriveType returns a string indicating the type of drive a drive letter
represents. In your programs, you can use this result in information displays.
However, you can also simply use the WinAPI function itself, along with the
defined constants. For example:

```
If GetDriveType("C:\") = DRIVE_FIXED Then
    ' has a C drive, local and installed
    Print "You have a hard drive!"
End If
```

This leads to a series of useful functions, such as those in Listing 6-14, that
return True if a drive has a certain attribute, or False if it does not.

```
Public Function IsRemote(sDrive As String) As Boolean
    IsRemote = (GetDriveType(sDrive) = DRIVE_REMOTE)
End Function
Public Function IsRemovable(sDrive As String) As Boolean
    IsRemovable = (GetDriveType(sDrive) = DRIVE_REMOVABLE)
End Function
Public Function IsFixed(sDrive As String) As Boolean
    IsFixed = (GetDriveType(sDrive) = DRIVE_FIXED)
End Function
Public Function IsCDROM(sDrive As String) As Boolean
    IsCDROM = (GetDriveType(sDrive) = DRIVE_CDROM)
End Function
Public Function IsRAMDisk(sDrive As String) As Boolean
    IsRAMDisk = (GetDriveType(sDrive) = DRIVE_RAMDISK)
End Function
```

Listing 6-14: Several functions that determine drive type

Drive Space

The WinAPI function GetDiskFreeSpace returns raw data that you can use, with
a little arithmetic, to determine the number of free bytes, used bytes, and total
bytes on any disk drive *providing the disk drive has less than 2 GB of space* (see
the next section for what you can do if you have more space than this).

```
Private Declare Function GetDiskFreeSpace Lib "kernel32" _
    Alias "GetDiskFreeSpaceA" ( _
    ByVal RootPathName As String, _
    SectorsPerCluster As Long, _
    BytesPerSector As Long, _
    NumberOfFreeClusters As Long, _
    TotalNumberOfClusters As Long) As Long
```

The declaration represents how Windows thinks about a drive. Windows manages drives such that they are broken up into logical pieces called sectors. Each sector contains some number of bytes. Sectors are grouped in clusters. You have probably seen the word *cluster* if you have ever used a disk defragmentation utility, which shows you a map, in clusters, as it works.

You may now be starting to understand the declaration for the GetDiskFreeSpace function. The total number of bytes on a disk drive is determined by its *total number of clusters _ sectors per cluster _ bytes per sector.* As a Visual Basic formula, the size (in bytes) of a drive can be represented as:

```
Size = TotalNumberOfClusters * SectorsPerCluster * BytesPerSector
```

The entire function is found in Listing 6-15:

```
Public Function DriveSize(ByVal DriveLetter As String)_
    As Long
        Dim BytesPerSector As Long
        Dim SectorsPerCluster As Long
        Dim NumberOfFreeClusters As Long
        Dim TotalNumberOfClusters As Long
        GetDiskFreeSpace DriveLetter, _
            SectorsPerCluster, _
            BytesPerSector, _
            NumberOfFreeClusters, _
            TotalNumberOfClusters
        DriveSize = TotalNumberOfClusters * _
                SectorsPerCluster * BytesPerSector
End Function
```

Listing 6-15: DriveSize returns a disk drive's total size in bytes

> *NOTE*
>
> *As with the example in Listing 6-13 (GetDriveType), you must pass the drive's full path to DriveSize.*

By using three of the arguments returned by GetDiskFreeSpace, DriveSize can return a particular drive's total size in bytes. Now, let's determine the drive's free and used space. GetDiskFreeSpace returns an additional argument named NumberOfFreeClusters. As you might expect, this extra piece of information is all we need.

FREE AND USED DRIVE SPACE

We can easily create another function that calculates the free space available on a disk drive. The Visual Basic formula is :

```
Available = NumberOfFreeClusters * SectorsPerCluster _
    * BytesPerSector
```

Listing 6-16 is a simple function to implement the formula.

```
Public Function DriveLeft(ByVal DriveLetter As String) _
    As Long
        Dim BytesPerSector As Long
        Dim SectorsPerCluster As Long
        Dim NumberOfFreeClusters As Long
        Dim TotalNumberOfClusters As Long
        GetDiskFreeSpace DriveLetter, _
            SectorsPerCluster, _
            BytesPerSector, _
            NumberOfFreeClusters, _
            TotalNumberOfClusters
        DriveLeft = NumberOfFreeClusters * SectorsPerCluster _
                * BytesPerSector
End Function
```

Listing 6-16: DriveLeft returns the free bytes available on a particular disk drive

Once you know the total size and available space, determining the amount of bytes used is easy. For example:

```
Print "You have used " & Format( _
Module1.DriveSize("C:\") - Module1.DriveLeft("C:\"), _
"###,###,###,###") & " bytes."
```

Drives Larger Than 2 GB

The GetDiskFreeSpace function does not work for drives larger than 2 GB (which you may recognize as the size limit of a long). For these drives, you need to use the GetDiskFreeSpaceEx function. Unfortunately, the GetDiskFreeSpaceEx function is not supported for versions of Windows before Windows 95 OSR2, so you need to use the GetVersion API to learn which version of Windows is running before deciding which function to call. However, if you have a version of Windows that supports the GetDiskFreeSpaceEx function, you can use it to determine the exact amount of available space. This function depends on storing a larger number in two Words (see Chapter 3). So, first, we set up a data structure that will hold each word (see Chapter 5):

```
Private Type LARGE_INTEGER
    lowWord As Long
    highWord As Long
End Type
```

Then, we use the VB Currency type, which can hold *very* large numbers. The information is converted to Currency via the following function:

```
Private Function CCurLargeInt(Lo As Long, Hi As Long) _
    As Currency
        'This function converts the LARGE_INTEGER data
        'type to the Currency data type which gives us
        'some room to spare
        Dim curLo As Currency, curHi As Currency
        If Lo < 0 Then
            curLo = 2 ^ 32 + Lo
        Else
            curLo = Lo
        End If
        If Hi < 0 Then
            curHi = 2 ^ 32 + Hi
        Else
            curHi = Hi
        End If
        CLargeInt = curLo + curHi * 2 ^ 32
End Function
```

Here's the Declare for GetFreeDiskSpaceEx:

```
Private Declare Function GetDiskFreeSpaceEx Lib _
"kernel32" Alias "GetDiskFreeSpaceExA" (ByVal _
    lpRootPathName As String, _
    lpFreeBytesAvailableToCaller As LARGE_INTEGER, _
```

```
lpTotalNumberOfBytes As LARGE_INTEGER, lpTotalNumberOfFreeBytes _
As LARGE_INTEGER) As Long
```

Finally, to show it off, you can use code similar to this:

```
Private Sub Form_Click()
    Dim lResult As Long
    Dim liAvailable As LARGE_INTEGER
    Dim liTotal As LARGE_INTEGER
    Dim liFree As LARGE_INTEGER
    Dim curAvailable As Currency
    Dim curTotal As Currency
    Dim curFree As Currency

    'Determine the Available Space, Total Size
    'and Free Space of a drive
    'using the non buggy GetFreeDiskSpaceEx
    lResult = GetDiskFreeSpaceEx("c:\", liAvailable, _
        liTotal, liFree)
    curAvailable = CCurLargeInt(liAvailable.lowWord, _
        liAvailable.highWord)
    curTotal = CCurLargeInt(liTotal.lowWord, _
        liTotal.highWord)
    curFree = CCurLargeInt(liFree.lowWord, _
        liFree.highWord)
    Print "Available Space:   " & _
    FormatNumber(curAvailable, 0) _
    & " bytes (" & FormatNumber(curAvailable / 1024 ^ 3) _
    & " G) " & vbCr & "Total Space:      " & _
    FormatNumber(curTotal, 0) & " bytes (" & _
    FormatNumber(curTotal / 1024 ^ 3) & " G) " & vbCr & _
    "Free Space:       " & FormatNumber(curFree, 0) _
    & " bytes (" & Format(curFree / 1024 ^ 3) & " G) "
End Sub
```

Drive Serial Number

Windows also stores other information about the drive. The volume serial
number is a value seen when you use a command prompt to do a Dir command
as shown below. The volume serial number in this case is 145C-1AE8:

```
C:\WINDOWS\DESKTOP>dir
Volume in drive C is C DRIVE
Volume Serial Number is 145C-1AE8
Directory of C:\WINDOWS\DESKTOP
.           <DIR>       01-01-96  1:08a .
..          <DIR>       01-01-96  1:08a ..
```

```
0 file(s)           0 bytes
2 dir(s)    482,172,928 bytes free
C:\WINDOWS\DESKTOP>
```

Other useful information that Windows maintains includes the volume name and whether the drive supports long filenames. In the above example, the volume name is C DRIVE.

Use the GetVolumeInformation WinAPI function to collect the additional information.

```
Private Declare Function GetVolumeInformation Lib _
    "kernel32" Alias "GetVolumeInformationA" (_
    ByVal lpRootPathName As String, _
        ByVal VolumeNameBuffer As String, _
        ByVal VolumeNameSize As Long, _
        VolumeSerialNumber As Long, _
        MaximumComponentLength As Long, _
        FileSystemFlags As Long, _
        ByVal FileSystemNameBuffer As String, _
        ByVal FileSystemNameSize As Long) As Long
```

NOTE

You must pass the drive's full path to GetVolumeInformation.

You can create a wrapper for GetVolumeInformation that returns any piece of information you want. For example, the DriveSerial function in Listing 6-17 returns the serial number of a drive.

```
Public Function DriveSerial(DriveLetter As String) _
    As String
        Dim VolumeNameBuffer As String
        Dim VolumeSerialNumber As Long
        Dim MaximumComponentLength As Long
        Dim FileSystemFlags As Long
        Dim FileSystemNameBuffer As String
        Dim FileSystemNameSize As Long
        VolumeNameBuffer = Space$(128)
        GetVolumeInformation DriveLetter, _
                             VolumeNameBuffer, _
                             Len(VolumeNameBuffer), _
                             VolumeSerialNumber, _
                             MaximumComponentLength, _
                             FileSystemFlags, _
                             FileSystemNameBuffer, _
                             FileSystemNameSize
        If InStr(VolumeNameBuffer, Chr$(0)) Then _
```

```
        DriveSerial = Left$(Hex$(VolumeSerialNumber), 4) _
        & "-" & Mid$(Hex$(VolumeSerialNumber), 5)
End Function
```

Listing 6-17: DriveSerial returns a drive's serial number

A note here on the code in Listing 6-17. The volume serial number is returned as a long integer. It has to be formatted into a Hex string to look like the serial number seen when you do a Dir from a command prompt. The last line of code does this, breaking the VolumeSerialNumber result into a pair of Hex strings with a dash between them.

Reading and Writing the Drive Name

GetVolumeInformation also returns the drive's name. The DriveName function in Listing 6-18 shows how.

```
Public Function GetDriveName(DriveLetter As String) _
    As String
        Dim i As Long
        Dim VolumeNameBuffer As String
        Dim VolumeSerialNumber As Long
        Dim MaximumComponentLength As Long
        Dim FileSystemFlags As Long
        Dim FileSystemNameBuffer As String
        Dim FileSystemNameSize As Long
        VolumeNameBuffer = Space$(128)
        GetVolumeInformation DriveLetter, _
                            VolumeNameBuffer, _
                            Len(VolumeNameBuffer), _
                            VolumeSerialNumber, _
                            MaximumComponentLength, _
                            FileSystemFlags, _
                            FileSystemNameBuffer, _
                            FileSystemNameSize
        i = InStr(VolumeNameBuffer, Chr$(0))
        If i > 0 Then GetDriveName = Left$(VolumeNameBuffer,_
        i - 1)
End Function
```

Listing 6-18: GetDriveName returns the drive's name

Listing 6-18 calls the GetVolumeInformation WinAPI function as Listing 6-17 does. In this case, however, you examine and process the VolumeNameBuffer argument.

It turns out that the drive name is not read-only! You can change it using the SetVolumeLabel WinAPI function.

> *NOTE*
>
> *As described earlier in the chapter under the Windows Application Programming Interface description, you need to strip the trailing null character from the string that GetVolumeInformation places in the VolumeNameBuffer argument.*

```
Private Declare Function SetVolumeLabel Lib "kernel32" _
    Alias "SetVolumeLabelA" (ByVal _
    RootPathName As String, _
    ByVal VolumeName As String) As Long
```

The subroutine SetDriveName in Listing 6-19 is complementary to the previous GetDriveName function.

```
Public Sub SetDriveName(ByVal DriveLetter As String, _
                        ByVal DriveName As String)
    SetVolumeLabel DriveLetter, DriveName
End Sub
```

Listing 6-19: SetDriveName subroutine changes the drive name

The SetVolumeLabel WinAPI function takes as its first argument the drive's full path. As its second argument, it takes a string value that contains the new name for the drive.

NEXT STEPS

The GetVolumeInformation WinAPI function returns additional information. One example is the FileSystemNameBuffer argument, which returns the name of the file system (such as NTFS or FAT 32). Create a function that uses GetVolumeInformation to return the file system name.

Chapter 7

Persistence: Remembering What You Can't Afford to Forget

I can't remember the number of times that I wanted to save something, and I can't remember the number of times I couldn't remember where I saved what I couldn't afford to forget....

Persistence

Persisting data means making data available to one or more programs after one program is done with the data. For example, when you install a program, Windows persists your username to the Windows Registry. Then, whenever a program wants to see who the current user is, the program can simply query the Registry to retrieve your name. This is data persistence.

Taking it a step farther, your own programs probably have all sorts of data that they need to persist—configuration information, options, and settings, just to name a few examples. Early versions of Windows persisted program data using Windows Information files (so-called INI files). Current Microsoft policy says that the Registry is where you should store information. The reason for this policy is that multiple users can share a computer, so applications should persist user preferences in the Registry where each user has his or her own section. In addition, a single Registry database is easier to backup, restore, and manage than are many small INI files. However, you can still use INI files as private data stores, and they offer some important benefits over the Registry.

There are two main storage means for persisting data, each with its own advantages:

1. The Windows Registry—The Registry offers powerful searching, reading, writing, and deleting options. You should use the Registry to store all settings that customize your software for each user. The Registry is the standard way to store information that will persist on the PC, and that a user cannot easily modify or locate.
2. INI files—INI files are also incredibly useful vehicles for persisting information. You can use them to store settings that will not change from user to user. You can create, update, and then delete INI files as needed, almost like a small, fast, personal database system. Also, unlike registry data, it is possible to edit INI files using any text editor—a potential convenience for users.

INI Files

An INI file is simply a text file that Windows knows how to parse for you. The entries in an INI file are based on key/value pairs:

Key = Value

where some key, followed by the equal sign, is then followed by the value to return for that key. It results in a very simple database of sorts. For example:

HANK=C:\WINDOWS\HANK.PWL.

If you were to query on the key HANK, you would get the value C:\WINDOWS|HANK.PWL. Imagine more entries in the INI file:

HANK=C:\WINDOWS\HANK.PWL
ROLFE=C:\WINDOWS\ROLFE.PWL
ADRIANA=C:\WINDOWS\ADRIANA.PWL

You query on the key and get the value. Very simple. This simple database is further expanded using optional section headings. For example:

[Password Lists]
HANK=C:\WINDOWS\HANK.PWL
ROLFE=C:\WINDOWS\ROLFE.PWL
ADRIANA=C:\WINDOWS\ADRIANA.PWL

The above sample has a section called Password Lists, and there are three keys in this section – HANK, ROLFE, and ADRIANA.

Reading a String Value from an INI File

GetPrivateProfileString is another WinAPI function that lets you read INI files.

```
Private Declare Function GetPrivateProfileString _
    Lib "kernel32" _
        Alias "GetPrivateProfileStringA" (ByVal _
        ApplicationName As String, ByVal _
        KeyName As Any, ByVal _
        Default As String, ByVal _
        ReturnedString As String, ByVal _
        Size As Long, ByVal _
        FileName As String) As Long
```

The arguments of GetPrivateProfileString enable you to specify a section (ApplicationName), a key (KeyName), a default return value (Default), and an INI file to read from (FileName).

To see how this function works, create a temporary file named test.ini in the root directory of your C drive using the Windows Notepad program. Paste in the file the password list shown in the previous section.

To use GetPrivateProfileString to read our password list example, you would use code similar to this:

```
GetPrivateProfileString "Password Lists", _
                        "HANK", _
                        "", _
                        ReturnedString, Len(ReturnedString),
"c:\test.ini"
```

After this call, the ReturnedString argument would hold the value c:\windows\hank.pwl. The ReturnedString variable must be preinitialized to sufficient length to hold the string.

A generic reading function may be written as shown in Listing 7-1:

```
Public Function iniGetString(Section As String, _
Key As String, Filename As String) As String

    Dim size As Long
    Dim returned As String
    returned = Space$(255)
    size = GetPrivateProfileString(Section, _
        Key, "", returned, Len(returned), Filename)
    If size > 0 Then iniGetString = Left$(returned, size)
End Function
```

Listing 7-1: iniGetString reads an entry from an INI file

The iniGetString function works by creating a variable that can contain up to 244 characters. The limit is arbitrary, however. Next, iniGetString calls GetPrivateProfileString to read the key. If the key is not found, the Default argument of GetPrivateProfileString has been set to an empty string (""). GetPrivateProfileString returns the length of the string read. The last job in iniGetString is trimming the returned value to the proper size.

The iniGetString can be used as follows to retrieve the value for the keyword HANK in the Password Lists section of the test.ini file you created earlier.

```
iniGetString("Password Lists", "HANK", "c:\test.ini")
```

NEXT STEPS

Consider passing another argument that specifies the default return value if a key is not found. (Hint: you need to set the Default argument.) Make the function read an argument of up to 1024 characters, enabling the storage of longer strings.

Reading a Numeric Value from an INI File

The iniGetString function returns a string. You can just as easily return a numeric value with a simple twist on the above function as shown in Listing 7-2:

```
Public Function iniGetNumber(Section As String, _
    Key As String, Filename As String) As Long

    Dim size As Long
    Dim returned As String
    returned = Space$(255)
    size = GetPrivateProfileString(Section, _
        Key, "", returned, Len(returned), Filename)
    If size > 0 Then iniGetNumber = _
        CLng(Left$(returned, size))
End Function
```

Listing 7-2: iniGetNumber returns a long integer value from an INI file

With the exception that the return result is *cast* to a long integer before returning, iniGetNumber works just like iniGetString.

To see how it works, add these lines to your test.ini file:

```
[Numbers]
TESTNUMBER = 55
```

The following statement can be used to retrieve the value of the TESTNUMBER key from the Numbers section in the INI file:

```
iniGetNumber("Numbers", "TESTNUMBER", "h:\t.ini")
```

With a little thought, you can create a generic INI read function that returns either a number or a string, as shown in Listing 7-3:

```
Public Function iniGet(Section As String, Key As String, _
        Filename As String) As Variant

    Dim size As Long
    Dim returned As String
    returned = Space$(255)
    size = GetPrivateProfileString(Section, Key, "", _
        returned, Len(returned), Filename)
    If size > 0 Then returned = Left$(returned, size)
    If IsNumeric(returned) Then
            iniGet = CDbl(returned)
    Else
            iniGet = returned
```

```
    End If
End Function
```

Listing 7-3: iniGet is a generic reading function that returns numeric or string data from an INI file

The iniGet function works just like the examples in Listings 7-1 and 7-2 work, with the exception that it checks the data type of the contents of the returned argument. If the contents are numeric, iniGet casts the result of the function to a Double; otherwise, the result defaults to a String.

NEXT STEPS

Consider handling more data types, for example, Date, Integer, Long, Currency, Byte etc.

Writing INI File Data

The corresponding partner to GetPrivateProfileString is WritePrivateProfileString, which lets you write (or create) an entry in an INI file.

```
Private Declare Function WritePrivateProfileString _
Lib "kernel32" Alias "WritePrivateProfileStringA" _
    (ByVal ApplicationName As String, ByVal KeyName As _
    Any, ByVal NewString As Any, ByVal FileName As String)_
As Long
```

The arguments for WritePrivateProfileString work the same way as they do for GetPrivateProfileStrings. To write to an INI file is as easy as reading from one, as Listing 7-4 illustrates:

```
Public Sub iniPutString(Section As String, _
                        Key As String, _
                        FileName As String, _
                        Value As String)
    WritePrivateProfileString Section, Key, Value, FileName
End Sub
```

Listing 7-4: IniPutString writes to an INI file

IniPutString simply writes the contents of Value into the Section containing the Key in the INI file named FileName. Very straightforward.

NEXT STEPS

Modify iniPutString to store both numeric and string data. Add support for other data types, as well. (Hint: You need to store everything as a string, and make your function(s) handle the conversion based on data type.)

Deleting INI Entries

A common requirement when working with INI files is to delete entries. You can remove the value part of a key/value pair by simply setting the value to an empty string, but the key and section still remain. However, Listing 7-5 illustrates a trick that lets you delete entire entries as well.

```
Public Sub Remove(Section As String, Key As String, _
    Filename As String)
        Const myNull = 0&
        WritePrivateProfileString Section, Key, _
            myNull, Filename
End Sub
```

Listing 7-5: Remove deletes an entire key/value pair in an INI file

The Remove function deletes an entire entry. After this call, the key will no longer be in the INI file. Remove works by passing a Null as the data, which tells Windows that you want to remove the entry completely.

NEXT STEPS

INI files are incredibly useful vehicles for persisting information. Consider creating a class module with properties for the Section, Key, and Filename. Create the class with a default name—perhaps App.Path & "\" & App.ExeName & ".ini"—that you can read from and write to. (Hint: See the code on the CD-ROM (\Chapter7\Chapter7.vbp) for a complete implementation of just such a class.)

The Windows Registry

The Windows Registry is a database along the lines of an INI file, but with proper indexing and more control. According to Microsoft, the Registry is where you should store information about your program. We believe that too much gets stored in the Registry, and that excessive use of the Registry helps degrade Windows performance, inducing instability. Most of the serious problems we have had with Windows come from loading up to much software, which, in turn, creates a huge Registry, which, in turn, takes forever to load and corrupts often. This is especially true under Windows 95.

Having unsuccessfully attempted to scare you away, we will now tell you how to add your own clutter to the Registry, and how to retrieve other Registry entries!

The Registry stores information in a hierarchical tree-like structure. This structure allows for sub entries to be made under entries. For example, one of the top-level storage locations in the Registry is titled HKEY_LOCAL_MACHINE. Under the HKEY_LOCAL_MACHINE entry, there may be stored information (strings, numbers etc.), just as in an INI file. However, and here is a major difference between the Registry and INI files, you can also create new entries under a Registry entry. In this regard, it is much more like the standard DOS file system of directories, subdirectories, and files. So, for example, the HKEY_LOCAL_MACHINE not only stores values, it can also have other entries that store information as well. For example, under HKEY_LOCAL_MACHINE there is a Config entry, which can store data and also have other entries under it.

> **TIP**
> *You can view Registry entries, using Regedit.exe (Regedt32.exe on Windows NT), which is included with Windows.*

Reading from and Writing to the Registry

You may know that Visual Basic provides methods for reading from and writing to the Registry. You may be wondering why we are explaining this to you when Visual Basic already has a function to read from and write to the Registry. The reason is that the built-in functions of GetSetting (retrieves Registry settings), SaveSetting (saves Registry settings), GetAllSettings (returns an array holding multiple settings), and DeleteSetting (deletes Registry settings) operate on a special place in the Registry—HKEY_CURRENT_USER\Software\VB and VBA Program Settings.

If you choose to use Visual Basic to persist your data using these Registry methods, you cannot read from or write to other places in the Registry. In this section, we discuss methods for generic Registry reading and writing.

READING FROM THE REGISTRY

As is the case with INI files, you read from and write to the Registry using WinAPI functions.

The WinAPI function for reading from the Registry is RegQueryValueEx.

```
Private Declare Function RegQueryValueEx Lib _
    "advapi32.dll" Alias "RegQueryValueExA" (ByVal _
                    Key As Long, ByVal _
                    ValueName As String, ByVal Reserved As Long, _
                    DataType As Long, ByVal _
                    Data As String, _
                    DataSize As Long) As Long
```

RegQueryValueEx takes as arguments a Key (similar to the Section argument of the WinAPI functions for INI files), a ValueName (similar to the Key argument for INI files), and a DataType argument. Because the terminology is confusing, the API wrapper functions will show you how they enable you to stay with terms familiar from INI files.

Unlike an INI file, the Registry is a real database, so you must open the Registry before reading its information. After reading, you must close the Registry. There are WinAPI functions for to open and close the Registry.

```
Private Declare Function RegCloseKey Lib "advapi32.dll" _
(ByVal hKey As Long) As Long
Private Declare Function RegOpenKey Lib "advapi32.dll" _
Alias "RegOpenKeyA" (ByVal hKey As Long, ByVal lpSubKey _
As String, phkResult As Long) As Long
```

The regGet function in Listing 7-6 opens the Registry, reads data, and then closes the Registry.

```
Public Function regGet(ByVal Group As Long, _
                       ByVal Section As String, _
                       ByVal Key As String) As String
    Dim lDataTypeValue As Long
    Dim sValue As String
    Dim GroupHandle As Long
    Dim size As Long
    RegOpenKey Group, Section, GroupHandle
    sValue = Space$(2048)
    size = Len(sValue)
    RegQueryValueEx GroupHandle, Key, 0&, _
    lDataTypeValue, sValue, size
    RegCloseKey GroupHandle
    regGet = Left$(sValue, size - 1)
End Function
```

Listing 7-6: regGet opens, reads, and closes any Registry entry

The regGet function works by opening the Registry using the RegOpenKey WinAPI function. RegOpenKey takes as arguments the group location in the Registry (one of the constant values: HKEY_CLASSES_ROOT, HKEY_CURRENT_USER, HKEY_LOCAL_MACHINE, etc.) and the subsection under that group (that the Registry refers to as a key). The Registry value name is set by the regGet function's key parameter. The function returns a value in GroupHandle, which is used by RegQueryValueEx to read any given key under that group.

The following sample code shows one way that you can use the regGet function:

```
Dim group As Long
Dim section As String
Dim key As String
group = HKEY_LOCAL_MACHINE
section = _
```

```
"Hardware\DESCRIPTION\System\CentralProcessor\0"
key = "VendorIdentifier"
Debug.Print regGet(group, section, key)
```

Using regGet with these values would return the manufacturer of the processor's name, for example, "AuthenticAMD".

Like most WinAPI functions, you need to declare the strings and size them before using them, so regGet creates a padded string before calling RegQueryValueEx. RegQueryValueEx returns the length of the string returned in the DataSize argument. regGet then removes the Null termination character (Chr$(0)) and all subsequent characters.

Next Steps

Consider adding code to read and parse different data types. (Hint: See the code module for this chapter (\Chapter7\Chapter7.vbp), which has a complete implementation for reading and writing all Registry data types.)

WRITING TO THE REGISTRY

Writing a value to the Registry is almost the same as reading one: the steps are to open the Registry, write your data, and then close the Registry. For opening the Registry, the WinAPI provides an alternative to RegOpenKey that can optionally be used only when writing—the RegCreateKey function. Just like RegOpenKey, RegCreateKey opens a Group and Section, but it creates them for you if they don't already exist.

NOTE
When writing to the Registry, you should always use RegCreateKey instead of RegOpenKey since RegCreateKey will create a key if its not there, while RegOpenKey will return an error if a key is not found. It's safest to assume that the group and section do not already exist.

```
Private Declare Function RegCreateKey Lib "advapi32.dll" _
    Alias "RegCreateKeyA" (ByVal hKey As Long, ByVal _
lpSubKey As String, phkResult As Long) As Long
```

After opening and/or creating the Group and Section, you need to write the actual data. Unlike the scenario for INI files, the WinAPI provides multiple functions that read and write a variety of data types to the Registry. The principal WinAPI function is RegSetValueExString, which is a declaration for the RegSetValueEx function designed to take a string value.

```
Private Declare Function RegSetValueExString Lib _
    "advapi32.dll" Alias "RegSetValueExA" (ByVal hKey As _
    Long, ByVal lpValueName As String, ByVal Reserved As _
```

```
Long, ByVal dwType As Long, ByVal lpValue As String, _
ByVal cbData As Long) As Long
```

RegSetValueExString writes a string value to a Group, Section, and Key location. It can be wrapped in a function, such as the regPut function shown in Listing 7-7:

```
Public Sub regPut(ByVal Group As Long, ByVal Section _
    As String, ByVal Key As String, ByVal Value As String)
        Dim GroupHandle As Long
        RegCreateKey Group, Section, GroupHandle
        RegSetValueExString GroupHandle, Key, 0&, 1&, _
                            Value, Len(Value)
        RegCloseKey GroupHandle
End Sub
```

Listing 7-7: regPut writes a string to the Registry

The regPut function works by opening (and creating, if needed) a Group and Section. Then it calls RegSetValueExString to store the string.

DELETING REGISTRY ENTRIES

NOTE
The code in this section can permanently disable your Registry, rendering your operating system inoperative, so be careful!

In the section on INI files, you learned how to set a Key's value to an empty string, and how to remove a key/value pair from the INI file altogether. With the Registry, there are more powerful (and more dangerous) WinAPI functions—you can delete Key entries, Sections, or entire Groups.

```
Private Declare Function RegDeleteKey Lib "advapi32.dll" _
    Alias "RegDeleteKeyA" (ByVal hKey As Long, ByVal _
    lpSubKey As String) As Long
```

RegDeleteKey removes a Key and its data. Be careful because in Windows 95 and 98, RegDeleteKey also deletes all subkeys. RegDeleteValue just removes a specified Key and its value.

```
Private Declare Function RegDeleteValue Lib _
    "advapi32.dll" Alias "RegDeleteValueA" (ByVal hKey _
    As Long, ByVal lpValueName As String) As Long
```

Using these two powerful WinAPI functions is straightforward: open the Registry, delete the item in question, and then close the Registry.

The DeleteKey function deletes a specified Section (and all its subkeys and values if used in Windows 95/98) from the Registry. The function requires a constant to define the security attributes required to delete Registry sections, a wise preventative. Thus, the Key should be opened with RegOpenKeyEx, which enables you to specify an access mask (RegOpenKey uses the default mask which, depending on your system configuration, may not enable you to delete the key). RegOpenKeyEx is declared as follows:

```
Declare Function RegOpenKeyEx Lib "advapi32.dll" Alias _
    "RegOpenKeyExA" (ByVal hKey As Long, ByVal lpSubKey As _
    String, ByVal ulOptions As Long, ByVal samDesired As _
    Long, phkResult As Long) As Long
```

See the code on the CD-ROM (\Chapter7\Chapter7.vbp) for a definition of these constants and how to use them. For example, the DeleteKey procedure, shown below, uses the KEY_ALL_ACCESS constant.

```
Public Function DeleteKey(ByVal Group As Long, _
              ByVal Section As String) As String
    Dim KeyValue As Long
    RegOpenKeyEx Group, vbNullChar, 0&, KEY_ALL_ACCESS, _
        KeyValue
    RegDeleteKey KeyValue, Section
    RegCloseKey KeyValue
End Function
```

Listing 7-8: DeleteKey deletes a Registry Key and its data

DeleteKey works by opening the Registry with a permission constant of KEY_ALL_ACCESS, which means that your program wants to receive full access to the Key, including the right to delete it. . It then deletes the Section, all its Keys, and their data.

The DeleteValue function in Listing 7-9 deletes a specified key/value pair from a specified Section.

```
Public Function DeleteValue(ByVal Group As Long, _
              ByVal Section As String, _
              ByVal Key As String) As String
    Dim KeyValue As Long
    RegOpenKey Group, Section, KeyValue
```

```
        RegDeleteValue KeyValue, Key
        RegCloseKey KeyValue
End Function
```

Listing 7-9: DeleteValue deletes a Registry Key's data

DeleteValue works by opening the Registry, deleting the Key and its data, and then closing the Registry.

Next Steps

Consider expanding your Registry manipulation routines to include additional data types beyond strings. Add a function to return an array of Keys and their values. Add a function to store an array of Keys and their data.

Chapter 8

Localization: The Art of Talking Like a Native

The Internet and the World Wide Web have made for a truly global village. People from literally anywhere in the world can use your software or view your Web pages. Unfortunately, most software displays content in the language of the author, not the user. Using only English puts your software off-limits to most of the world. And if your Web site is for commercial purposes, using an English-only solution effectively limits your potential market. However, Visual Basic and Windows offer powerful localization capabilities that let you write once and run in any language Windows supports—the secrets follow.

Localization

There are two main ways to localize your software. The first solution is to create a separate version of your software for every language you choose to support, a technique called *static localization*. Obviously, this is slow and expensive. On the Web, some sites do provide links to pages in other languages, but these translated pages are usually out of sync with the primary language pages because it is difficult to constantly translate pages and rarely possible to keep up with the original source. The better solution is *dynamic localization*—to create software that localizes itself as the need arises—which is what this chapter is all about. All you need is Visual Basic and knowledge of some of Windows' more obscure features.

ActiveX Components That Adapt

If your Web application uses Visual Basic-authored ActiveX controls, ActiveX documents, or ActiveX DLLs, then you can you can easily localize your Web site by localizing the components that your Web page uses to display information to the user. Even Web sites that do not use ActiveX components on the client side (in order to maintain compatibility with non-Microsoft browsers) can take this approach by using components on the server side and generating Web content using Active Server Pages (ASP) or Visual Basic Web classes.

Once you know how to localize ActiveX components, you can use them to localize both Web sites and applications.

To begin with, Windows has a wide range of localization features. Although most developers never use them, one localization feature—the locale ID—provides the key to creating self-localizing components.

Microsoft has many different versions of Windows localized for international markets all over the world. Windows internally maintains information about the language of Windows itself, as well as the user's language preference. Each major language region of the world is referred to as a *locale*. Microsoft has assigned each locale an identifier, or *locale ID*.

By using the locale ID that Windows maintains, a program can determine the user's language preference.

Microsoft chose to include in Visual Basic the capability to detect the locale ID, and also to detect when the locale ID changes. Visual Basic thus enables you to create components that can dynamically detect and respond to the language preference of the user viewing your Web page or running your application.

From Visual Basic to Self-Localizing ActiveX Controls

Visual Basic enables you to create an ActiveX control using the Visual Basic UserControl project template. A Visual Basic UserControl contains an object property named Ambient. The UserControl.Ambient object provides access to information about the container of the ActiveX control.

One item of information contained in the Ambient object is a property named LocaleID, which is the Windows locale ID for the current ActiveX control host. For example, if your ActiveX control were running under Internet Explorer, Ambient.LocaleID would return the locale ID that Internet Explorer is currently using. For ActiveX hosts that do not directly support this property, Visual Basic inserts the current Windows locale ID.

The Ambient.LocaleID property is a long integer value that specifies the language and country of the user. It is easier to think about locale IDs as hexadecimal values; for example, US English is hex &H409 and German is hex &H407.

Also included in the UserControl object is an event named UserControl_AmbientChanged. This event occurs whenever an ambient property changes. So, for example, when the locale ID of the host changes, this event triggers and passes the value LocaleID to the PropertyName argument of the event procedure.

Listing 8-1 shows how you can determine whether the locale ID changes while a program that's using your ActiveX control is running. When run under US English Windows, this code displays 409.

```
Private Sub UserControl_AmbientChanged(PropertyName _
    As String)
        Select Case PropertyName
        Case "LocaleID"
```

```
        MsgBox "The locale is " & Hex(Ambient.LocaleID)
      End Select
End Sub
```

Listing 8-1: AmbientChanged shows the locale ID of the client application

By themselves, the Ambient.LocaleID property and AmbientChanged event cannot make your control change languages; they only enable you to track which language is in use by the client. However, if you combine them with a resource file, you have the opportunity to dynamically detect, and then modify, your control's textual displays. As shown in Listing 8-2, you can respond to changes in the locale ID by examining the value of the Ambient.LocaleID property.

```
Private Sub UserControl_AmbientChanged(PropertyName _
    As String)
      Select Case PropertyName
      Case "LocaleID"
          Select Case Hex(Ambient.LocaleID)
          Case 409 ' US English
              ResourceOffset = 1000
      Case 407 ' German
          ResourceOffset = 2000
      Case 406 ' French
          ResourceOffset = 3000
      Case Else
          ' default to US English
          ResourceOffset = 1000
      End Select
    End Select
End Sub
```

Listing 8-2: AmbientChanged event procedure generates an offset to a resource file

Each language supported sets the ResourceOffset variable, which represents an offset to a string table that you included in the project's resource file. In this manner, if the locale ID changes, you change the offset so that it points to the section for the new language and reload your text strings. All text displayed to the user should be loaded from the resource file based on the offset currently in use.

> *NOTE*
> *Once you can detect and respond to locale ID changes in the control's host, you can add as many languages as you want to support.*

Creating Resource Files

The easiest way to create resource files is to use Microsoft Visual C++. Create a new Resource Script File and insert a string table. Then just add the necessary strings.

If you don't have Visual C++, don't despair. Visual Basic comes with the program RC.EXE, which can compile a resource script file. You can create a resource script file using a text editor such as Notepad. Here is a sample of a simple resource script with two string tables. You can actually put all of your strings in a single string table, but it is customary to separate them by language to make the script easier to read.

```
STRINGTABLE DISCARDABLE
BEGIN
    1000 "This is the base for the English language strings"
    1001 "Here is another English language string"
END

STRINGTABLE DISCARDABLE
BEGIN
        2000    "German strings start here"
END
```

Save the file with the extension .RC. After you have defined a script, you can compile it using the RC.EXE program. Find the program on your system (it is typically in one of the BIN directories in your Visual Studio directory tree. If your script is named tres.rc, you would compile it with the command line:

```
rc tres.rc
```

This creates a file with the extension .RES. You can add this file to your project by using the Project menu's Add File command. The .RES file will appear in your project window as a "related document."

You can then use the LoadResString command to load strings from the resource file. The following code loads string #1000 from the resource file and prints it in the immediate window:

```
Dim LocalString As String
LocalString = LoadResString(1000)
Debug.Print LocalString
```

Creating Self-Localizing ActiveX DLLs and Documents

As you might already know, the Ambient object is found only in the Visual Basic UserControl object. But what if you want to create and use an ActiveX document or an ActiveX DLL rather than an ActiveX control? True, you cannot use the same code, but you can use WinAPI functions to retrieve the same information.

The GetSystemDefaultLCID and GetUserDefaultLCID WinAPI functions are the keys to implementing self-localizing capabilities in programs that do not have an Ambient object. GetSystemDefaultLCID returns the default locale ID of the system (Windows) while GetUserDefaultLCID returns the locale ID of the user's chosen language. The only time that these values are different is when a user explicitly asks to run in a language other than the one the user specified when Windows was installed—a rare occurrence.

```
Declare Function GetSystemDefaultLCID Lib "kernel32" _
Alias "GetSystemDefaultLCID" () As Long
Declare Function GetUserDefaultLCID Lib "kernel32" _
Alias "GetUserDefaultLCID" () As Long
```

Using Visual Basic you can create an ActiveX document or an ActiveX DLL that takes advantage of these functions to implement the same functionality shown in the ActiveX control example. A sample program that initializes an ActiveX document by setting the UserDocument object to the user's current system language is shown in Listing 8-3:

```
Option Explicit
Private Declare Function GetUserDefaultLCID Lib _
    "kernel32" () As Long
Private Sub UserDocument_Initialize()
        ' add languages we will support
```

```
            Combo1.AddItem "English"
            Combo1.AddItem "Français"
            Combo1.AddItem "Deutsch"
            Combo1.AddItem "Italiano"
            Combo1.AddItem "Español"
            ' this is the start of the documents life, so lets
            ' read the LCID and set our pointer appropriatly
            Select Case Hex(GetUserDefaultLCID)
                Case 409 ' US English
                    ResourceOffset = 1000
                Case 412 ' French
                    ResourceOffset = 2000
                Case 407 ' German
                    ResourceOffset = 3000
                Case 416 ' Italian
                    ResourceOffset = 4000
                Case 410 ' Spanish
                    ResourceOffset = 5000
                Case Else
                    ' default to US English
                    ResourceOffset = 1000
            End Select
End Sub
```

Listing 8-3: A self-localizing UserDocument object

The code in Listing 8-3 determines the user's default locale ID for the
UserDocument when loaded in the browser.

Using the techniques presented so far in this chapter, you can create
ActiveX controls, ActiveX Documents, and ActiveX DLLs that adapt to the
viewer's preferences. You can support as many languages as you want and
you can provide an interface option to enable users to view your data in any
supported language, even if the Windows locale is different. While using the
project's resource file to contain multiple language strings is a popular
approach to localize software, trying to shoehorn multiple languages into a
single resource file adds its own complexity. Aside from the need to sometimes
manage large resource files, each new language or string requires that you
recompile and redistribute the component.

To move further into localization, another technique is required. Using the
same programs we've already created, we can add code that loads (or tries to
load) DLL resource files on the fly. You then create a separate resource file for
each supported language. This way you can create your program and then add
resource files without having to recompile your program. You can add languages
without a single change to your program.

Self-localization can save many hours of development time—you will find yourself localizing in days instead of months. Further, future maintenance work is reduced because you don't need to maintain multiple code bases of your product—you simply maintain a series of resource files.

Self-localization has other advantages as well. If you write programs for use in other countries, you already know that localization is not as simple as just changing the words displayed by your interface. In many countries, the colors, graphics, and other icons of your interfaces may not be understood because most of the world's people do not use the English alphabet.

For a set of products I worked on (Modern GuardX and Modern TrialX), we needed to provide localized versions for Europe, as well as for the Far East (Hong Kong, China, Korea, Japan, etc.) and other non-English-speaking countries such as Israel.

Simply placing multiple language strings in a resource file does not work in this sort of environment, as the physical fonts used are different. For example, the Japanese language character set for Windows includes three different character sets: Katakana, Hiragana, and Kanji. This is an extreme case, but many countries do not use the same default Windows fonts as used in US Windows—and therein lies the problem you encounter when localizing for many foreign markets.

The traditional answer would have been to hire a translation firm, wait several months, spend many tens of thousands of dollars, and get a completely new product in the language of choice. Aside from the time and cost of this process, we would have had multiple code bases to support, as each language version of the products would have been compiled as a separate program.

Because we have spent a number of years in the software business and had localized numerous products, we believed that there had to be a better way. After spending quite some time studying how Windows implements non-English languages and character sets, we came upon a solution that provides some tremendous benefits—the language DLL.

Implementing Language DLLs

A *language DLL* is a Visual Basic-authored ActiveX Dynamic Link Library that provides a standard object interface. Via this interface, the calling program has access to the resource file included in the ActiveX DLL project. By declaring an instance of the language DLL and using its GetResString method instead of using the Visual Basic LoadResString method, your program can load strings from the DLL's resource file. You can also code a GetResPicture method to replace the Visual Basic LoadResPicture method.

As the following code shows, the DLL code is almost trivial:

```
Option Explicit
Public Function GetResPicture(ByVal Index As Long, _
    Fmt As Long) As Picture
```

```
        Set GetResPicture = LoadResPicture(Index, Fmt)
End Function
Public Function GetResString(ByVal Index As Long) _
    As String
        GetResString = LoadResString(Index)
End Function
```

The above code simply creates public methods that enable access to the DLL's resource file. Then, in the calling program, the following syntax is used to read the DLL's strings or pictures (assuming the instance of the language DLL is referenced through a Visual Basic object variable named LangDLL):

```
PropertyPage.Caption = LangDLL.GetResString(504)
```

At the highest level, using a language DLL enables your program (or control) to load any language set required. This is essentially equivalent to using multiple resource strings in a traditional resource file. So, why is this approach better? Because when you combine the language DLL with the capability to detect the default language that Windows is using, your code can dynamically load the proper DLL—without asking the user to choose a language.

The key to this dynamic adaptability is the WinAPI function GetSystemDefaultLCID. GetSystemDefaultLCID returns a long integer value that indicates the default language of the Windows installation running the calling program. This is the same value returned from the Visual Basic UserControl object's Ambient.LocaleID property; GetSystemDefaultLCID, however, is available to any Visual Basic project, not just to controls. GetSystemDefaultLCID is also available at any time during your program, including any part of control initialization.

As stated earlier, GetSystemDefaultLCID returns a coded reference to the Windows default language; for example, for US English it returns 1033 (HEX 409) and for German it returns 1031 (HEX 407). GetSystemDefaultLCID thus provides a way to determine the language your program is running on. Now, we need to connect GetSystemDefaultLCID to the language DLL. This is done by naming the DLL using the three-digit hex value that GetSystemDefaultLCID returns.

For example, if the product is named TRXT100.OCX, you can create an English language DLL titled TRXT409.DLL and a German language DLL titled TRXT407.DLL. In fact, you can create a language DLL for any language you want your program to support.

When the program loads, it calls an initialization routine that determines the locale ID using GetSystemDefaultLCID, and then it creates the filename of the language DLL by merging the locale ID into the name of the DLL. The routine then checks for a DLL with the proper name, and if it finds it, loads that DLL and sets a public object to reference it. Now, all coded access to the language DLL will automatically read strings and images from the language DLL instead of the program's own resource file—your program just self-localized. The Listing 8-4 implements this technique.

```
Option Explicit
Dim LangDll As Object

Const OFS_MAXPATHNAME = 128
Const OF_EXIST = &H4000

' OpenFile() Structure
Type OFSTRUCT
        cBytes As Byte
        fFixedDisk As Byte
        nErrCode As Integer
        Reserved1 As Integer
        Reserved2 As Integer
        szPathName(OFS_MAXPATHNAME - 1) As Byte
End Type
Const MAX_PATH = 260

Private Declare Function GetSystemDefaultLCID _
    Lib "kernel32" () As Long
Private Declare Function GetSystemDirectory Lib _
    "kernel32" Alias "GetSystemDirectoryA" _
    (ByVal lpBuffer As String, ByVal nSize As Long) As Long

Private Declare Function OpenFile Lib "kernel32" _
    (ByVal lpFileName As String, lpReOpenBuff As OFSTRUCT, _
    ByVal wStyle As Long) As Long

Public Sub SetLocale()
        Dim strProgID As String
        Dim buffer As String
        Dim ret As Long
        Dim SystemDir As String
        Dim typOfStruct As OFSTRUCT
        Dim sFilename As String
        Dim LID As Long
    On Error Resume Next
    ' get localeID
    LID = GetSystemDefaultLCID
    ' get system dir + language DLL for me
    buffer = Space$(MAX_PATH)
    ret = GetSystemDirectory(buffer, Len(buffer))
    SystemDir = Left$(buffer, _
        InStr(buffer, Chr$(0)) - 1) + "\"
    ' get name DLL, ex TRXL407.DLL
    sFilename = SystemDir + _
```

```
                    Left$(UCase$(App.EXEName), 4) _
                    + "L" + Hex$(LID) + ".DLL"
     ' is there a language DLL in the sys dir?
     If Len(sFilename) > 0 Then
         OpenFile sFilename, typOfStruct, OF_EXIST
         If typOfStruct.nErrCode = 0 Then
             ' try to load that object
             strProgID = Left$(UCase$(App.EXEName), 4) + _
                     "L" + Hex$(LID) + ".Localizer"
             Set LangDll = CreateObject(strProgID)
         End If
     End If
     ' if lang DLL not found use default
     If LangDll Is Nothing Then Set LangDll = Me
End Sub
```

Listing 8-4: Code that dynamically attempts to load and connect to a language DLL

The code in Listing 8-4 uses the GetSystemDirectoryWinAPI function to determine the path of the Windows System directory. It then checks for the existence of the language DLL in that directory. If a file with the proper name is found in the Windows System directory, the Visual Basic CreateObject method is used to attempt to load the DLL.

If the language DLL is not found, or if the load fails, the LangDLL object will be empty (Nothing), in which case the routine sets LangDLL to Me, which in effect points the LangDLL object to this program's resource file.

The language DLL implementation shown in Listing 8-4 enables you to maintain a single code base for your program or control, while automatically self-localizing if it finds an appropriate language DLL. This alone makes for a much easier localization and a more customized user experience. Adding a new language is a simple matter of distributing a new resource DLL.

Resource files alone, however, do not a localization make.

Setting Default Fonts

While the language DLL implementation solves about half of the localization challenge, a significant amount of work still remains. If the country where your software runs does not use the English alphabet, you need to modify the Font property of every single object in your program that displays a font. Windows takes care of updating the font of title bars of windows, menus, and message boxes, but you have to modify each Label, Textbox, Frame, and other objects or controls that have a Font property.

It's the WinAPI, of course, that provides a way around the Windows default font. The Windows default font is guaranteed to be in the native language of the Windows version, and to be the font face that Windows uses in title bars of windows, menus, and message boxes. The GetTextFace WinAPI function returns the name of this font face, for example, Ms Sans Serif. Using GetTextFace requires a fair bit of work, but it is easily encapsulated into a function, as Listing 8-5 illustrates:

```
Option Explicit
DefLng A-Z

Type TEXTMETRIC
            tmHeight As Long
            tmAscent As Long
            tmDescent As Long
            tmInternalLeading As Long
            tmExternalLeading As Long
            tmAveCharWidth As Long
            tmMaxCharWidth As Long
            tmWeight As Long
            tmOverhang As Long
            tmDigitizedAspectX As Long
            tmDigitizedAspectY As Long
            tmFirstChar As Byte
            tmLastChar As Byte
            tmDefaultChar As Byte
            tmBreakChar As Byte
            tmItalic As Byte
            tmUnderlined As Byte
            tmStruckOut As Byte
            tmPitchAndFamily As Byte
            tmCharSet As Byte
End Type

Private Const DEFAULT_GUI_FONT = 17
Const LOGPIXELSX = 88        '  Logical pixels/inch in X
Private Const LOGPIXELSY = 90        '  Logical pixels/inch in Y

Private Declare Function GetTextMetrics Lib "gdi32" _
    Alias "GetTextMetricsA" (ByVal hDC As Long, _
    lpMetrics As TEXTMETRIC) As Long
Private Declare Function GetTextFace Lib "gdi32" _
    Alias "GetTextFaceA" (ByVal hDC As Long, ByVal nCount _
    As Long, ByVal lpFacename As String) As Long
Private Declare Function SelectObject Lib "gdi32" _
    (ByVal hDC As Long, ByVal hObject As Long) As Long
Private Declare Function CreateWindowEx Lib "user32" _
    Alias "CreateWindowExA" (ByVal dwExStyle As Long, _
    ByVal lpClassName As String, ByVal lpWindowName As _
```

```
        String, ByVal dwStyle As Long, ByVal x As Long, _
        ByVal y As Long, ByVal nWidth As Long, ByVal _
        nHeight As Long, ByVal hWndParent As Long, ByVal hMenu _
        As Long, ByVal hInstance As Long, lpParam As Any) As Long

    Private Declare Function GetDC Lib "user32" (ByVal hWnd _
        As Long) As Long
    Private Declare Function GetStockObject Lib "gdi32" _
        (ByVal nIndex As Long) As Long
    Private Declare Function GetDeviceCaps Lib "gdi32" _
        (ByVal hDC As Long, ByVal nIndex As Long) As Long
    Private Declare Function ReleaseDC Lib "user32" _
        (ByVal hWnd As Long, ByVal hDC As Long) As Long

    Private Declare Function DestroyWindow Lib "user32" _
        (ByVal hWnd As Long) As Long

    Public Property Get DefaultFont() As StdFont
    ' This procedure gets the stock GUI
        On Error Resume Next
        Dim GuiFont As Long, OldFont As Long
        Dim ret As Long
        Dim hDC As Long
        Dim TYP_METRICS As TEXTMETRIC
        Dim FontFaceName  As String
        Dim hWnd As Long
        Dim dwExStyle, lpClassName, lpWindowName
        Dim dwStyle, x, y, nWidth, nHeight
        Dim hWndParent, hMenu, hInstance, lpParam
        ' instantiate font
        Set DefaultFont = New StdFont
        ' create a window
        hWnd = CreateWindowEx(dwExStyle, "STATIC", _
        "localizer_win", dwStyle, x, y, nWidth, _
        nHeight, hWndParent, hMenu, hInstance, lpParam)
        ' get dc of new window
        hDC = GetDC(hWnd)
        ' Get font handle for DEFAULT_GUI_FONT
        GuiFont = GetStockObject(DEFAULT_GUI_FONT)
        ' Set GuiFont to window
        OldFont = SelectObject(hDC, GuiFont)
        ' Get fontface name
        FontFaceName = Space$(255)
```

```
        ret = GetTextFace(hDC, 255, FontFaceName)
        FontFaceName = Left$(FontFaceName, _
        InStr(FontFaceName, Chr$(0)) - 1)
        ' get font metrics
        ret = GetTextMetrics(hDC, TYP_METRICS)
        ' assign font face name
        DefaultFont.Name = FontFaceName
        ' TYP_METRICS.tmInternalLeading is used to
        ' reduce the cell size to the point size.
        DefaultFont.Size = ((TYP_METRICS.tmHeight - _
            TYP_METRICS.tmInternalLeading) * 72) / _
            GetDeviceCaps(hDC, LOGPIXELSY)
        ' clean up
        ret = SelectObject(hDC, OldFont)
        ret = ReleaseDC(hWnd, hDC)
        DestroyWindow hWnd
End Property
```

Listing 8-5: GetTextFace retrieves the name of the Windows default font

The code in Listing 8-5 returns the default font used by Windows. This may then be applied to your own forms and controls in your Form_Load event(s). The localization class includes the procedure in Listing 8-6 that, given an object such as a form, steps through every control and applies the default font to it.

```
Public Sub SetDefaultFont(Obj As Object)
    On Local Error Resume Next
    Dim ctl As Control
    Dim myFont As New StdFont
    Set myFont = DefaultFont
    For Each ctl In Obj.Controls
        ctl.Font.Name = myFont.Name
        ctl.Font.Size = myFont.Size
        ctl.Font.Charset = myFont.Charset
        ctl.Font.Weight = myFont.Weight
        ctl.Font.Bold = myFont.Bold
        ctl.Font.Italic = myFont.Italic
        ctl.Font.Strikethrough = myFont.Strikethrough
        ctl.Font.Underline = myFont.Underline
    Next
    Set myFont = Nothing
End Sub
```

Listing 8-6: SetDefaultFont sets an object to use the Windows default font

NOTE
Why does the code in Listing 8-6 take the time to set each property of the Font object, rather than just setting the entire object? Because setting the entire object affects all objects that use that Font. The unexpected result would be that when you, for example, set the FontBold property of one control to True, all controls using the same Font object would also turn bold, which is not good.

Handling Other Languages

Now that your program can dynamically load the proper resource file via a language DLL and dynamically switch the font of all objects, your localization efforts are almost done. Aside from actually translating the resource strings used in each language DLL, there is another thing you should do—make sure that the Textbox, Labels, and Caption fields of your controls are the proper size.

Most other languages use more space than English. For example, in English it's common to have an OK button. In Spanish, OK is loosely translated as Aceptar, which requires 350 percent more room on the button. This also holds true with text-entry fields. In general, make your buttons larger than they need to be for English. This horizontal expansion also impacts your placements of labels and captions as well as for the positioning of multiple OptionButtons and CheckBoxes. Again, you need to leave as much as 400 percent more space for the captions as you would normally.

Horizontal expansion is not the only issue; some languages expand vertically as well. For example, Kanji uses about 130 percent more vertical space than English, thus you need to make your text entry fields and captions taller than you would normally. After you make the needed adaptations, working this way seems natural and you quickly learn to design your interfaces with much more room, which results in a cleaner and less-cluttered look, which has value itself.

Chapter 9

Working with Networks

Most programs written today interact with a network. Whether the network is a company intranet, a Windows NT server-based network, a peer-to-peer network, or the Internet, the inclusion of network access in your programs places an expanded range of control and information at your fingertips—if you know where to look.

Accessing a Network

Most applications require access to data that may be stored remotely and accessed via network connections. It is important, therefore, to determine whether a network is available to your program before attempting to access network resources. It follows that the very first step in working with Windows networking is to make sure a network is present. Without a network present, there is no sense trying to access network features such as setting drive mappings, drive types, network printers, and so on. So, first things first—let's create a function that returns True if a network is present and False if a network is not present.

Determining Whether a Network Is Present

For this task, and for many other Windows networking tasks, we need to use the WinAPI. As you learned in Chapter 6, the WinAPI is a bit harder to use than native Visual Basic, but sometimes there is just no other way to get the job done. Such is the case with determining whether a network is present. The WinAPI function of choice for this task is GetSystemMetrics.

```
Private Declare Function GetSystemMetrics Lib "user32" (_
                        ByVal nIndex As Long) As Long
```

GetSystemMetrics is a truly powerful function, with literally dozens of different uses. GetSystemMetrics takes an argument indicating what aspect of Windows to return information about. To determine whether or not a network is present, we will use the SM_NETWORK constant.

```
Private Const SM_NETWORK = 63
```

As Listing 9-1 illustrates, all you need to do is create a wrapper function around GetSystemMetrics that returns True or False when used with the SM_NETWORK constant.

```
Const SM_NETWORK = 63
Private Declare Function GetSystemMetrics Lib "user32" _
(ByVal nIndex As Long) As Long

Public Function Network() As Boolean
    Network = GetSystemMetrics(SM_NETWORK) And 1
End Function
```

Listing 9-1: GetSystemMetrics returns True if a network is present or False if there is no network present

Reading the Username

Once you know a network is present, you can do other interesting things, such as reading the username of the current user. There are occasions when you will want to maintain a list of the users who access your software. Getting the username is easy, once you know the correct WinAPI function. The WNetGetUser WinAPI function returns the username.

```
Private Declare Function WNetGetUser Lib "mpr.dll" _
    Alias "WNetGetUserA" (_
        ByVal lpName As String, _
        ByVal lpUserName As String, _
        lpnLength As Long) As Long
```

WNetGetUser is one of a series of network functions built into Windows and accessible via the WinAPI. The NetUserName function shown in Listing 9-2 works by creating a buffer string for WNetGetUser to write the username to. Then it makes the actual call to WNetGetUser, and removes any terminating null from the username returned. Finally, NetUserName returns the user name as its return result.

```
Public Function NetUserName() As String
    Dim j As Long
    Dim UserName As String
    UserName = Space$(255)
    j = WNetGetUser("", UserName, Len(UserName))
    j = InStr(UserName, Chr$(0))
    If j > 0 Then NetUserName = Left$(UserName, j - 1)
End Function
```

Listing 9-2: NetUserName returns the name of the currently logged on Windows user

Reading the Computer Name

Every computer on a network requires a unique computer name. This is the name shown in the Windows Explorer window. You normally set this name using the Network applet of the Windows Control Panel. You can read this value at any time using the GetComputerName WinAPI function.

```
Private Declare Function GetComputerNameA Lib _
"kernel32" ( ByVal lpBuffer As String, _
        nSize As Long) As Long
```

GetComputerNameA returns the name of this computer. All we need to do is wrap it in a Visual Basic function such as that in Listing 9-3.

```
Public Property Get ComputerName() As String
    Dim sComputerName As String
    Dim j As Long
    sComputerName = Space$(256)
    GetComputerNameA sComputerName, Len(sComputerName)
    j = InStr(sComputerName, Chr$(0))
    If j > 0 Then ComputerName = _
        Left$(sComputerName, j - 1)
End Property
```

Listing 9-3: GetComputerName returns the name that identifies the computer to a network

Notice that ComputerName was made a property. This was done because, in addition to reading the computer name, you can also set the computer name programmatically, as shown in the next section.

Setting the Computer Name

Just as you can read the computer name, you can also set it. The WinAPI function to set the computer name is SetComputerNameA.

```
Private Declare Function SetComputerNameA _
    Lib "kernel32" ( ByVal lpComputerName As String) As Long
```

After assigning the name, you need to reboot the machine to have the new name recognized. Under Windows 95/98, if the name passed to SetComputerName contains characters outside the standard character set, no error is generated, whereas Windows NT generates an error. Also, Windows NT requires that you have Administrator authority to set the computer name.

The ComputerName Let property shown in listing 9-4 encapsulates the WinAPI into an easier to use Property.

```
Public Property Let ComputerName(ByVal NewComputerName _
    As String)
        SetComputerNameA NewComputerName
End Property
```

Listing 9-4: SetComputerName sets the name that identifies the computer to a network

NEXT STEPS

Check out the ExitWindowsEx function, which you can use to restart the system after changing the computer name.

Finding the Next Free Network Drive

When working with network drives and drive letters, you will sometimes need to map a drive letter to a drive on a remote computer, which is called a network resource. Mapping a network resource makes it appear to the user that the resource is actually on the local system. Doing this without involving the user requires a bit of WinAPI wizardry.

The NextDrive function cycles through each of the drives on the system. When it finds a drive that is not already mapped or a known type (e.g., RAM, CD-ROM, Floppy, Fixed, or Network), it returns a string composed of that drive letter followed by a colon, for example, E:. Once armed with the drive letter you can then map a drive to the letter, as discussed in the next section.

To make NextDrive work we need to use the GetDriveType WinAPI function. As you learned in Chapter 6, GetDriveType takes a drive's full path and returns a numerical value indicating the type of drive the drive letter represents.

```
Declare Function GetDriveType Lib "kernel32" _
Alias "GetDriveTypeA" (ByVal nDrive As String) As Long
```

If GetDriveType returns a result of 1, then the drive path passed does not map to a drive. This, then, is what we want—the first free drive letter on a computer.

The NextDrive function in Listing 9-5 works by getting the drive types one by one, starting with the A: drive and working toward Z:, which is the last possible drive. The code only takes potential drives after the C: drive because not all systems have a B: drive, and we don't want to get stuck trying to map a network resource to the B: drive.

```
Function NextDrive() As String
    Dim DriveNum As Long
```

```
      Dim DriveType As Long
      For DriveNum = 65 To 90
          DriveType = GetDriveType(Chr$(DriveNum) & ":\")
          If DriveType = 1 And DriveNum > 67 _
              Then Exit For
      Next
      NextDrive = Chr$(DriveNum) + ":"
  End Function
```

Listing 9-5: NextDrive returns the next free drive letter after the C: drive

Connecting to a Network Resource

Mapping a drive makes it appear to be part of the local system. Windows provides a number of WinAPI functions for mapping and unmapping network drives. This chapter looks at the simplest of these functions.

The WNetAddConnection WinAPI function lets you map a drive letter to a network resource. This lets you connect a local drive letter, such as that returned from the NextDrive function in Listing 9-5, to a network resource.

```
Private Declare Function WNetAddConnection Lib "mpr.dll" _
    Alias "WNetAddConnectionA" ( _
    ByVal lpszNetPath As String, _
    ByVal lpszPassword As String, _
    ByVal lpszLocalName As String) As Long
```

WNetAddConnection takes first the name of the network resource, such as \\server\drive. The second argument is the name of the local device, such as F:. If the resource is password protected, as determined by the network administrator for the resource you are connecting to, you can specify a password for use in making the connection. If you pass an empty string, then the network will use the best password it has available, which includes no password, some default password, or a cached password. If in doubt, pass an explicit password.

The MapDrive procedure in Listing 9-6 shows how to implement the WNetAddConnection WinAPI function.

```
Const WN_SUCCESS = 0
Public Sub MapDrive(sDrive As String, sResource As String)
    If WNetAddConnection(sResource, "", _
    Left$(sDrive, 2)) = WN_SUCCESS Then
        ' worked ok
    Else
        Err.Raise vbObjectError + 513, , _
```

```
        "Could not map drive"
    End If
End Sub
```

Listing 9-6: MapDrive maps a local, free drive letter to a network resource

The code in Listing 9-6 has three items of interest. First, no password is specified in the second argument, although you could specify one if it was required by the network resource. Second, only the two leftmost characters of the local drive are used. This is because WNetAddConnection expects a drive letter and a colon, not the closing slash. Third, if the WinAPI function succeeds, the return value is WN_SUCCESS (or 0). Any other result indicates a failure of some sort. In this example, we simply raise an error to indicate that something was wrong.

Using MapDrive is easy. For example, if we had a server named gateway, with a drive named c, we could map the local F: to the remote \\gateway\c$ drive as follows:

```
MapDrive "F:", "\\gateway\c$"
```

NEXT STEPS

Consider adding an optional password to the MapDrive procedure to handle sharing. Look into the WNet error codes in the win32api.txt file that comes with Visual Basic, and implement verbose help instead of just raising an error.

Disconnecting from a Network Resource

The complementary functionality to MapDrive is presented in UnMapDrive. Just as you can map a local drive to a network resource, you can also disconnect a mapped drive from a resource using the WNetCancelConnection WinAPI function. The UnMapDrive function shown in Listing 9-7 removes the drive mapping created using MapDrive or any other process. All that is required is the local drive letter of the mapped resource, for example, F:.

```
Declare Function WNetCancelConnection Lib "mpr.dll" _
Alias "WNetCancelConnectionA" (ByVal lpszName As String, _
ByVal bForce As Long) As Long

Public Sub UnMapDrive(sDrive As String)
    If WNetCancelConnection(Left$(sDrive, 2), 0) _
        = WN_SUCCESS Then
        ' worked ok
    Else
        Err.Raise vbObjectError + 514, , _
```

```
        "Could not unmap drive"
    End If
End Sub
```

Listing 9-7: UnMapDrive unmaps a local drive letter from a network resource

The WNetAddConnection and WNetCancelConnection WinAPI functions are simple to use but have been superceded by newer functions, including WNetAddConnection2 and WNetAddConnection3. These functions offer additional capabilities, including the capability to map other devices such as printers. An example of this is shown in Chapter 16.

Network Dialogs

Up to now, you've seen how to use certain WinAPI functions to connect and disconnect network resources. These functions work well if you know the local drive letters and network resources in advance. But what if you want to grant your users the ability to map drives or access other network resources? Luckily, the WinAPI contains additional functions that enable you to do just that by implementing a set of predefined dialogs.

The WNetConnectionDialog WinAPI function displays a connection dialog similar that shown in Figure 9-1:

Figure 9-1: The built-in Windows dialog for mapping a network drive

The WNetConnectionDialog WinAPI function is declared as follows:

```
Private Declare Function WNetConnectionDialog Lib _
    "mpr.dll" ( ByVal hWnd As Long, ByVal dwType As Long) _
    As Long
```

By including the capability to display a variety of dialogs, WNetConnectionDialog enables users to connect to various types of network resources. You indicate which dialog to show by the constant you pass in the second argument. For displaying the Map Network Drive dialog shown in Figure 9-1, use the RESOURCETYPE_DISK constant shown in Listing 9-8, which has a value of 1. The first argument is the handle of the owning window, for example, Form1.hWnd, or zero (0) to use the DeskTop window.

```
Const RESOURCETYPE_DISK = 1
Public Function ConnectNetworkDialog() As Boolean
    ConnectNetworkDialog = _
    WNetConnectionDialog(0&, RESOURCETYPE_DISK) = _
        WN_SUCCESS
End Function
```

Listing 9-8: The RESOURCETYPE_DISK constant displays the built-in Windows dialog for mapping a network drive

The code in Listing 9-8 returns True (–1) if the connection was successful or False (0) if the connection was unsuccessful.

WNetConnectionDialog also has the capability to display a printer connection dialog for mapping a local printer designation, such as LPT1, to a network printer. The code is the same as for mapping a network drive, with the exception that a different constant is used in the call to WNetConnectionDialog. The constant for showing the printer connection dialog is RESOURCETYPE_PRINT, which has a value of 2.

Using RESOURCETYPE_PRINT displays a dialog like that shown in Figure 9-2:

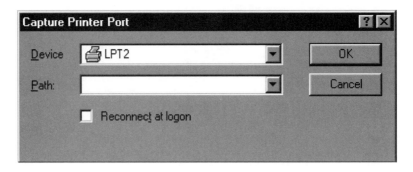

Figure 9-2: The built-in Windows dialog for connecting to a printer resource

The ConnectPrintDialog function shown here uses this variant of the WNetConnectionDialog function:

```
Public Function ConnectPrintDialog() As Boolean
    ConnectPrintDialog = _
    WNetConnectionDialog(0&, RESOURCETYPE_PRINT) = _
        WN_SUCCESS
End Function
```

The Internet Explorer API: Access to the Internet Without a Browser

You have probably posted data for forms many times, and every time you posted data, you were probably using an Internet Browser. You go to a Web site, fill out a form, and click a Submit button. As you wait, if you watch the URL monitor in your browser, you can see that your browser is connecting to a form-handling CGI (Common Gateway Interface) program or ASP (Active Server Pages) page (which works just like a form-handling CGI program).

If you have Windows, Internet Explorer, and Visual Basic, then you can use the Internet Explorer API to open Internet channels and send information to a server without using a browser. For example, suppose you want to read an HTML page into your program as data. The Internet Explorer API enables you to do this and other Internet-related functions in your programs.

All the Internet Explorer API functions are contained in three DLLs: Wininet.dll, Inloader.dll, and Schannel.dll. These latter two DLLs are required for Wininet.dll. Table 9-1 lists the names of the API functions and what they do.

Table 9-1: Internet Explorer API Functions

FUNCTION NAME	DESCRIPTION
InternetOpen	Opens an Internet TCP/IP pathway.
InternetConnect	Uses the TCP/IP pathway to connect to a server.
HttpOpenRequest	Connects to a resource on the server.
HttpSendRequest	Posts information to the resource on the server.
InternetReadFile	Reads a response from the server resource.
InternetCloseHandle	Closes a handle returned from one of the API Open functions.

Communicating with a server over the Internet requires three logical components.

First, you need a program that can format and send data to the server, which we'll call the *data source.* This is a program you write using, in this case, Visual Basic. The actual Internet code is small and will probably just be a single module in your program.

Second, you need a program on the server that can read your data, process it, and respond to the data, which we'll call the data sink. Normally, this would be a CGI program, an ASP program, or Visual Basic Web class application. For CGI applications, all you need to do is examine the environment variables and read and write to the server's standard in and out ports. While you can create CGI programs using VB, most Web programmers who use Windows-based servers use VB to create components that are accessed from ASP pages.

Third, and most important, you need a suite of protocols that can handle all the messy communication details. This last part—the protocols—is the part built in Internet Explorer in the form of Wininet.dll and its dependency DLLs,

Inloader.dll and Schannel.dll. These include the HyperText Transport Protocol (HTTP and HTTPS) and the Transmission Control Protocol-Internet Protocol (TCP/IP) upon which HTTP is based.. HTTP is a protocol that communicates between a server and a client (usually a Web server and an Internet browser, respectively).

This chapter focuses on creating the data source, or client side of the equation. Chapter 17 teaches you to create Internet applications (the server lside of the equation) using Visual Basic.

After an Internet pipeline, or channel, to the server is established using TCP/IP and HTTP, the data source program can read and write to the channel using standard Visual Basic file reading and writing code. In fact, it helps to think about the Internet channel as if it was a file—you open it, you read and write to it, and then you close it. The data source program has seven requirements:

1. Install the required run-time files on the user's system.
2. Open an Internet channel.
3. Connect to the Internet server.
4. Connect to the data sink on the Internet server.
5. Post form data to the data sink.
6. Read the response from the data sink.
7. Close all the handles.

Installing the Run-Time Files

The entire process of communicating with a server over the Internet will work only for users that have an Internet Service Provider (ISP) and a valid connection or account. The process will work for any machine with Internet Explorer (IE) installed on it. For machines without IE installed, the Wintinst.exe self-installer is provided by Microsoft. Wintinst.exe is small (about 400 KB) and will update a machine without IE with the required system files. Wintinst.exe will not install IE nor will it change any system settings with regard to browser settings.

Internet Explorer API Redistributable Components

First, a few words about using the Internet Explorer API. Prior to Internet Explorer 4.x, Microsoft distributed a self-extracting executable named Wintinst.exe that installed the Internet Explorer core files. Wintinst.exe came as a part of the ActiveX SDK, and was also found on MSDN. Wintinst.exe contained the core system files required for Internet communication. Wintinst.exe did not include a browser, just three critical files: Wininet.dll, Inloader.dll, and Schannel.dll. These three files can still be found on the Microsoft MSDN Web site or the ActiveX SDK, in the Wintinst.exe setup program, which is included on the CD-ROM, in the Chap9 directory, that accompanies this book.

Recently, Microsoft has changed its position on the distribution of its new Internet channel DLLs. The new Microsoft position is that you should use the IE 5.0 Internet Explorer Administration Kit (IEAK) and that you must install at least a minimal-function browser if you are going to use the IE core system files. However, you can still find and use Wintinst.exe under the previous ActiveX SDK license, and the previous license grants the right to use the existing Wintinst.exe! Instead of megabytes of redistributables, we use a few hundred KB.

Also note that you only need to install the IE core system files for those machines without them, and there are not very many copies of Windows 9x or Windows NT that do not include them.

Opening an Internet Channel

Let's take a look at the first Internet Explorer API function you need—InternetOpen, which opens an Internet channel.

```
Declare Function InternetOpen Lib _
"wininet.dll" Alias "InternetOpenA"( _
ByVal sUserAgent As String, _
ByVal lAccessType As Long, _
ByVal sProxyName As String, _
ByVal sProxyBypass As String, _
ByVal lFlags As Long) As Long
```

The arguments to InternetOpen control many aspects of the channel. The arguments that we care about are sUserAgent and lAccessType. The scUserAgent argument is used by the system to track your sessions. Because it is a user-defined string, we just use the application name. lAccessType defines the kind of Internet connection we want to set up in cases where a proxy server is in use. Setting lAccessType to the INTERNET_OPEN_TYPE_PRECONFIG constant (which has a value of 0) tells InternetOpen to use the client machine's existing Internet connection definition.

The basic code to open an Internet channel is as follows:

```
Const INTERNET_OPEN_TYPE_PRECONFIG = 0
Dim scUserAgent As String
scUserAgent = App.ExeName
hOpen = InternetOpen(scUserAgent, _
    INTERNET_OPEN_TYPE_PRECONFIG, "", "", 0)
```

InternetOpen returns a long integer value, which, if not zero, is the handle for future operations with the channel. Store the result of InternetOpen –because you will need it for the remaining steps in the process of communicating with a server over the Internet. You will also need to close the channel using the InternetCloseHandle API when you are finished using the connection.

Connecting to the Internet Server

After an Internet channel is open, you need to connect to an Internet server. To do so, you use the URL (Uniform Resource Locator) of the server to which you want to connect, for example, www.yourdomain.com. The API function for this is InternetConnect.

```
Declare Function InternetConnect _
Lib "wininet.dll" Alias "InternetConnectA"( _
ByVal hInternetSession As Long, _
ByVal sServerName As String, _
ByVal nServerPort As Integer, _
ByVal sUsername As String, _
ByVal sPassword As String, _
ByVal lService As Long, _
ByVal lFlags As Long, _
ByVal lContext As Long) As Long
```

InternetConnect takes a URL and establishes a session to the server resource specified. InternetConnect takes several arguments, including the channel handle from InternetOpen, the server name, the server port to connect to, and the service type. The INTERNET_SERVICE_HTTP constant is used for the latter argument, which specifies that you wish to use the HTTP protocol for the connection. One of the more bizarre aspects of this function is that you always use the INTERNET_INVALID_PORT_NUMBER constant as the server port number to connect to; this tells the function to use the default port number for the chosen service.

```
Const INTERNET_INVALID_PORT_NUMBER = 0
Const INTERNET_SERVICE_HTTP = 3
Dim Server As String
Server = "http://www.yourdomain.com"
hConnection = InternetConnect(hOpen, _
Server, INTERNET_INVALID_PORT_NUMBER, _
"", "", INTERNET_SERVICE_HTTP, 0, 0)
```

Just like InternetOpen, InternetConnect also returns a long integer, which, if not zero, is a handle to the session opened with the server. So, don't lose the hConnection value!

Connecting to the Data Sink

The next step is to specify the resource to which we actually want to connect; in this case, a CGI program running on the server.

```
Declare Function HttpOpenRequest Lib "wininet.dll" _
    Alias "HttpOpenRequestA"( _
    ByVal hHttpSession As Long, _
```

```
ByVal sVerb As String, _
ByVal sObjectName As String, _
ByVal sVersion As String, _
ByVal sReferer As String, _
ByVal lpAny As Long, _
ByVal lFlags As Long, _
ByVal lContext As Long) As Long
```

While HttpOpenRequest takes a lot of arguments, for working with CGI programs all we need to worry about is sVerb, sObjectName, and lFlags. sVerb is a string that indicates the type of operation you want to perform after the connection is made. When working with CGI programs, the value to use is the string POST. The sObjectName parameter is a string with the name of the resource you want to access; in this case, the CGI program name. The code to connect to a CGI program named sample.exe in the /cgi-bin directory of the www.yourdomain.com domain is:

```
Const INTERNET_FLAG_KEEP_CONNECTION = 4194304
Dim CGI As String
CGI = "/cgi-bin/sample.exe"
hURL = HttpOpenRequest(hConnection, "POST", _
CGI, "", "", 0, _
INTERNET_FLAG_KEEP_CONNECTION, 0)
```

If HttpOpenRequest is successful, it returns another long integer handle with a value greater than zero.

Posting Form Data

At this point, we have opened a TCP/IP channel to the Internet, connected to a server and established a session, and started an instance of the form handler (the CGI program named sample.exe) running on the server. The final step is to send some data to the form handler. This is almost trivial now that the connection is established. The HttpSendRequest API function passes your data to the server, which, in turn, passes it to the form handler.

```
Declare Function HttpSendRequest Lib _
"wininet.dll" Alias "HttpSendRequestA" ( _
ByVal hHttpRequest As Long, _
ByVal sHeaders As String, _
ByVal lHeadersLength As Long, _
ByVal sOptional As String, _
ByVal lOptionalLength As Long) As Integer
```

Essentially, HttpSendRequest posts a specially formatted string containing form data to the CGI program running on the server over the TCP/IP session established. You can also pass a header to the server that tells the server what kind of data to expect, such as binary data, multipart forms, or other nontextual information. However, in this implementation we use the default type of data, which is HTML.

HttpSendRequest returns a value not equal to zero if it fails. Thus, about all it takes to send data to an HTML form handler is to call the API function and pass your data and the length of the string containing the data. In the code below, the data is contained in a variable named m_cPostBuffer.

```
If HttpSendRequest(hURL, "", 0, _
    m_cPostBuffer, Len(m_cPostBuffer)) Then
    '// it worked!
End If
```

We just achieved our objective, or at least most of it! The process is fairly easy to implement once you figure out the sequence of calls and get the arguments typed correctly.

There are still a few important details to discuss. Perhaps the most important detail is that the HTML protocol expects its data in a very specific format. The m_cPostBuffer variable used above to pass information to the form handler has two important criteria it must meet.

First, the data must be in the form of *field name=field value*. For example, if you have a data field named Company with a value of Modern Software, the string needs to be Company=Modern Software. Multiple fields are concatenated using the ampersand (&) character. For example, imagine a field named Last_Name with a value of Marquis. The new string would be Company=Modern Software&Last_Name=Marquis. This process continues for all the data fields that you wish to pass to the form handler.

Second, after the data string is built, you need one more step before it's ready to send using HttpSendRequest: it must be URL encoded. The HTTP protocol defines very specifically what characters it will transport, and what it cannot transport. There are a number of reasons why many characters cannot be passed as plain text, but the easiest answer is because your data will (or may) get corrupted. So, instead, we encode the data, replacing forbidden characters with a code set composed of allowed characters. Then, at the server end a decoding process is performed exchanging the codes for the forbidden characters. In the example above, there is a forbidden space (ASCII 32, hex 20) between Modern and Software. Under the HTML specification, spaces must be replaced with a plus character (+). So, the URL-encoded data to pass to HttpSendRequest would be Company=Modern+Software&Last_Name=Marquis. (See Listing 9-10, later in this chapter, for a complete URL-encoding function). The UrlEncode function in Listing 9-10 does the job of converting data from raw to URL encoded for you before it is sent to the server. (If you will be parsing and using the data on the server, you might need a complementary UrlDecode routine in your CGI programs.)

Reading the Response

After going through the trouble of opening an Internet channel, connecting to an Internet server, connecting to the data sink on the Internet server, and formatting and posting your data to the data sink, it would be nice to read a response from the data sink. If you are writing your own data sink (CGI form handler), then you can create any response that you want. Your CGI program can run calculations, access a database, perform any action you want, and then return the results to you as a URL-encoded string.

As you might expect, there is an WinAPI function for reading the response from the data sink—it's called InternetReadFile and the metaphor of reading a disk file should be very apparent.

```
Private Declare Function InternetReadFile _
Lib "wininet.dll" ( _
ByVal hFile As Long, _
ByVal sbuffer As String, _
ByVal lNumBytesToRead As Long, _
lNumberOfBytesRead As Long) As Integer
```

InternetReadFile reads the response from the data sink just like you would read a file. It reads a fixed number of bytes at a time, and when the "end" of the server response is found, it concludes. Note the lNumberOfBytesRead argument in the declaration. This is not a typo; ByVal is not used. InternetReadFile returns information to you not in its return result, but rather in the lNumberOfBytesRead argument directly.

The process is to call InternetReadFile over and over in a loop until it returns no more data, at which point the process is complete. Then, you simply return the data collected.

```
'setup a buffer of 1024 chars
lNumBytesToRead = 1024
sbuffer = Space$(lNumBytesToRead)
'while there is data to read…
Do While _
    InternetReadFile(hURL, sbuffer, _
    lNumBytesToRead, lNumberOfBytesRead)
    'lNumberOfBytesRead returns the number
    'of bytes actually read
    If lNumberOfBytesRead = 0 Then
        Exit Do    'no more data to read
    Else  'data was returned, concatenate
        'to result
        Result = Result & _
        Left$(sbuffer, lNumberOfBytesRead)
    End If
```

```
        'since the API changes the value
        'of lNumBytesToRead, reset it
        lNumBytesToRead = 1024
        'make a new buffer
        sbuffer = Space$(lNumBytesToRead)
Loop
'done reading, trim results and return
PostForm = Trim$(Result)
```

The data collected will be in HTML format, with familiar HTML coding such as <BODY> and so on. You will need to parse the data, bypassing <HEAD>, <p>, and the other HTML codes, to extract the data that you care about. In our implementation, the CGI program returns a string in the body of the HTML code much like the string passed to the CGI program. In other words, the response is similar to *fieldname1=fieldvalue&fieldname2=fieldvalue*. This way the result can easily be parsed.

Closing All the Handles

The final step is to use the CloseHandle WinAPI function to close all the open handles and release the resources used.

```
Private Declare Function _
InternetCloseHandle Lib "wininet.dll" _
(ByVal hInet As Long) As Integer
```

You'll recall from earlier sections that handles were returned by the API functions that opened the Internet channel, connected to the Internet server, and connected to the data sink. InternetOpen returned a handle in the hOpen variable, InternetConnect returned a handle in hConnection, and HttpOpenRequest returned a handle in hURL, respectively. Closing the handles is easy.

```
InternetCloseHandle hURL
InternetCloseHandle hConnection
InternetCloseHandle hOpen
```

Putting the Pieces Together: A Complete Data-Source Program

All of the sample code you've seen up to now fits together in the example that follows. We've also added an error handler that closes all open handles; unlike Visual Basic, the Internet Explorer API will not clean up for you! Also, when you open a connection, you can keep it open as long as you want. In our case, we wanted a clean stable "in and out" implementation, so we created the code shown in Listing 9-9. The PostForm function posts data to a form handler, and returns the result of the post in the function result. Normally, the response from the server is a text stream—an HTML page of some sort.

```
Const INTERNET_FLAG_KEEP_CONNECTION = &H400000

Public Function PostForm(ByVal Server As String, _
                    ByVal CGI As String) As String
        On Error GoTo myError
        Dim hOpen As Long, hConnection As Long
        Dim hURL As Long
        Dim sbuffer As String
        Dim lNumBytesToRead  As Long
        Dim lNumberOfBytesRead As Long
        Dim Result As String
        Dim scUserAgent As String
    scUserAgent = App.EXEName
    ' open internet connection
    hOpen = InternetOpen(scUserAgent, _
    INTERNET_OPEN_TYPE_PRECONFIG, "", "", 0)
    If hOpen <> 0 Then
        hConnection = InternetConnect(hOpen, Server, _
        INTERNET_INVALID_PORT_NUMBER, "", "", _
        INTERNET_SERVICE_HTTP, 0, 0)
        If hConnection <> 0 Then
            hURL = HttpOpenRequest(hConnection, "POST", _
                CGI, "", "", 0, _
                INTERNET_FLAG_KEEP_CONNECTION, 0)
            If hURL <> 0 Then
                If HttpSendRequest(hURL, "", 0, _
                    m_cPostBuffer, Len(m_cPostBuffer)) Then
                        lNumBytesToRead = 1024
                        sbuffer = Space$(lNumBytesToRead)
            Do While InternetReadFile(hURL, sbuffer, _
                lNumBytesToRead, lNumberOfBytesRead)
                        If lNumberOfBytesRead = 0 Then
                            Exit Do
                        Else
                            Result = Result & _
                                Left$(sbuffer, _
                            lNumberOfBytesRead)
                        End If
                        lNumBytesToRead = 1024
                        sbuffer = Space$(lNumBytesToRead)
                    Loop
                    PostForm = Trim$(Result)
                Else
                Err.Raise vbObjectError + 504, , _
                    "HttpSendRequest"
                End If
```

```
            Else
                Err.Raise vbObjectError + 505, , _
                    "HttpOpenRequest"
            End If
        Else
            Err.Raise vbObjectError + 506, , _
                InternetConnect"
        End If
    Else
        Err.Raise vbObjectError + 507, , "InternetOpen"
    End If

myExit:
    InternetCloseHandle hURL
    InternetCloseHandle hConnection
    InternetCloseHandle hOpen
    Exit Function
myError:
    Resume myExit
End Function
```

Listing 9-9: PostForm uses the Internet Explorer API to post form data to a CGI program on an Internet server, and to then read the program's response

The code in Listing 9-10 encodes the text about to be sent to the server. The encoding is called URL-encoding, which is used to replace certain reserved characters with a code. At the server, these codes are replaced with the character again.

```
Private Function UrlEncode(sText As String) As String
    Dim sResult As String
    Dim sFinal As String
    Dim sChar As String
    Dim i As Long
    For i = 1 To Len(sText)
        sChar = Mid$(sText, i, 1)
        If InStr(1, abcdefghijklmnopqrs_
            tuvwxyzABCDEFGHIJKLMNOPQR_
            STUVWXYZ0123456789", _
        sChar) <> 0 Then
            sResult = sResult & sChar
        ElseIf sChar = " " Then
            sResult = sResult & "+"
        ElseIf True Then
            sResult = sResult & "%" & Right$("0" _
                & Hex(Asc(sChar)), 2)
```

```
            End If
            If Len(sResult) > 1000 Then
                sFinal = sFinal & sResult
                sResult = ""
            End If
        Next
        UrlEncode = sFinal & sResult
End Function
```

Listing 9-10: UrlEncode performs URL encoding of data

The sample program titled Chap9.vbp, found on the CD-ROM, is a working example of executing a server script and reading its contents using the Internet Explorer API. Running this sample is very simple—connect to the Internet and run Chap9.VBP.

Chapter 10

Reliable and Flexible Data Validation

"Garbage in, garbage out" is one of the older sayings in the computer industry, and it is absolutely true. If you let garbage data in your system, you have garbage data to work with and no result will be reliable. However, if you don't allow some flexibility in how the user enters data, users will complain and eventually stop using your system. This chapter shows you how to be both firm and flexible in enforcing data integrity in what users enter in your applications.

Validation of Numeric Data

Now that Visual Basic provides a wealth of conversion functions, validating numbers is easier than ever. Each function attempts to convert data regardless of format into the type of data you need—effectively testing the validity of the original data. No longer do you have to do all sorts of calculations to determine whether an entry is a number. Just use one of the built-in conversion functions—IsNumeric, TypeName, or VarType—to check the contents of the entry box.

IsNumeric

The IsNumeric function tests data to determine whether it is numeric. The function won't distinguish among varieties of numeric data; for instance, it won't tell you whether a number is a Currency or an Integer value. Instead, it returns a single True or False result. It is up to you to test further for a specific data type. You can use IsNumeric in the Immediate window to test various data values, as shown here:

```
Print IsNumeric(50.2123)
True
Print IsNumeric(ABC123)
True
Print IsNumeric(&HABC123)
True
Print IsNumeric("ABC123")
False
```

You might be wondering why ABC123 came up as a True instead of a False. This is because ABC123 is not a valid hexadecimal number when it lacks the prefix "&H" that tells Visual Basic to expect a hexadecimal number. You'll probably notice that it does not matter whether the number in these examples is enclosed in quotes or not. This is because Visual Basic automatically attempts to convert strings to numbers when a function expects a numeric parameter. If it succeeds, the IsNumeric function returns True. This automatic type conversion can be confusing. In fact, some Visual Basic programmers call this "evil type coercion" because it is not always obvious whether you are dealing with a string or a number.

The following code causes an error:

```
Print IsNumeric($50,000,000.02)
```

because the comma is a special character that separates function parameters, as far as Visual Basic is concerned. If, however you placed the value in a string, it would work because Visual Basic would treat the commas as part of the number, and not as a separator between function parameters.

```
Print IsNumeric("$50,000,000.02")
True
```

Because Visual Basic uses commas to separate parameters or variables, and the $ to indicate the presence of string variables, you should avoid using these characters when you want to hard code values in your code. In this example, you would use the value 50000000.02.

TypeName

The TypeName function is new to Visual Basic 6. TypeName accepts any data or variable and returns, as a text string, the data type of the variable or data. For instance, if you use the TypeName function on an array of integers, TypeName returns Integer(). You can use TypeName in immediate mode to experiment with the data types that result for literal values. For example:

```
Print TypeName(True)
Boolean
Print TypeName(25)
Integer
Print TypeName(1000000)
Long
Print TypeName(52.1)
Double
Print TypeName(1.4E+06)
Double
Print TypeName("Test")
String
```

When evaluating literal values, the result isn't always accurate. For instance, you might want to place the value 25 in a variable of type Byte instead of Integer. Similarly, 52.1 can be placed in a Single, Decimal, or Double variable. However, if you declare a variable and use TypeName on the variable, you'll always get the correct result. (The exception is a Variant variable, which causes an unpredictable result just like a literal value does.) Table 10-1 lists the results returnable by the TypeName function, which are also shown in the online help for this function:

Table 10-1: Strings Returned by the TypeName Function

STRING	MEANING
"Empty"	Used when the variant variable has not been initialized
"Null"	Used when the data in a variant variable is not valid
"Integer"	Integer value
"Long"	Long Integer value
"Single"	Single-precision floating-point number
"Double"	Double-precision floating-point number
"Currency"	Currency value
"Date"	Date value
"String"	String
"Object"	Object
"Error"	Used when the variable represents an error value
"Boolean"	Boolean value
"Decimal"	Decimal value
"Byte"	Byte value
"Unknown"	Displays if the data type is unknown, which could be a user-defined type that you've created or it could be an error
"Nothing"	Used for object variables that don't refer to objects
object type	Prints the name of the object type if the variable is of that type, such as FileSystemObject

VarType

The VarType function is similar to the TypeName function except that it returns a predefined constant that indicates the data type of the variable/data being evaluated instead of a string. Although you can think of VarType as equivalent to TypeName with a bit less intelligence, VarType is preferable in certain instances. For example, because it returns numbers it is more efficient for use in programs that need to perform different operations based on the data type (numeric comparisons are faster than string comparisons). It is also easier to determine if a variable is an array—any result larger or equal to 8192 is an array. VarType is used in the same manner as TypeName and is used when you need a number returned instead of a string. Table 10-2 lists the constants that VarType returns.

Table 10-2: Constants Returned by the VarType Function

CONSTANT	VALUE	MEANING
vbEmpty	0	Empty
vbNull	1	Null
vbInteger	2	Integer
vbLong	3	Long
vbSingle	4	Single
vbDouble	5	Double
vbCurrency	6	Currency
vbDate	7	Date
vbString	8	String
vbObject	9	Object
vbError	10	Error
vbBoolean	11	Boolean
vbVariant	12	Variant (returned only for an array of Variant)
vbDataObject	13	Data access object
vbDecimal	14	Decimal value
vbByte	17	Byte value
vbUserDefinedType	36	Variant that contains a user-defined type
vbArray	8192	Array

Because the constant names returned by VarType are defined in the Visual Basic for Applications library, they are available to your applications. The tricky part of using this function is in evaluating a variable that holds an array. The VarType function returns the vbArray constant summed with the constant for the data type of the elements. This means that if the result of VarType is greater than vbArray, you have to subtract vbArray from the result to determine what type of data the array holds.

Validation of Dates

Validating dates is a bit more work because there are many more formats that are valid and common, even within a single country. Consider, for example, a favorite day of accountants, and look at all the common formats that are used for it:

April 15, 2000
15 April 2000
15 Apr 00
April 15th, 2000
April 15th, '00

```
4/15/00
4/15/2000
04/15/2000
4-15-00
```

Of course, if you restrict your users to just one of these formats, they'll complain and want more. The best approach is to allow any of these and to validate anything the user enters. Using the built-in functions provided for working with dates, this approach is pretty easy and provides more flexibility for your users. Conveniently, you can use the TypeName and VarType functions already described to validate variables, because the Date data type is recognized by both functions. To validate literal values as well as variables, Visual Basic provides the IsDate function.

To see why the TypeName and VarType function can't work on literals, consider the following two examples:

```
Print TypeName (4-15-99)
Integer
Print TypeName ("4-15-99")
String
```

The literal 4-15-99 is interpreted as the number –110 (4 minus 15 minus 99). The literal "4-15-99" is a string, and the TypeName function does not try to evaluate strings (unlike the IsNumeric function that you saw earlier).

IsDate

Quite simply, the IsDate function looks at a value or a variable and determines whether it is a date/time value or not. The sample code shown below shows some of the examples that you can try to test the function. Date/time values that are hard-coded in your code should be surrounded with pound signs (#). Visual Basic knows that literals surrounded by # characters are dates in the same way that it knows that literals surrounded by quotes are strings. This is especially critical if you are entering dates such as 4/15/99, which look like two division operations to VB.

```
Print IsDate(#4/15/99#)
True
Print IsDate(#December 15, 1999#)
True
Print IsDate(#15:22#)
True
Print IsDate(#2:23 PM#)
True
Print IsDate(#4-15-99#)
True
```

All of the following examples will cause an error or return False:

```
Print IsDate(#January 32, 1999#)
Raises an error (invalid date)
Print IsDate(4/15/99)
False
Print IsDate(#4.4.99#)
Raises an error
Print IsDate(#Thursday, April 15, 1999#)
Raises an error
```

Although the third example is a perfectly valid form of date in other countries, IsDate works in conjunction with your international settings and only allows dates in the format of your own country. This is important if you are writing internationalized applications that need to validate dates because your local country's format may be different from that of the rest of the world. For this reason, it is always best to rely on Visual Basic's date validation rather than to try to write your own.

Validation of Text Entries

Validating text has an upside and a downside. The upside is that it's easy to determine whether the user has entered anything at all because you can just check a text box against an empty string (""). The downside is that it's not so easy to determine whether the text that was entered is valid. In some cases, you don't care and don't need to worry about it. In other cases, however, you have to look at exactly what the user entered and make sure it fits your requirements.

Text Length

Developers need to consider three questions regarding the length of the text that the user has entered:

1. Has any text been entered at all?
2. Has any maximum length been exceeded?
3. Has a specific, required length been entered correctly?

The first question you normally address is whether any text has been entered at all; that is, it is at least one character long. You can do this in a couple of ways. You can either compare the text box to an empty string ("") or you can check the length of the string with the Len function. This is pretty easy, but it often gets left out until the testers have at your code, so it's good to put it on your to-do list.

The second question you normally address, especially when dealing with a database, is to verify that some maximum length has not been exceeded. Database text fields are normally given a maximum length that you cannot exceed, so you need to make sure that the user doesn't think that more data can be entered. The easiest way to enforce this is to set the MaxLength property of the TextBox control. Once this property is set, there is no way for the user to exceed the length, and the second question is taken care of.

The third question may or may not apply. Depending on the data being entered, you may have several valid lengths that can be entered. Consider, for example, the US ZIP code. Some people only remember the first five digits. However, bulk mailers always use the full 10 characters (9 digits plus a dash) because they get a break on postage if the whole ZIP code is provided. This is a perfect example of two specific, valid lengths for the same data. This particular type of validation is demonstrated in the example later in the chapter, in the "Putting It All Together" section.

Text Content

The next issue that comes up during text validation is the content of the text that the user entered. This issue has two forms:

- Characters entered in the text
- Format of the text

These two items are related, as well. For instance, if the user is entering a US phone number, all of these characters might be valid in the user's mind:

- ( )—for the area code
- -
- x—indicating an extension after the number
- space character to separate the sections instead of a dash
- .—for the people who type phone numbers such as 415.555.1212

If you start talking about international numbers, you have to include the plus sign, which is commonly used to indicate the country code. Of course, the format in other countries is different than the common formats used for the US phone numbers. In fact, in some countries the number of digits in a phone number varies from city to city! Remember this if you are building internationalized applications: users in other countries don't have US-style area codes, and people in the US don't have city or region codes.

This type of validation requires both a list of valid characters and a specified format to deal with. The example later in the chapter, in the "Putting It All Together" section, shows how to handle these requirements.

Validating Other Types of Data

While numeric, date, and text cover most of the data-entry spectrum, there are three extras that you might have to deal with:

1. Yes/No responses
2. Pick one from a set list of items
3. Enable the user to either pick an item or enter a new one

These situations are best handled with a combination of form controls and a little bit of error handling. Yes/No is a perfect opportunity to use a CheckBox control, because that's what it is designed for. Having the user enter either a Y or an N is just asking for trouble down the road. Give them a box—it's easier to understand and the user doesn't have to guess what you want.

Picking from a list calls for a drop-down list box using the ComboBox control. The only trick here is to make sure that the user picks an item from the list, because it is possible for the user to skip the control entirely. After the user picks an item, the box removes the option of having no item selected. This is an extra bit of error checking provided by the built-in ComboBox control.

The last situation, allowing the user to either pick or create an item, is the hardest to handle. There are several possibilities:

- The user picks an item from the list. No problem.
- The user skips the control and doesn't pick or enter anything. This could cause an error.
- The user enters an item already in the list. This shouldn't be a problem because the control can be automatically positioned to that item in the list.
- The user enters a new item. The item has to be checked for validity against whatever rules were established for your database.

All of these cases for these three situations are discussed in the example in the next section.

Putting It All Together

Now that you've learned about some of the kinds of validation that are needed, we can build an example that incorporates the best practices for validating data of all these different types. The example is set up in a modular way, so that you can reuse the independent pieces in your own applications. With the preliminaries out of the way, let's get started.

Building the Data-Entry Form

We're going to build a typical data-entry form that you've probably seen hundreds of times in other applications. It will include all the cases we just talked about and will show you how to deal with each one to prevent errors and to make data entry as intuitive as possible for the user.

The form we're building is shown in Figure 10-1.

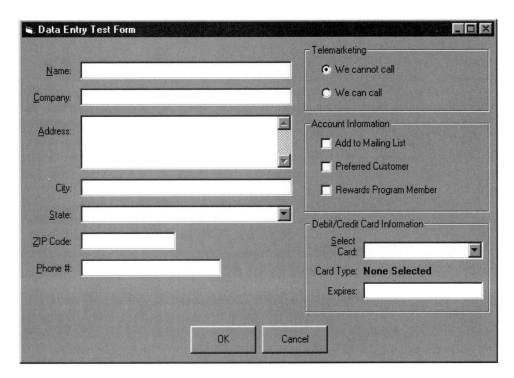

All of the data types discussed earlier are represented:

- Date validation will be done on the expiration date for the credit card.
- Text entry validation will be done in all the text boxes. Most will be checked for length, both minimum and maximum.
- ZIP code is checked for two valid lengths.
- Phone number is checked for a valid length and then reformatted.
- Option buttons enforce the selection of an item.
- Check boxes allow for selection of yes/no data.
- Drop-down lists are used in the two different ways mentioned earlier: the State list is static, but the Select Card list can be expanded with a new item.
- Credit card number is validated for length as well as to check whether the number is valid.

Setting Essential Properties

Some controls on the form require that you set certain properties for the form to work properly. Table 10-3 includes these essential properties. Feel free to choose any text for the Name properties; however, the rest of this section is based on the names shown in the table. Also, all labels (except for the one next to Card Type) are part of a control array named lblStatic. This is because these are pieces of static text that will not be manipulated through code. In addition, the tab order has been set from top to bottom on the left column, followed by top to bottom on the right column. This is because it follows the way the data would be collected:

Table 10-3: Form and Control Properties

TextBox	(Name)	txtName
	MaxLength	40
	Text	???
TextBox	(Name)	txtCompany
	MaxLength	60
	Text	???
TextBox	(Name)	txtAddress
	MaxLength	240
	MultiLine	True
	ScrollBars	2—Vertical
	Text	???
TextBox	(Name)	txtCity
	MaxLength	40
	Text	???
ComboBox	(Name)	cboState
	Style	2—Dropdown List
TextBox	(Name)	txtZIP
	MaxLength	10
	Text	???
TextBox	(Name)	txtPhone
	MaxLength	25
	Text	???
OptionButton	(Name)	optNoCalls
	Value	True
	Caption	???
OptionButton	(Name)	optCallOK
	Caption	???
CheckBox	(Name)	chkMailingList
	Caption	???
CheckBox	(Name)	chkPreferred
	Caption	???

CheckBox	(Name)	chkRewards
	Caption	???
ComboBox	(Name)	cboCreditCardNumber
	Style	0—Dropdown Combo
	Text	Empty—No Value
Label	(Name)	lblCreditCardType
	Caption	???
TextBox	(Name)	txtExpirationDate
	MaxLength	10
	Text	???
CommandButton	(Name)	cmdOK
	Caption	???
CommandButton	(Name)	cmdCancel
	Cancel	True
	Caption	???

Enforcing Character Validation

Some of the boxes should only have numbers put in them, or just numbers with a limited set of punctuation. This validation is pretty easy to do, once you've figured out the characters to allow. Looking at the fields on the form, there are some places where we can restrict by character:

- ZIP Code—numbers and the dash character
- Phone #—numbers, dashes, parentheses, spaces, and an X (for extension). International numbers are not being supported, so we don't have to use the plus sign (for international codes). If you need international numbers, make the appropriate changes.
- Select Card—digits and the dash character

For these boxes, we've allowed a little bit of flexibility in how the number is entered. We'll also manipulate some of the data after they are entered, so that, for example, all phone numbers will internally have the same format. For now, we just need to restrict the characters to these ranges. To make this easier, we're going to create a function to validate an input character against a range defined by the particular field.

To make the code work, first add these constants to the Declarations section of your form. These constants list all the valid characters for each of the three input fields.

```
Const ValidZIPCharacters = "0123456789-"
Const ValidPhoneCharacters = "0123456789()- xX+"
Const ValidCCCharacters = "0123456789-"
```

Next, let's create a function to check the input keystroke against this range. Because this function is called exclusively from the KeyPress event procedure of each text box, we can let it return either a zero (which effectively eliminates the

character entered by the user) or the original value, which has no visible effect.
The IsCharValid function is shown here:

```
Private Function IsCharValid(intChar As Integer, _
    strRange As String) As Integer

    If intChar < 32 Then
        '
        ' have to allow control characters through, such
        ' as the backspace character
        '
        IsCharValid = intChar
    ElseIf InStr(1, strRange, Chr(intChar), vbTextCompare) > 0 Then
        IsCharValid = intChar
    Else
        IsCharValid = 0
    End If

End Function
```

The first test in the IsCharValid function enables control characters, such as
those generated by the backspace and Enter keys, through the function. If you
don't do this, the user won't be able to erase or move with the cursor keys while
in a text box.

The second test looks for the input character in the range provided by the
caller. This is where the constants you created come into play. Each of the boxes
has a specific range that is allowed. If the input character isn't in the range, it is
thrown out by this function.

Here's how you use this function to validate the ZIP code box, for example.
The US ZIP code has either five or nine digits. If it has nine digits, the groups are
separated by a dash into subgroups of five and four digits.

```
Private Sub txtZIP_KeyPress(KeyAscii As Integer)
    KeyAscii = IsCharValid(KeyAscii, ValidZIPCharacters)
End Sub
```

Because IsCharValid returns a zero for an invalid character, you can simply
hook up the IsCharValid return value to the KeyAscii parameter of the event
handler. The other two text boxes (Phone # and Select Card) are just as easy to
set up. The code for these boxes is shown here:

```
Private Sub cboCreditCardNumber_KeyPress(KeyAscii As Integer)
    KeyAscii = IsCharValid(KeyAscii, ValidCCCharacters)
End Sub
Private Sub txtPhone_KeyPress(KeyAscii As Integer)
    KeyAscii = IsCharValid(KeyAscii, ValidPhoneCharacters)
End Sub
```

> *NOTE*
> *This approach misses the case where the user pastes data from the clipboard. One way to deal with this is to catch the ^V key and validate the entire string against the condition (you'll want another function that examines the clipboard text one character at a time, setting KeyAscii to zero if any of the characters aren't valid). Or to disable pasting entirely (which customers won't appreciate). Either way - this should be dealt with.*

These simple validations will keep bad characters out of the boxes, making it easier to validate them further later.

Reformatting Input Data

As was mentioned earlier, people enter the same data in many different ways, all of which are perfectly valid. For instance, an expiration date might be entered:

    Dec 2000
    12/2000
    12/00
    12/31/00

These are all valid, and we need to take this into account when writing our code. However, after the data are entered, there's no reason we can't change the data to our own format. This section shows you how to use the Validate event of several controls to reformat the input data into a common format, no matter how the user entered the data.

The first box containing data to reformat is the Expires box. This box must allow a date to be entered in nearly any format. Once the date is entered, we will reformat it in MM/YYYY format. The code to do this is shown here:

```
Private Sub txtExpirationDate_Validate(Cancel As Boolean)

    If Not IsDate(txtExpirationDate.Text) Then
        MsgBox "Please enter a valid date.", vbExclamation
        Cancel = True
    Else
        txtExpirationDate = Format(txtExpirationDate, "MM/YYYY")
    End If

End Sub
```

If an invalid date is entered, a message box displays indicating that. When the message box is closed, setting the Cancel parameter to True will cause the focus to be returned to the date text box. If the date is valid, the Format function reformats whatever date is entered to the format we've chosen (MM/YYYY) and puts it in the box.

The next box to reformat is the ZIP Code box. The correct format for a ZIP code is either NNNNN or NNNNN-NNNN. We'll create code in the Validate event to make sure that one or the other of these formats was entered, and if the dash is in the wrong place, we'll move it to the right place. Add the following code to your form to take care of these cases:

```
Private Sub txtZIP_Validate(Cancel As Boolean)
    Dim strTemp As String
    strTemp = Replace(txtZIP.Text, "-", "")
    If (Len(strTemp) <> 5 And Len(strTemp) <> 9) _
        Or Not(IsNumeric(strTemp))Then
        MsgBox "Please enter either a five or nine digit ZIP code.", _
            vbExclamation
        Cancel = True
        Exit Sub
    End If

    If Len(strTemp) = 9 Then
        txtZIP = Left(strTemp, 5) & "-" & Right(strTemp, 4)
    End If

End Sub
```

The final reformat that we'll do is the Phone # box. There are a number of valid formats for phone numbers.

nnn-nnnn
nnn-nnn-nnnn
1-nnn-nnn-nnnn
1-nnn-nnnn
nnn-nnnn xnnnn

There are many other variations of this, as well. The rules that we'll use for reformatting phone numbers are:

1. All numbers will at least be in the format (nnn) nnn-nnnn. Numbers entered without area codes will have a default area code prepended to them.
2. Any extensions will be listed as xnnnnn following the phone number.
3. If an initial 1 is added to the number, it will be removed, because users already know to dial a 1 for long distance.

With these rules in mind, let's create the validation code.

```
Private Sub txtPhone_Validate(Cancel As Boolean)
    Dim strTemp As String
    Dim strPhone As String
```

```
Dim strExtension As String
Dim intResult As Integer

Const DefaultAreaCode = "703"
'
' Remove all the grouping characters for
' now. We'll add them back in later.
'
strTemp = Replace(txtPhone, "(", "")
strTemp = Replace(strTemp, ")", "")
strTemp = Replace(strTemp, "-", "")
strTemp = Replace(strTemp, " ", "")
strTemp = Replace(strTemp, "X", "x")


'
' Break up the digits into the number and
' the extension, if any.
'
intResult = InStr(1, strTemp, "x", vbTextCompare)
If intResult > 0 Then
    strExtension = Mid(strTemp, intResult + 1)
    strPhone = Left(strTemp, intResult - 1)
Else
    strPhone = strTemp
End If

If Left(strPhone, 1) = "1" Then
    strPhone = Mid(strPhone, 2)
End If

If Len(strPhone) <> 7 And Len(strPhone) <> 10 Then
    MsgBox "Please enter a valid telephone number.", vbExclamation
    Cancel = True
    Exit Sub
End If

'
' Prepend the default area code
'
If Len(strPhone) = 7 Then
    strPhone = DefaultAreaCode & strPhone
End If

'
' Build the new phone number
'
txtPhone = "(" & Left(strPhone, 3) & ") " _
```

```
                    & Mid(strPhone, 4, 3) & "-" _
                    & Right(strPhone, 4)

                '
                ' Add the extension, if any
                '
                If strExtension <> "" Then
                    txtPhone = txtPhone & " x" & strExtension
                End If

        End Sub
```

We created a default area code of 703, which you can change to your liking. If you're going to be using the application in different locations, you may want to store that information with the application user's profile, similar to the way that Windows stores your favorite locations for dialing.

We first get rid of all the grouping and separator characters, except for the X, which marks the beginning of an extension. We do convert uppercase Xs to lowercase for purposes of comparison.

Next, we parse out the phone number and the extension. If there is a leading 1, it's removed. The phone system is such that you can't have a 1 as the first number of either an area code or a phone number prefix. We will then either have a 10-digit phone number or a 7-digit phone number. If we don't have either, there is an error and we bail out immediately.

For seven-digit phone numbers, we prepend the default area code, and then we build the final number with a little bit of string manipulation. The extension we found, if any, is added back to the number. You can use any of the following test cases to see the validation in action:

- 5551212—will prepend 703 and create (703) 555-1212
- 15551212—same result as previous case
- 5551212 x 1 2 3 4—becomes (703) 555-1212 x1234—spaces are removed
- 17035551212 x 1 2 3 4—same as previous case
- Any numbers that aren't 7 or 10 digits—trapped error

The end result of this code makes it easier for the user to enter data, because the user knows that the computer is smart enough to change the data to whatever format was selected for use in the system.

The Select Card box could be reformatted; however, there are too many formats being used for credit cards, so we'll simply use the code in the next section to validate the card number and card type.

Credit Card Validation

While we aren't going to write the code to dial up a bank to actually perform a credit card transaction, we are going to do some validation of the credit card number and determine the type of credit card. Every credit card (at least the major ones) has a built-in formula in the card number to help determine immediately if the card number is valid. Because every transaction costs the credit card processors money to perform, it's in their best interest to have a "sanity check" built into the number to help prevent wasteful transactions.

Aside from this built-in formula, there are also ranges of numbers assigned to all the major credit cards. These ranges don't include "private label" cards, such as those used at department stores, but the ranges do include cards such as VISA, MasterCard, and so on.

You'll see how to build the two functions that will both validate a number and, for valid card numbers, display the credit card type in the label assigned for that purpose.

The call to these functions goes in the Validate event procedure of the combo box, and is shown here:

```
Private Sub cboCreditCardNumber_Validate(Cancel As Boolean)
    If IsValidCreditCardNumber(cboCreditCardNumber.Text) Then
        lblCreditCardType = DetermineCardType(cboCreditCardNumber.Text)
    Else
        MsgBox "This is not a valid credit card number."
        lblCreditCardType = ""
        Cancel = True
    End If
End Sub
```

The first function, **IsValidCreditCardNumber**, is shown here:

```
Private Function IsValidCreditCardNumber(strCCNum As String) As Boolean

    Dim i As Integer
    Dim intTotal As Integer
    Dim intTempTotal As Integer

    For i = Len(strCCNum) To 2 Step -2
        intTotal = intTotal + CInt(Mid(strCCNum, i, 1))
        intTempTotal = CInt(Mid(strCCNum, i - 1, 1)) * 2
        If intTempTotal > 9 Then
            intTotal = intTotal + intTempTotal - 9
        Else
            intTotal = intTotal + intTempTotal
```

```
        End If
    Next i

    If Len(strCCNum) Mod 2 = 1 Then
        intTotal = intTotal + CInt(Left(strCCNum, 1))
    End If

    IsValidCreditCardNumber = (intTotal Mod 10 = 0)

End Function
```

Reading through this function, you can learn how the built-in algorithm works:

1. Working backwards from the last digit of card, add the digit to the calculation total variable.
2. Multiply the digit to the left by two. If the result is greater than 9, subtract 9 from the result and add it to the total. Otherwise, just add the value to the total.
3. Repeat step 2 until you reach the beginning of the card.
4. If you have an odd number of digits, add the first digit of the card to the total.
5. If the result is a multiple of 10, the card is valid. Otherwise, it's not.

Try this function with any card in your wallet or purse and you should see a valid result. The second part of the validation is to determine the card type. The card companies have gotten together and created ranges for their cards. Most are pretty simple, but there are a few cards from outside the US that have slightly more complex ranges, as this function shows:

```
Private Function DetermineCardType(strCCNum As String) As String

    Dim intHeader As Integer
    Dim enmCardType As CreditCardTypes

    enmCardType = Unknown

    Select Case CInt(Left(strCCNum, 1))
    Case 1
        intHeader = CInt(Left(strCCNum, 4))

        If intHeader = 1800 And Len(strCCNum) = 15 Then
```

```
            enmCardType = JCB
        End If

Case 2
    intHeader = CInt(Left(strCCNum, 4))

    If (intHeader = 2014 Or intHeader = 2149) _
        And Len(strCCNum) = 15 Then
        enmCardType = enRoute
    End If

    If intHeader = 2131 And Len(strCCNum) = 15 Then
        enmCardType = JCB
    End If

Case 3
    Select Case CInt(Left(strCCNum, 3))
    Case 340 To 379
        If Len(strCCNum) = 15 Then
            enmCardType = AmericanExpress
        End If
    Case 360 To 369
    Case 380 To 389
        If Len(strCCNum) = 14 Then
            enmCardType = DinersClub
        End If
    Case 300 To 305
        If Len(strCCNum) = 16 Then
            enmCardType = JCB
        ElseIf Len(strCCNum) = 14 Then
            enmCardType = DinersClub
        End If
    Case 306 To 399
        If Len(strCCNum) = 16 Then
            enmCardType = JCB
        End If
    End Select

Case 4
    If Len(strCCNum) = 13 Or Len(strCCNum) = 16 Then
```

```
            enmCardType = VISA
        End If

    Case 5
        intHeader = CInt(Left(strCCNum, 2))

        If (intHeader >= 51 And intHeader <= 55) _
            And Len(strCCNum) = 16 Then
            enmCardType = MasterCard
        End If

    Case 6
        intHeader = CInt(Left(strCCNum, 1))

        If intHeader = 6 And Len(strCCNum) = 16 Then
            enmCardType = Discover
        End If

    End Select

    Select Case enmCardType
    Case Unknown
        DetermineCardType = "Unknown"
    Case AmericanExpress
        DetermineCardType = "American Express"
    Case Discover
        DetermineCardType = "Discover/NOVUS Cards"
    Case MasterCard
        DetermineCardType = "MasterCard"
    Case VISA
        DetermineCardType = "VISA"
    Case DinersClub
        DetermineCardType = "Diners Club"
    Case JCB
        DetermineCardType = "JCB"
    Case enRoute
        DetermineCardType = "enRoute"
    End Select

End Function
```

The key to this function is the first digit of the card. As you can see from the code, 4, 5, and 6 are pretty straightforward; 1, 2, and 3 have many smaller ranges within them, all of which should be self-explanatory.

To save ourselves some work in this function, we define an enumerated type to hold all the valid credit card types. When the function is nearly done, we map those values back to text strings to return to the caller. The enumerated type should be added to the declarations section of your form. It looks like this:

```
'
' Using the enumerated type makes it
' a bit easier in the code to identify
' a particular card. The text name of
' the card is only determined once.
'
Enum CreditCardTypes
    AmericanExpress = 1
    Discover = 2
    MasterCard = 3
    VISA = 4
    DinersClub = 5
    JCB = 6
    enRoute = 7
    Unknown = 8
End Enum
```

One nice thing about the Visual Basic coding environment is that it will supply a list of these values whenever you are about to assign a value to a variable of the enumerated type. For instance, the enmCardType variable is declared of type CreditCardTypes. As you type the code, VB will provide a list of available constants whenever you press the equal sign after typing the variable name. This lets you stick to the list without having to remember all the values.

You might be asking why we didn't also include an enumerated type for the String names, because we have to map the numeric values back anyway. The reason is simple: VB only allows integers to be in enumerated types. Other languages do support strings and other data types in enumerated types; however, we have to live with our conversion code at the end to get the result.

After you've added all the code, you can try typing in a credit card number and watch the card type display in the window. Invalid card numbers will result in an error message and a card type won't be displayed.

Wrapping Up

The last bits of validation needed in this form are fairly trivial compared to the work we've already done. Depending on your requirements, you may need to make sure that the other fields are not blank. You already know that they won't be too long, but VB can't force the user to enter something into the fields. You can add the above validation code to the Click event of the OK button. After you've validated the fields, you can add your own code to perform the crux of your application, such as saving the data to a database.

Depending on how complex your validation rules are, you may want to add ToolTips to your controls. This enables the user to place the mouse cursor over a box and get more information about what goes in it. If you have specific requirements, such as to not use bad characters, you can add this to the ToolTipText property of the controls in question.

By carefully guiding the user to provide the correct input, the validation is made much easier, and the data going into the database is as reliable as you can make it without driving to the customer's home to verify that the person and the address exists. Performing extensive validation like this on input data will make your applications more reliable and the data trustworthier.

Chapter 11

Working with the Operating System

At one time or another your application will need to know how much memory or what kind of processor is installed on the user's PC. In fact, as the evolution of software moves forward, it becomes increasingly important for your application to understand the platform it's running on.

Retrieving System Information

At some point, we need to know how much memory is installed on a PC, or we need to retrieve battery information for laptops. When writing software, you need to know these types of detail. For example, if your system is slow, you might want to present a wait dialog or splash screen during a long process. System information also includes the mode that Windows started in and information about the CPU. Knowing these details enables you to handle various conditions gracefully.

Through use of the WinAPI, Windows can provide your application with significant information regarding system configuration and status. This chapter demonstrates some of the WinAPI functions that retrieve this type of information.

Determining the Amount of Memory

All developers need to worry about memory. As applications and their run-time support file requirements grow ever larger, how much memory is available becomes a critical issue. Insufficient memory can reduce any program to a crawl. Luckily, the WinAPI function GlobalMemoryStatus provides all the memory information you need.

```
Private Declare Sub GlobalMemoryStatus Lib "kernel32" _
        (lpBuffer As MEMORYSTATUS)
```

GlobalMemoryStatus takes as an argument a user-defined type called MEMORYSTATUS. After the call to GlobalMemoryStatus, the members of the MEMORYSTATUS argument contain information about the computer's memory.

You must declare the MEMORYSTATUS type in the declarations section of a Visual Basic code module, as shown here:

```
Private Type MEMORYSTATUS
    dwLength As Long
    dwMemoryLoad As Long
    dwTotalPhys As Long
    dwAvailPhys As Long
    dwTotalPageFile As Long
    dwAvailPageFile As Long
    dwTotalVirtual As Long
    dwAvailVirtual As Long
End Type
```

Some members of MEMORYSTATUS contain the total physical memory installed and the available physical memory. Other members contain information about virtual memory, which is system memory used by Windows when it runs out of conventional memory. For our purposes, the members that we are interested in are dwMemoryLoad, dwTotalPhys, and dwAvailPhys.

The dwMemoryLoad member contains a value betweeen 0 and 100, which value represents the approximate amount of memory currently in use. Zero (0) means no memory is in use, while 100 means that all memory is in use. Use this value as a relative gauge of how "loaded" the PC is. One way that you could use this value is this: If the PC has a load of 75 or higher, your software either will not start or will display a warning to the user.

The dwTotalPhys member contains the total bytes of physical memory installed. Use this value to determine the amount of memory the PC has. You might then decide, for example, that your software cannot run on a machine that has less than 64 MB of memory.

The dwAvailPhys member contains the total bytes of physical memory currently available. Unlike dwMemoryLoad, this member contains the actual amount of memory in bytes.

To determine the total number of bytes of memory the PC has, use code similar to that in Listing 11-1:

```
Public Function MemoryTotal() As Long
    Dim memsts As MEMORYSTATUS
    GlobalMemoryStatus memsts
    MemoryTotal = memsts.dwTotalPhys
End Function
```

Listing 11-1: MemoryTotal returns the number of bytes of memory installed on a computer

While total memory is useful, more often than not what you really want to know is how much memory is available to your program. Listing 11-2 shows how easy it is to determine this information using GlobalMemoryStatus.

```
Public Function MemoryAvailable() As Long
    Dim memsts As MEMORYSTATUS
    GlobalMemoryStatus memsts
    MemoryAvailable = memsts.dwAvailPhys
End Function
```

Listing 11-2: MemoryAvailable returns the number of bytes of physical memory available to your program

Determining How Windows Started

Windows can start in one of three modes. Knowing which mode Windows started in by tells you whether all drivers and resources were loaded, which knowledge can make your software more reliable. There are three possible start modes:

- Normal mode
- Safe mode
- Safe mode with network support

Normal mode, as you might expect, indicates that Windows started without any problems. If Windows experiences a Registry problem during startup, it may start in safe mode. During this safe mode startup period, the user can decide if they want to attempt to load configuration files and drivers for peripherals. If the network drivers loaded correctly during a safe mode startup, the system will run in safe mode with network support.

If you have read this book in order, the GetSystemMetrics WinAPI function is familiar to you. It is one of the more useful WinAPI functions for Visual Basic developers. GetSystemMetrics can return a wealth of information about the user interface, as well as peripheral information such as network installations and mouse configurations. It can also return a value that indicates how the user's Windows session started.

```
Declare Function GetSystemMetrics Lib "user32" _
Alias "GetSystemMetrics" (ByVal nIndex As Long) As Long
```

GetSystemMetrics takes one of several constants to indicate exactly what information it should return. The constant to use to determine the Windows start mode is SM_CLEANBOOT.

```
Const SM_CLEANBOOT = 67
```

When passed SM_CLEANBOOT, GetSystemMetrics returns a value from 0 to 2 that represents the start mode of the current Windows session. The StartMode function 11-3 shows how to encapsulate this WinAPI into a function.

```
Public Function StartMode() As Integer
    StartMode = GetSystemMetrics(SM_CLEANBOOT)
End Function
```

Listing 11-3: StartMode indicates which start mode Windows is running under

If StartMode returns 0, Windows is in normal mode, which means that all drivers and devices are available. A return value of 1 indicates that Windows is in safe mode, which means that there is a severe system problem, the user configuration files have been skipped, no nonsystem device drives are loaded, and there is no network support. A return value of 2 means that Windows is in safe mode and that network support is loaded.

Getting and Setting Environment Variables

Windows maintains a number of environment variables, such as the PATH and TEMP variables, which you might need. These variables are set in the Autoexec.bat file or in the Windows NT environment settings. You can use WinAPI functions to access an environment variable, write data to the variable, or delete the variable.

> *NOTE*
> *Before you can access an environment variable, you must first create it—and no WinAPI function performs this task. You must actually edit the Autoexec.bat file or set the Windows NT variable..*

The WinAPIs for reading and writing environment variables are GetEnvironmentVariable and SetEnvironmentVariable and are declared as follows:

```
Declare Function GetEnvironmentVariable Lib "kernel32" _
    Alias "GetEnvironmentVariableA" ( _
    ByVal lpName As String, _
    ByVal lpBuffer As String, _
    ByVal nSize As Long) As Long
Declare Function SetEnvironmentVariable Lib "kernel32" _
    Alias "SetEnvironmentVariableA" ( _
        ByVal lpName As String, _
        ByVal lpValue As String) As Long
```

Getting an Environment Variable

The GetVariable function in Listing 11-4 works by taking as an argument the name of the environment variable to retrieve. For example, PATH would be used to retrieve the current system path. It calls the GetEnvironmentVariable WinAPI function, which returns a value greater than 0 if it succeeds. In that case, GetVariable strips off the trailing null terminator and returns the remaining string as the function result.

```
Public Function GetVariable(sVariable As String) As String
    Dim result As Long
    Dim tmp As String
    tmp = Space$(1024)
    result = GetEnvironmentVariable(sVariable, tmp, _
            Len(tmp))
    If result = 0 Then
        ' failed return nothing
    Else
        GetVariable = Left$(tmp, result)
    End If
End Function
```

Listing 11-4: GetVariable returns the string value of an environment variable

> *NOTE*
>
> *The Visual Basic Environ statement is equivalent to the GetEnvironmentVariable WinAPI function; VB, however, does not provide a function to delete or modify an environment variable.*

Setting an Environment Variable

You can set an environment variable to any arbitrary value using the SetEnvironmentVariable API function shown in Listing 11-5. Be aware, however, that if you change an environment variable, you might affect other programs that rely on that variable.

```
Public Sub SetVariable(sVariable As String, sValue _
        As String)
    SetEnvironmentVariable sVariable, sValue
End Sub
```

Listing 11-5: SetVariable sets an environment variable to a value

SetVariable works by simply passing the environment variable name, such as PATH or TMP, and the new contents for the environment variable to the SetEnvironmentVariable WinAPI function.

Deleting an Environment Variable

You can set an environment variable to an empty string, as shown in the
KillVariable procedure in Listing 11-6. This is a variation of the SetVariable
procedure. KillVariable works by simply setting the environment variable to an
empty string.

```
Public Sub KillVariable(sVariable As String)
    SetEnvironmentVariable sVariable, ""
End Sub
```

Listing 11-6: KillVariable deletes an environment variable

Shutting Down and Restarting Windows

If your application requires the capability to restart itself, it might also need the
capability to restart Windows. For example, the SetComputerName WinAPI
function (discussed in Chapter 9) requires that Windows restart before the new
computer name takes effect. Conveniently, the ExitWindowsEx WinAPI function
can log off the user, shut down Windows, and restart the system.

```
Declare Function ExitWindowsEx Lib "user32" Alias _
    "ExitWindowsEx" ( ByVal uFlags As Long, _
    ByVal dwReserved As Long) As Long
```

ExitWindowsEx takes different actions based on the uFlags argument you
pass to it. Defined constants for this argument are listed in Table 11-1:

Table 11-1: Constants Passable to ExitWindowsEx

CONSTANT	VALUE	ACTION TAKEN BY EXITWINDOWEX
EWX_LOGOFF	0	Logs off the user and closes down applications as if the user selected Shut Down on the Windows Start menu, and then chose the Close All Programs and Log On as a Different User option.
EWX_SHUTDOWN	1	Performs a shut down sequence as if the user selected Shut Down on the Windows Start menu, and then chose the Shut Down the Computer option.
EWX_REBOOT	2	Shuts down and restarts the system as if the user selected Shut Down on the Windows Start menu, and then chose the Restart the Computer option.
EWX_POWEROFF	8	Shuts down and turns off the computer. Available only for systems that support the Windows automatic power off feature.

Shutting Down Windows

The ShutDown function in Listing 11-7 exits Windows by passing the EWX_SHUTDOWN constant to ExitWindowsEx.

```
Public Sub ShutDown()
    Dim dwReserved As Long
    ExitWindowsEx EWX_SHUTDOWN, dwReserved
End Sub
```

Listing 11-7: ShutDown initiates a Windows shut down

Restarting Windows

The Reboot function in Listing 11-8 works by calling ExitWindowsEx with the EWX_REBOOT constant.

```
Public Sub Reboot()
    Dim dwReserved As Long
    ExitWindowsEx EWX_REBOOT, dwReserved
End Sub
```

Listing 11-8: Reboot reboots Windows

> *NOTE*
>
> *On Windows NT or 2000 systems, the process must have the SE_SHUTDOWN_NAME privilege set to shutdown or restart the system.*

Retrieving Hardware Information

All flavors of Windows can run on a number of different computing platforms. Windows runs on chips from Intel, DEC, AMD, IBM, and others. These CPUs all offer widely differing performance characteristics. Windows lets you determine the CPU type, the number of CPUs, and the relative performance capabilities of the CPU type. Knowing the CPU type or the CPU's capabilities enables you to inform the user about their platform when support is needed, and also enables you to determine whether your software should be run at all. For example, a very memory/processor intensive application might not be recommended for an Intel 386-class CPU.

Determining the CPU Type

Depending on your application, you might need to know about the user system's processor, or your application might require a certain type of processor. The WinAPI function that obtains this information is GetSystemInfo.

```
Private Declare Sub GetSystemInfo Lib "kernel32" (lpSystemInfo As
SYSTEM_INFO)
```

GetSystemInfo returns information in the lpSystemInfo parameter, which is of the SYSTEM_INFO user-defined type whose members are populated with information about the system. You must declare SYSTEM_INFO in the declarations section of a Visual Basic code module.

```
Private Type SYSTEM_INFO
    dwOemID As Long
    dwPageSize As Long
    lpMinimumApplicationAddress As Long
    lpMaximumApplicationAddress As Long
    dwActiveProcessorMask As Long
    dwNumberOfProcessors As Long
    dwProcessorType As Long
    dwAllocationGranularity As Long
    dwReserved As Long
End Type
```

There are constants to use with SYSTEM_INFO that help you identify what information is contained in the members of the parameter after a call to GetSystemInfo. For determining CPU type these constants are defined as:

```
Const PROCESSOR_INTEL_386 = 386
Const PROCESSOR_INTEL_486 = 486
Const PROCESSOR_INTEL_PENTIUM = 586
Const PROCESSOR_MIPS_R4000 = 4000
Const PROCESSOR_ALPHA_21064 = 21064
```

To determine the type of CPU, we examine the dwProcessorType member after a call to GetSystemInfo, as shown in the CPUName function in Listing 11-9:

```
Public Function CPUName() As String
    Dim lpSystemInfo As SYSTEM_INFO
    GetSystemInfo lpSystemInfo
    Select Case lpSystemInfo.dwProcessorType
    Case PROCESSOR_INTEL_386
        CPUName = "386"
    Case PROCESSOR_INTEL_486
        CPUName = "486"
    Case PROCESSOR_INTEL_PENTIUM
        CPUName = "Pentium"
    Case PROCESSOR_MIPS_R4000
```

```
        CPUName = "MIPS"
    Case PROCESSOR_ALPHA_21064
        CPUName = "Alpha"
    End Select
End Function
```

Listing 11-9: CPUName returns the type of CPU the PC has

> NOTE
>
> *The GetSystemInfo function detects processor types, but does not distinguish between compatible processors from different manufacturers. Thus, an AMD K6 processor is treated as if it were an Intel Pentium processor.*

Determining the Number of CPUs

Even though Visual Basic itself does not implement multiprocessing, knowing whether more than one processor is available may help you make decisions about how your software loads and runs; for example, whether or not to assign threads you create to a specific processor. GetSystemInfo returns the number of processors in the dwNumberOfProcessors member of the SYSTEM_INFO parameter. The CPUCount Function 11-10 illustrates encapsulating this WinAPI.

```
Public Function CPUCount() As Integer
    Dim lpSystemInfo As SYSTEM_INFO
    GetSystemInfo lpSystemInfo
    CPUCount = lpSystemInfo.dwNumberOfProcessors
End Function
```

Listing 11-10: CPUCount returns a number indicating how many CPUs are installed in the system

> NOTE
>
> *The GetSystemInfo function detects the number of processors that can be used by the operating system, not necessarily the number installed. Thus, GetSystemInfo will return 1 for Windows 95/98 even on a multiprocessor system, because Windows 95/98 can only use one processor.*

Determining CPU Performance Capabilities

Windows can provide a value that indicates whether the CPU is "slow." This is a subjective decision Windows makes using an internal formula. At best, this lets you make a somewhat informed decision about how your software should load and run.

To determine this information, use the GetSystemMetrics WinAPI function and the SM_SLOWMACHINE constant as shown in Listing 11-11:

```
Declare Function GetSystemMetrics Lib "user32" Alias_
"GetSystemMetrics" (ByVal nIndex As Long) As Long
Private Const SM_SLOWMACHINE = 73
Public Function IsSlow() As Boolean
    IsSlow = GetSystemMetrics(SM_SLOWMACHINE)
End Function
```

Listing 11-11: GetSystemMetrics returns True only for a "slow" CPU

Retrieving the Flavor of Windows and the Operating System Version

Because some WinAPI calls are found only under specific versions of Windows, it is very important to be able to dynamically determine whether your program is running under Windows 95/98 or Windows NT. When working with the WinAPI, you often also need to determine the operating system version. The key to retrieving this information is the GetVersionEx WinAPI function.

```
Declare Function GetVersionEx Lib "kernel32" Alias _
"GetVersionExA" (lpVersionInformation As OSVERSIONINFO) _
As Long
```

GetVersionEx uses takes a parameter of the OSVERSIONINFO user-defined type, and populates the parameter with major and minor versions, build number, platform information, and an additional custom or OEM-defined operating system field. You must declare OSVERSIONINFO in the declarations section of a Visual Basic code module.

```
Type OSVERSIONINFO
    dwOSVersionInfoSize As Long
    dwMajorVersion As Long
    dwMinorVersion As Long
    dwBuildNumber As Long
    dwPlatformId As Long
    szCSDVersion As String * 128
End Type
```

> *NOTE*
> *The dwOSVersionInfoSize field of the OSVERSIONINFO structure must be set to the size of the structure before calling GetVersionEx.*

Identifying Windows 95/98

The Win95or98 function in Listing 11-12 returns True if the operating system is Windows 95/98, or False if the system is not Windows 95/98.

```
Function Win95or98() As Boolean
    Dim typOS As OSVERSIONINFO
    Const VER_PLATFORM_WIN32_WINDOWS = 1
    typOS.dwOSVersionInfoSize = Len(typOS)
    GetVersionEx typOS
    Win95or98 = typOS.dwPlatformId = _
        VER_PLATFORM_WIN32_WINDOWS
End Function
```

Listing 11-12: Win95or98returns True only if the operating system is Windows 95/98

Identifying Windows NT

Detecting Windows NT is as easy as detecting Windows 95/98. Just call GetVersionEx, as shown in Listing 11-13, and check whether the dwPlatformId member of the OSVERSIONINFO parameter is VER_PLATFORM_WIN32_NT.

```
Function WinNT() As Boolean
    Dim typOS As OSVERSIONINFO
    typOS.dwOSVersionInfoSize = Len(typOS)
    GetVersionEx typOS
    WinNT = typOS.dwPlatformId = _
        VER_PLATFORM_WIN32_NT
End Function
```

Listing 11-13: WinNT returns True only if the operating system is Windows NT

Identifying the Operating System Version

After the operating system is identified, you need to determine its version. For Windows 95/98 this is not so important, but for Windows NT this is often a major requirement because the differences between operating system versions is great. To retrieve the major version number, simply call GetVersionEx and check the dwMajorVersion member of the OSVERSIONINFO parameter. Windows 2000 returns 5, NT version 4 returns the value 4, and NT version 3 returns 3.

The WinNT4 example shown in Listing 11-14 determines whether the program is running under Windows NT version 4.

```
Public Function WinNT4() As Boolean
    Dim typOS As OSVERSIONINFO
    typOS.dwOSVersionInfoSize = Len(typOS)
    GetVersionEx typOS
```

```
        If typOS.dwPlatformId = VER_PLATFORM_WIN32_NT Then
            ' this is Windows NT, get version
            WinNT4 = typOS.dwMajorVersion = 4
        End If
End Function
```

Listing 11-14: WinNT4returns True only if the operating system is Windows NT version 4

Chapter 12

Windows Help Systems—From the Inside

Usually, you'll want your Visual Basic applications to be capable of providing users with help. Visual Basic itself offers rudimentary help constructs, but Windows help offers much greater functionality.

WinHelp

WinHelp, the original help system, is built into the operating system. WinHelp is a standard Windows program named Winhelp.exe. WinHelp provides a single WinAPI function, named WinHelp, through which you can control any aspect of the help system. This chapter assumes that you are familiar with help systems and how to create help systems using the Windows help compiler.

In early versions of Windows, a program had to implement help by including code that waited for the user to press the F1 (or other) key or by handling a request for help from a menu. Windows 95 made the process easier with a new message—WM_HELP—that is automatically sent to Win32 programs when the user presses the F1 key. Visual Basic is capable of detecting this message and automatically displaying help for the currently active form, control, or menu entry. All you have to do is set the help filename in the Project Settings dialog box for your application. Next, set the HelpContextID and WhatsThisHelp properties for the forms, controls, and menu items to which you want to attach help.

Despite Visual Basic's support for online help, there may times when you want your program to automatically launch the online help. This can be done using the WinHelp API function, which is declared as follows:

```
Declare Function WinHelp Lib "user32" Alias "WinHelpA" ( _
ByVal hwnd As Long,  _
ByVal lpHelpFile As String, _
ByVal wCommand As Long, _
dwData As Any) As Long
```

Through the parameters to WinHelp, you indicate the help file to use and what actions to perform. Let's examine the WinHelp arguments before discussing the code required to perform the WinHelp tricks (see Table 12-1).

Table 12-1: WinHelp Parameters

PARAMETER	MEANING
hwnd	The handle to the window (form or control) that this help is for
lpHelpFile	The name of the help file that contains the help you wish to display
wCommand	A value indicating what WinHelp is supposed to do; for example, pop up context sensitive help, display contents, display a help page, or display the search windows
dwData	An optional parameter whose exact value depends on the wCommand parameter

---

Displaying a Help Page

Now that we have introduced the WinHelp WinAPI function and its arguments, let's get busy with some code! First things first; let's write a procedure that displays a particular help page, in this case Windows Help On Help. This is handy for a program designed for novice Windows users. It is a built-in help page that explains how help works. For this sample, we use a wCommand value of HELP_HELPONHELP. This command works only if the Winhlp32.hlp file is found. Winhlp32.hlp is a system file installed on all 32-bit versions of Windows, and is usually found in the \Windows\Help folder.

Create a new Visual Basic project and add a class file. Name the class myHelp and then add the following code to the class module:

```
Private Declare Function WinHelp Lib "user32" _
Alias "WinHelpA" (ByVal hwnd As Long, ByVal lpHelpFile _
As String, ByVal wCommand As Long, dwData As Any) As Long
Public Owner As Long
Public HelpFile As String
```

The Owner variable is a shared variable that is used to indicate the handle, if any (it can be left empty), of the owner form or control you are displaying help for. The HelpFile variable is a shared variable used to indicate the name of the help file you plan to work with. You can specify the complete path to a help file or just the name of the help file if it is located in your Windows directory.

The HelpOnHelp function in Listing 12-1 displays the built-in Windows help for new users.

```
Private Const HELP_HELPONHELP = 4
Public Sub HelpOnHelp()
    Dim result As Long
    result = WinHelp(Owner, HelpFile, HELP_HELPONHELP, "")
End Sub
```

Listing 12-1: Windows' built-in help

To use the HelpOnHelp function, create a form and use the class as shown in Listing 12-2:

```
Option Explicit
Dim hlp As New myHelp
Private Sub Form_Load()
    hlp.Owner = Me.hwnd
    hlp.HelpFile = ""
    hlp.HelpOnHelp
End Sub
```

Listing 12-2: Setting up and calling myHelp class

You don't need to specify the name of the help file (which is winhlp32.hlp) or its path—Windows will find it if it is installed when you use the HELP_HELPONHELP option.

Running this code displays help on using help, as shown in Figure 12-1:

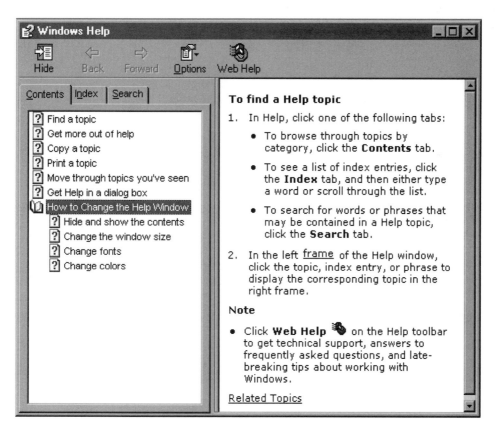

Figure 12-1: Help on Help window

Closing a Help Window

It is good programming etiquette to always close any help windows that you've opened before your program ends. The windows will not automatically close when your program ends. To close an open help window, use WinHelp with the wCommand parameter set to HELP_QUIT. The procedure in Listing 12-3 shows how to do this. Add the code in Listing 12-3 to the help class created in Listing 12-2:

```
Private Const HELP_QUIT = 2
Public Sub Quit()
    Dim result As Long
    result = WinHelp(Owner, HelpFile, HELP_QUIT, 0)
End Sub
```

Listing 12-3: The Quit function closes a help window

Now you can add the code in Listing 12-4, which calls the Quit function, to the Form_Unload event of your test form.

```
Private Sub Form_Unload(Cancel As Integer)
    hlp.Quit
End Sub
```

Listing 12-4: Calling the Quit function to close a help file

Now you understand the basics of using WinHelp. You simply pass to WinHelp what function it is to perform, and close the help file before your program exits. But the devils are in the details, as they say, so let's forge on.

Context-Sensitive Help

The HELP_FINDER command tells WinHelp to display a help file's table of contents, which is contained in the CNT file associated with the help file. The code shown in Listing 12-5 causes the topics of a help file to display, enabling the user to browse and select a topic to display:

```
Private Const HELP_FINDER = 11
Public Sub Topics()
    Dim result As Long
    result = WinHelp(Owner, HelpFile, HELP_FINDER, 0)
End Sub
```

Listing 12-5: Displaying help file's table of contents using Windows API calls

NOTE
Displaying an older help file, that does not have an associated CNT file, requires using the HELP_CONTENTS command, which has a value of 3, instead of the HELP_FINDER command.

Now, in your program, add a command button and add the event procedure code shown in Listing 12-6 to the command button.

```
Private Sub Command1_Click()
    hlp.Quit    ' close any open file
    hlp.HelpFile = "windows.hlp "
    hlp.Topics
End Sub
```

Listing 12-6: Displaying the Windows help file table of contents using the Help Class

The code shows the recommended steps for displaying the topics of a help file: close any open help file, set the new help file (in this case, to the Windows help file), and display the table of contents.

Showing a Specific Help Page

The HELP_CONTEXT command tells WinHelp to display a specific help topic or page. You indicate the context-id of the help page using the dwData argument of WinHelp.

To enable the user to look up a specific page, add the code in Listing 12-7 to your help class module.

```
Private Const HELP_CONTEXT = 1
Public Sub Context(ContextID As Long)
    Dim result As Long
    result = WinHelp(Owner, HelpFile, HELP_CONTEXT, ByVal ContextID)
End Sub
```

Listing 12-7: Looking up a specific help topic

NOTE
In the call to WinHelp, you must precede the ContextID parameter with the ByVal keyword. This is one of those tricky details that exist because WinAPI function calls were designed for C programmers.

Now, in your sample for displaying a specific help page, add a button and the event procedure code in Listing 12-8 to that button.

```
Private Sub Command2_Click()
    hlp.Quit
    hlp.HelpFile = "C:\YourHelp.hlp"
    hlp.Context 100
End Sub
```

Listing 12-8: Displaying a help page by context-id

This code closes any open help file, sets the new help file, and then displays help context-id 100.

Displaying Help in a Pop-up Window

The HELP_CONTEXTPOPUP command tells WinHelp to display a help page in a shadowed, pop-up window instead of the help files-defined window type. To display a help page in this manner, add the code in Listing 12-9 to your class file (Listing 12-2).

```
Private Const HELP_CONTEXTPOPUP = 8
Public Sub PopUp(ContextID As Long)
    Dim result As Long
    result = WinHelp(Owner, HelpFile, _
        HELP_CONTEXTPOPUP, ByVal ContextID)
End Sub
```

Listing 12-9: Displaying a help page in a pop-up shadowed window

Searching Help

WinHelp has several commands that work with find strings in a help file. The first of these is HELP_KEY. HELP_KEY tells WinHelp to display the topic that matches the keyword passed in the dwData argument. If the keyword is not found, or there is more than one match, then WinHelp displays the "Topics Found" dialog. To search for a keyword, add the code in Listing 12-10 to your Help class file.

```
Private Const HELP_KEY = 257
Public Sub HelpKey(sKey As String)
    Dim result&
    result = WinHelp(Owner, CStr(HelpFile), _
        HELP_KEY, ByVal sKey)
End Sub
```

Listing 12-10: Finding a help topic using a keyword

The code in Listing 12-11 displays the topic in the Windows help file that has the keyword "web."

```
Private Sub Command3_Click()
    hlp.HelpFile = " Windows.hlp"
    hlp.HelpKey "web"
End Sub
```

Listing 12-11: Searching for a specific keyword

You can use multiple keywords, but semicolons must separate them. For example, the code in Listing 12-12 displays the Windows 95/98 troubleshooting help page for PC card conflicts.

```
Private Sub Command3_Click()
    hlp.HelpFile = " Windows.hlp"
    hlp.HelpKey "troubleshooting;PC"
End Sub
```

Listing 12-12: Searching for multiple keywords

Another handy WinHelp search command is HELP_PARTIALKEY. Contrary to what its name implies, it does not display any help directly; instead, it displays the Search dialog box, enabling your users to search for help on their own. HELP_PARTIALKEY searches the K keyword-table of a help file.

The K keyword-table is an optional table of strings that a help file author can include in a help file. These are often related words used to help users "zero in" on the exact help they need. HELP_PARTIALKEY tells WinHelp to find the keyword(s) passed; however, if no keyword is passed (the string parameter is empty), or if there is more than one match, WinHelp displays the Search dialog box.

To search the K keyword-table, add the code in Listing 12-13 to your class file (Listing 12-2).

```
Private Const HELP_PARTIALKEY = 261
Public Sub SearchFor(sKey As String)
    Dim result As Long
    result = WinHelp(Owner, HelpFile, HELP_PARTIALKEY, ByVal sKey)
End Sub
```

Listing 12-13: Searching the K keyword-table and displaying the Search dialog box

When using the Listing 12-13 code, leave the sKey argument empty ("") to display the Search dialog.

Making Sure Your Help File Is the One That's Visible

Windows supports multitasking; that is, users can switch to another program whenever they wish. Users can also load different help files while using other programs.WinHelp uses the HELP_FORCEFILE command to help synchronize your program with the Windows help system. Using HELP_FORCEFILE ensures that WinHelp is displaying your help file by opening your help file if another help file has been opened as Listing 12-14 illustrates.

```
Private Const HELP_FORCEFILE = 9
Public Sub EnsureVisible()
    Dim result As Long
    result = WinHelp(Owner, HelpFile, HELP_FORCEFILE, 0)
End Sub
```

Listing 12-14: Using the HELP_FORCEFILE command to ensure synchronization between a program and WinHelp

Displaying the Help Window Where You Want

WinHelp provides a technique for positioning an open help file window. The process requires declaring a HELPWININFO structure that contains members for position information in Windows coordinates (see Table 12-2). Other members indicate how large to make the help window and how to draw the help window:

Table 12-2: HELPWININFO Structure Members Defined

MEMBER	MEANING
Size	Must be set to the size of the structure variable before passing to WinHelp; for example, THWI.Size = Len(THWI)
UpperLeftX	X-coordinate position of the upper-left corner where the window should be drawn
UpperLeftY	Y-coordinate position of the upper-left corner where the window should be drawn
Width	The new width of the window
Height	The new height of the window
ShowStyle	How to show the window; this member must be one of the ShowWindow API constants (see Table 12-3)
WinNamePtr	A pointer to the name of the window; not used with Visual Basic

You must declare the structure in the class module:

```
Private Type HELPWININFO
    Size As Long
    UpperLeftX As Long
    UpperLeftY As Long
```

```
    Height As Long
    Width As Long
    ShowStyle As Long
    WinNamePtr As long
End Type
```

The UpperLeftX, UpperLeftY, Height, and Width members represent where to place the window on the screen. For use with WinHelp, the screen is divided into a grid with 1024 increments or units in each direction. To move a window to the upper-left corner of the screen, for example, you set the UpperLeftX and UpperLeftY members each to a value of 0. To make this same window 400 units wide and 500 units tall, you set Width to 400 and Height to 500. The ShowWindow member determines how to show the window. This member must be one of the API constants (see Table 12-3).

> **TIP**
> *The measurement system just described is unique to WinHelp. Do not confuse the 1024 _ 1024 grid with pixels!*

Table 12-3: ShowWindow API constants that can be placed in the ShowStyle member of the HELPWININFO structure

CONSTANT	VALUE	MEANING
SW_HIDE	0	Hides the window
SW_MINIMIZE	6	Minimizes the window
SW_SHOWNORMAL	1	Activates the window and restores it to its original size and position
SW_RESTORE	9	Same as SW_SHOWNORMAL
SW_SHOW	5	Activates the window, bringing it to the top of the z-order using current window coordinates
SW_SHOWMAXIMIZED	3	Activates and maximizes the window
SW_SHOWMINIMIZED	2	Activates and minimizes the window
SW_SHOWMINNOACTIVE	7	Displays the window as an icon without focus

It's now easy to display a help window where you want. Simply set up the HELPWININFO structure with the required position, size, and display style, and call WinHelp for an open window as shown in Listing 12-15:

```
Private Type HELPWININFO
    Size As Long
    UpperLeftX As Long
    UpperLeftY As Long
    Width As Long
    Height As Long
    ShowStyle As Long
```

```
        WinNamePtr As Long
End Type
Dim THWI As HELPWININFO
Private Const HELP_SETWINPOS = 515
Public Sub SetPosition(UpperLeftX As Long, _
        UpperLeftY As Long, _
        Width As Long, Height As Long)
    Dim result As Long
    With THWI
        .Size = Len(THWI)
        .UpperLeftX = UpperLeftX
        .UpperLeftY = UpperLeftY
        .Width = Width
        .Height = Height
        .ShowStyle = 1
    End With
    result = WinHelp(Owner, HelpFile, _
        HELP_SETWINPOS, THWI)
End Sub
```

Listing 12-15: A complete implementation of the WinHelp positioning capability

> **NOTE**
> *You pass the HELPWININFO structure to WinHelp by reference, not by value!*
> *Therefore, don't use the ByVal keyword with the dwData argument.*

Putting It All Together

Listing 12-16 is the complete code for the entire WinHelp class. See chap12.vbp on the book's CD-ROM for the code and a sample program showing how to use the class.

```
DefInt A-Z
Option Explicit
Private Declare Function WinHelp Lib "user32" Alias _
"WinHelpA" (ByVal hwnd As Long, ByVal lpHelpFile As _
String, ByVal wCommand As Long, dwData As Any) As Long
Private Type HELPWININFO
    Size As Long
    UpperLeftX As Long
    UpperLeftY As Long
    Width As Long
    Height As Long
    ShowStyle As Long
    WinNamePtr As Long
End Type
```

```
Dim THWI As HELPWININFO
Private Const HELP_SETWINPOS = 515
Private Const HELP_FORCEFILE = 9
Private Const HELP_PARTIALKEY = 261
Private Const HELP_CONTEXT = 1
Private Const HELP_KEY = 257
Private Const HELP_QUIT = 2
Private Const HELP_HELPONHELP = 4
Private Const HELP_CONTENTS = 3
Private Const HELP_FINDER = 11
Private Const HELP_CONTEXTPOPUP = 8
Public Owner As Long
Public HelpFile As String
Public Sub SearchFor()
    Dim result As Long
    result = WinHelp(Owner, HelpFile, _
        HELP_PARTIALKEY, ByVal "")
End Sub

Public Sub HelpOnHelp()
    Dim result As Long
    result = WinHelp(Owner, HelpFile, HELP_HELPONHELP, "")
End Sub
Public Sub Contents()
    Dim result As Long
    result = WinHelp(Owner, HelpFile, HELP_CONTENTS, 0&)
End Sub
Public Sub HelpKey(sKey As String)
    Dim result&
    result = WinHelp(Owner, CStr(HelpFile), HELP_KEY, _
        ByVal sKey)
End Sub
Public Sub Context(ContextID As Long)
    Dim result As Long
    result = WinHelp(Owner, HelpFile, HELP_CONTEXT, _
        ByVal ContextID)
End Sub
Public Sub Quit()
    Dim result As Long
    result = WinHelp(Owner, HelpFile, HELP_QUIT, 0)
End Sub
Public Sub Topics()
    Dim result As Long
    result = WinHelp(Owner, HelpFile, HELP_FINDER, 0)
End Sub
Public Sub PopUp(ContextID As Long)
```

```
        Dim result As Long
        result = WinHelp(Owner, HelpFile, HELP_CONTEXTPOPUP, _
            ByVal ContextID)
End Sub
Public Sub SetPosition(UpperLeftX As Long, _
        UpperLeftY As Long, Width As Long, Height As Long)
    Dim result As Long
    With THWI
        .Size = Len(THWI)
        .UpperLeftX = UpperLeftX
        .UpperLeftY = UpperLeftY
        .Width = Width
        .Height = Height
        .ShowStyle = 1
    End With
    result = WinHelp(Owner, HelpFile, HELP_SETWINPOS, _
            THWI)
End Sub
Public Sub EnsureVisible()
    Dim result As Long
    result = WinHelp(Owner, HelpFile, HELP_FORCEFILE, 0)
End Sub
```

Listing 12-16: The complete WinHelp class

Chapter 13

Multiple Document Interface Forms

The earliest Visual Basic applications were little more than DOS programs with a friendly, if simple, user interface. You chained each form to the next one, and you probably included a form or two containing a menu of buttons. Now with Windows, however, Visual Basic enables you to create multiwindow applications with richer functionality by providing Multiple Document Interface (MDI) forms.

MDI Form Basics

An *MDI form* is a form that holds other forms. *MDI child forms* are forms that exist inside of the MDI form. Visual Basic lets you use only a single MDI form per application. This is a limit imposed by the Windows architecture. You can, however, continue to use standard forms in your application; for example, for splash screens or custom dialog boxes.

But the point of adding an MDI form via the Project|Add MDI Form option is to populate that form with MDI child forms, which is done by setting the MDIChild property to True *after* the MDI form is added. When Visual Basic displays a child form, it will be displayed within the MDI form's frame, and the value of the ActiveForm property will be a reference to the active child form not a reference to the parent form. The Arrange method enables you determine how the visible MDI child forms appear and when you minimize an MDi child form, its icon appears inside the MDI form. When an MDI child form has the focus, its menus replace the menu of the MDI form automatically.

There are a few restrictions on MDI child forms:

- MDI child forms cannot be shown modally. A modal form is one that requires action by the user before the program proceeds. They can only be shown nonmodally (that is, using the Show method with no arguments) within the MDI parent's frame. If you change the AutoShowChildren property to False, you will need to use the Show method with no arguments.
- A form cannot be changed at run-time from being an MDI child form to being a non-MDI child. This can only be done at design-time.

It is a difficult to distinguish an MDI child form from the parent MDI form in the Project Explorer. There is only a subtle difference in the image (usually called a *glyph*) that appears. For the MDI form, it is a big form with a duller small form next to it; for the MDI child form, it is the reverse.

> **TIP**
>
> *You will often use the New operator to create an MDI child form at run-time by cloning an MDI child form you added at design time.*

To help tell them apart, the names of MDI and standard forms are normally given different prefixes. In this chapter, standard forms are prefixed with the usual frm prefix, but the MDI form will be prefixed with mdi. (Granted, you can only have one MDI form, so you could use the frm prefix and name the MDI form frmMDI.)

Finally, there is a restriction on what kind of controls you can add to an MDI form: only controls that can be aligned to one of the sides of the MDI form may be added (for example, Coolbar, PictureBox, StatusBar and Toolbar).

The order of the life-cycle events for an MDI application take some getting used to because they depend on which form is designated the Startup form. For example, if the MDI form is the Startup form and it loads the child form in its Load event (which is very common), you get:

1. Parent form Initialize
2. Parent form Load
3. Child form Initialize
4. Child form Load
5. Parent form Resize
6. Child Form Resize
7. Child form Paint
8. Parent form Activate
9. Child form Activate
10. Child form GotFocus

On the other hand, if the child form is the Startup form, you get:

1. Child form Initialize
2. Parent form Initialize
3. Parent form Load
4. Child form Load
5. Parent form Resize
6. Child Form Resize
7. Parent form Activate
8. Child form Activate
9. Child form GotFocus
10. Child form Paint

When the MDI form is unloaded, all its child forms are unloaded as well and you get this sequence of events:

1. Parent form QueryUnload
2. Child form QueryUnload
3. Child form Unload
4. Parent form Unload
5. Child form Terminate
6. Parent form Terminate

Sharing System Resources

One of the best things about an MDI form is that it can contain commonly used resources that can be shared across all the forms in the application. For example, if you're using the Common Dialog control, you can put a single control on the MDI form and make it available to the rest of the child forms in the application. This saves valuable system resources by not wasting memory on duplicate controls. You can also use the MDI form to manage what would otherwise be global variables that hold data connections, status indicators, and so on.

To demonstrate how to handle this type of sharing, we're going to create a very simple note viewer application. This application will enable you to load multiple text files into MDI child windows. We'll build on this application as we proceed through the chapter. To get started, do the following:

1. Start a new Standard EXE project and add an MDI form to it.
2. Name the MDI form mdiMain, and rename the form that's already included from Form1 to frmFile.
3. Mark frmFile as an MDI child by setting the MDIChild property to True.
4. On the frmFile form, add a single text box and name it txtContent. This box will be used to hold the contents of the file that is loaded.
5. Position the text box so that you have a margin around the top and the left. (Don't worry about resizing the box to fill the form. In the next step, we add code to perform that task.)
6. Add the following code to resize the text box so it fills the form:

```
Private Sub Form_Resize()
    On Error Resume Next
    txtContent.Width = Me.ScaleWidth - 120
    txtContent.Height = Me.ScaleHeight - 120
End Sub
```

> **NOTE**
> The error trap essentially ignores when the width is set negative, so we just skip ahead instead of worrying about it.

7. Set the Scrollbars property of the text box to Vertical. Set the MultiLine property to True, so that text will wrap properly.
8. Add these menu items to the MDI parent form so that the last three are submenu items of the main File menu:

CAPTION	NAME
&File	mnuFile
&Open	mnuFileOpen
—	mnuFileSeparator
E&xit	mnuFileExit

9. Add a Common Dialog control to the MDI form, and name it cdlCommon. You can put the control directly on the MDI form.

> *NOTE*
> *While it might be obvious that the user will use these menu items to load a selected file into a new child window, you might wonder why an item with just a hyphen as its caption is included. The reason is that using a hyphen as the value of the Caption property of a menu item is the way to create a separator bar—in this case, between the Open and Exit choices. And even though the separator bar won't have any associated code, it still has to have a unique name.*

To finish things off, add the following code to the application. It uses the FileSystemObject, which is part of the Microsoft Scripting Runtime library. Be sure to add a reference to the library in your project, otherwise this project won't work properly.

```
Option Explicit
Private Sub mnuFileExit_Click()
    Unload Me
End Sub

Private Sub mnuFileOpen_Click()
    On Error GoTo EH

    Dim frmNew As frmFile
    Dim objFSO As New Scripting.FileSystemObject
    Dim objStream As Scripting.TextStream

    cdlCommon.CancelError = True
    cdlCommon.DialogTitle = "Open File"
```

```
cdlCommon.Flags = cdlOFNHideReadOnly
cdlCommon.Filter = "All Files (*.*)|*.*|" _
    & "Text Files (*.txt)|*.txt|" _
    & "HTML Files (*.htm;*.html)|*.htm;*.html"
cdlCommon.FilterIndex = 2
cdlCommon.ShowOpen

Set frmNew = New frmFile

Set objStream = objFSO.OpenTextFile(cdlCommon.FileName)
frmNew.txtContent = objStream.ReadAll
objStream.Close
Set objFSO = Nothing

frmNew.Show
Exit Sub

EH:
    If Err.Number = cdlCancel Then
        Exit Sub
Else
    MsgBox "Error occurred: " & Err.Description _
        & " (#" & Err.Number & ")"
End If

End Sub
```

This code is pretty straightforward. First, we provide an event procedure (mnuFileExit_Click) to let the user exit the application by selecting the Exit choice from the menu. The mnuFileOpen_Click event procedure contains the bulk of the menu logic. This procedure sets up the Common Dialog control to prompt for a file name. We really want to allow only text and HTML files to be read, but if the user picks a different type of file, we're not doing any validation on the file name for now. We then use the OpenTextFile method of the FileSystemObject to open a text stream (ordinary text file). Next, we read all the text from the file into the text box on a new instance of the frmFile MDI child form. We then show the file and exit the subroutine. The error handler is here to handle the case in which the user presses the Cancel button on the Common Dialog. If any other error triggers the trap, for now it is simply displayed to the user.

There's one final step to complete before testing the application: change the StartupForm property to point to the MDI form instead of the frmFile child form. This way, when the application is run, you'll first see the MDI form with its menu. You can open as many files as you wish to see how the forms are loaded into the MDI form. When you're done viewing a document, you can just click the close button (the X button) to exit the particular document.

Sharing in the Real World

There were a few things we did in the example in the previous section that are not ideal for a larger application including:

- The MDI form accesses a control of the child form directly. As you learned in Chapter 12, this violates encapsulation. We should, instead, provide a public property on the child form so that the MDI form can modify the data that way.
- The child form is not aware of its parent or the functions that are available to it. The child form doesn't know when an Open request has been made. If the user selects a menu choice that is applicable to the child form, it is not notified of the choice, which makes it impossible to react to the requested action.
- All of the work is being done in the MDI form to load the data for the child form. Because the MDI form might be responsible for many types of file open tasks, the child form should be responsible for using the Common Dialog and for opening and reading the file. The MDI child form can handle all its own requests and needs. Thus, it can be a "self-sufficient" entity within the MDI parent form.

Let's modify the application to eliminate these potential problems. First, the Common Dialog control on the MDI form needs a Property Get to serve as an accessor method so that the child forms can use it when necessary. Add this code to the MDI form:

```
Public Property Get ComDlg() As CommonDialog
    Set ComDlg = cdlCommon
End Property
```

This code lets child forms have access to the Common Dialog control for use in Open File dialogs or in whatever dialogs are necessary, without having to have code in the MDI form that is specific for a particular file type.

The next change we have to make will let the child form know about its parent and have the capability to get to the parent's resources. In addition, the child form will be capable of opening and loading the file itself. To do this, we create a public method on the MDI child form called Display. That code is shown here:

```
Public Sub Display(mdiInput As MDIForm)
    On Error GoTo EH

    Dim objFSO As New Scripting.FileSystemObject
    Dim objStream As Scripting.TextStream
    Show
    Set m_mdiMain = mdiInput
    With m_mdiMain.ComDlg
        .CancelError = True
        .DialogTitle = "Open File"
```

```
    .Flags = cdlOFNHideReadOnly
    .Filter = "All Files (*.*)|*.*|" _
        & "Text Files (*.txt)|*.txt|" _
        & "HTML Files (*.htm;*.html)|*.htm;*.html"
    .FilterIndex = 2
    .ShowOpen
    Me.Caption = .FileName
    Set objStream = objFSO.OpenTextFile(.FileName)
End With

txtContent = objStream.ReadAll
objStream.Close
Set objFSO = Nothing

Exit Sub

EH:
    If Err.Number = cdlCancel Then
        Unload Me
        Exit Sub
    Else
        MsgBox "Error occurred: " & Err.Description _
            & " (#" & Err.Number & ")"
    End If

End Sub
```

You should also add the following variable declaration to the Declarations section of the MDI child form.

```
Private m_mdiMain As MDIForm
```

The code in the Open file Click event becomes much simpler now.

```
Private Sub mnuFileOpen_Click()
    Dim frmNew As New frmFile
    frmNew.Display Me
End Sub
```

In the new version of the code, the MDI form only has to create a new instance of the child form. The child form then accesses the MDI form's ComDlg property to show the Open File dialog. Everything else is the same from there until the error handler, which unloads the child window if the user doesn't select a file. The other change is that the filename is shown in the window's caption.

The final change to make is to share the FileSystemObject. Because each window needs to use the FileSystemObject to open files, we can simply open a single FileSystemObject in the MDI form and share it. The accessor for it is basically the same as the Common Dialog control.

```
Public Property Get FSO() As Scripting.FileSystemObject
    Set FSO = m_objFSO
End Property
```

You should also add the following declaration to the form:

```
Private m_objFSO As Scripting.FileSystemObject
```

Next, you need to create the FSO object and make sure it is cleaned up, so add this code to the MDI form:

```
Private Sub MDIForm_Load()
    Set m_objFSO = New Scripting.FileSystemObject
End Sub
Private Sub MDIForm_Unload(Cancel As Integer)
    Set m_objFSO = Nothing
End Sub
```

The final changes you need to make go in the code on the child form so that the child form can use the shared FileSystemObject. First, remove the declaration for the FSO object in the Display method because it's now a duplicate. The additional code needed is marked in bold here:

```
Public Sub Display(mdiInput As MDIForm)d
    On Error GoTo EH

    Dim objStream As Scripting.TextStream
    Dim strFilename As String

    Show
    Set m_mdiMain = mdiInput
    With m_mdiMain.ComDlg
        .CancelError = True
        .DialogTitle = "Open File"
        .Flags = cdlOFNHideReadOnly
        .Filter = "All Files (*.*)|*.*|" _
            & "Text Files (*.txt)|*.txt|" _
            & "HTML Files (*.htm;*.html)|*.htm;*.html"
        .FilterIndex = 2
        .ShowOpen
        strFilename = .FileName
    End With
```

```
    Set objStream = m_mdiMain.FSO.OpenTextFile(strFilename)
    txtContent = objStream.ReadAll
    objStream.Close
    Me.Caption = strFilename
    Exit Sub

EH:
    If Err.Number = cdlCancel Then
        Unload Me
        Exit Sub
    Else
        MsgBox "Error occurred: " & Err.Description _
            & " (#" & Err.Number & ")"
    End If

End Sub
```

Using this code, the child form can now make use of the FileSystemObject owned by the MDI form!

Managing Menus

An MDI form is designed to manage multiple documents, which means that the MDI form will often have a menu and/or a toolbar that is shared between the documents. While the toolbar is associated only with the MDI form, menus are a bit different. An MDI form can have its own menus, as can the MDI child forms within its frame. However, when you show an MDI child form that has a menu, the child's menu will replace the MDI form's menus. Any command selected from the menu at that point will be sent to the child window. While this may sound like a benefit, look at the downside:

- All menus that are common across the application have to be copied to each child form that has its own menu. There is no easy way to do this other than manually editing the text of the form in Notepad.
- All common code in those common menus has to be replicated across all the child forms. Alternatively, you can call the MDI form to handle those menu choices, but you still have to have event procedures for every menu choice in every child window.

As you can see, there is a lot of work involved in putting menus on child forms. You can do it, but this section teaches a more efficient way to manage menus for child forms. In spite of how it looks, you can define a child-specific menu without having to copy all the common menus and related code.

At this point, you haven't seen much by way of communication between the MDI form and its child forms. You've seen only how the child form is started from the MDI form and is capable of accessing some shared resources.

However, by adding further communication capabilities, your MDI application's child forms will be capable of using shared as well as custom menu items.

Shared Menu Items

First, let's add a method to save changes to the files you open. In VB's menu editor, add a Save menu choice to the File menu, and give it the control name mnuFileSave. Here is the code you need to add to the form:

```
Private Sub mnuFileSave_Click()
    If Me.ActiveForm Is Nothing Then Exit Sub
    If TypeOf Me.ActiveForm Is frmFile Then
        Me.ActiveForm.Save
    End If
End Sub
```

This code first checks any nonempty forms to make sure that the active child form is of the frmFile type. This ensures that when we call the Save method, it will actually work. If we don't first check what type of form it is, it's possible to get an error. To actually perform the save operation, add the following code (for brevity we are leaving off the error trapping you would need in production-level file-saving code):

```
Public Sub Save()
    Dim objStream As Scripting.TextStream

    With m_mdiMain.FSO
        Set objStream = .OpenTextFile(Me.Caption, ForWriting, True)
        objStream.Write txtContent
        objStream.Close
    End With

End Sub
```

For this code, we use the child form's caption to retrieve the filename to write the information back to. We could also store the filename in a local variable instead of just using the form's caption, or we could add a public property to the child formthat sets and gets the name of the file to use.

This application can also provide New File and Save As, which work in a similar way. In addition, we need provide for the case in which the user hasn't saved the file yet and doesn't have a filename yet. To make these changes, first add the menu choices to the MDI form:

CAPTION	NAME PROPERTY
&New	mnuFileNew
Save &As...	mnuFileSaveAs

> **TIP**
> *You can place the menu items in any order, but New normally comes first
> while Save As follows Save.*

Next, rename the Display method on the child form to OpenFile. You should
also change the code in the mnuFileOpen event handler to:

```
Private Sub mnuFileOpen_Click()
    Dim frmNew As New frmFIle
    frmNew.OpenFile Me
End Sub
```

> **NOTE**
> *We didn't rename the Display method to Open because we can't; Open is a
> reserved word.*

To handle the case in which a new file is being created, add this code to the
MDI form. This code will call a method called NewFile on the child form whose
code you'll see momentarily.

```
Private Sub mnuFileNew_Click()
    Dim frmNew As New frmFile
    frmNew.NewFile Me
End Sub
```

> **NOTE**
> *Like the word Open, the word New is a reserved word, so we use NewFile as the
> method for the child form.*

Add this code to the child form:

```
Public Sub NewFile(mdiInput As MDIForm)
    Show
    Set m_mdiMain = mdiInput
    Me.Caption = "New File"
End Sub
```

The words "New File" in the caption of the child form is the signal that the
file hasn't been saved yet. After it is saved, we'll put the full pathname into the
caption of the form.

The rewritten Save routine on the child form needs to be changed quite a bit. Also, it is a bit different from the NewFile routine because it must test for a filename and, if necessary, retrieve a new filename, as shown here:

```
Public Sub Save()
    On Error GoTo EH
    Dim objStream As Scripting.TextStream
    If Me.Caption = "New File" Then
        With m_mdiMain.ComDlg
            .CancelError = True
            .DialogTitle = "Save File"
            .Flags = cdlOFNHideReadOnly
            .Filter = "All Files (*.*)|*.*|" _
                & "Text Files (*.txt)|*.txt|" _
                & "HTML Files (*.htm;*.html)|*.htm;*.html"
            .FilterIndex = 2
            .ShowSave
            Me.Caption = .FileName
        End With
    End If

    With m_mdiMain.FSO
        Set objStream = .OpenTextFile(Me.Caption, ForWriting, True)
            objStream.Write txtContent
            objStream.Close
    End With
    Exit Sub
EH:
    If Err.Number = cdlCancel Then
        Exit Sub
    Else
        MsgBox "Error occurred: " & Err.Description _
            & " (#" & Err.Number & ")"
        Unload Me
    End If
End Sub
```

The SaveAs routine on the MDI form is basically the same as the Save routine. The code is as follows:

```
Private Sub mnuFileSaveAs_Click()
    If Me.ActiveForm Is Nothing Then Exit Sub
    If TypeOf Me.ActiveForm Is frmFile Then
        Me.ActiveForm.SaveAs
    End If
End Sub
```

The code in the child form is basically the same for SaveAs as the Save method. However, this code doesn't check the current filename before saving the data. The code is as follows for the child form:

```
Public Sub SaveAs()
    On Error GoTo EH
    Dim objStream As Scripting.TextStream
    With m_mdiMain.ComDlg
        .CancelError = True
        .DialogTitle = "Save File"
        .Flags = cdlOFNHideReadOnly
        If Me.Caption <> "New File" Then
            .FileName = Me.Caption
        End If
        .Filter = "All Files (*.*)|*.*|" _
            & "Text Files (*.txt)|*.txt|" _
            & "HTML Files (*.htm;*.html)|*.htm;*.html"
        .FilterIndex = 2
        .ShowSave
        Me.Caption = .FileName
    End With

    With m_mdiMain.FSO
            Set objStream = .OpenTextFile(Me.Caption, ForWriting, True)
            objStream.Write txtContent
            objStream.Close
    End With
    Exit Sub
EH:
    If Err.Number = cdlCancel Then
            Unload Me
            Exit Sub
    Else
            MsgBox "Error occurred: " & Err.Description _
                & " (#" & Err.Number & ")"
    End If
End Sub
```

The application now handles all the file functions that are typical in word processing applications, and all the relevant code is wrapped in the child form's code. A good change that you can make to this code is to move the common save code to a subroutine. We didn't do that here but it's something that could be done very easily.

Semishared Menu Items

The previous section demonstrated how a common menu can signal multiple child forms. But what if the child form needs its menu tailored to be more relevant to what is going on in the child form? Luckily, communication between forms can also occur in the reverse direction. Each child form can signal the MDI form to change its menu in a particular fashion. Specifically, the child form can inform the parent when it is capable of accepting commands such as Cut, Copy, and Paste.

First, add an Edit menu and the following submenu items to the MDI form's menus:

CAPTION	NAME PROPERTY
&Edit	mnuEdit
Cu&t	mnuEditCut
&Copy	mnuEditCopy
&Paste	mnuEditPaste

Disable each of these submenu items by clearing its Enabled checkbox. That way, the items will be available only when activated by a child form.

Each child form is responsible for activating the menu items it wants to activate. This is done using one class module that acts as a coordinator for a class specific to each menu. Because there is only one menu that needs to be handled (the Edit menu), only two class modules are needed. Let's call the coordinator class module MDIMenus and the class responsible for the Edit menu EditMenus. Here's the code for the MDIMenus coordinating class:

```
Option Explicit

Private m_objEdit As EditMenus

Public Property Set Edit(ByVal vData As EditMenus)
    Set m_objEdit = vData
End Property

Public Property Get Edit() As EditMenus
    Set Edit = m_objEdit
End Property

Private Sub Class_Initialize()
    Set m_objEdit = New EditMenus
End Sub

Private Sub Class_Terminate()
    Set m_objEdit = Nothing
End Sub
```

The EditMenus code is shown here:

```
Option Explicit
Private m_blnCut As Boolean
Private m_blnCopy As Boolean
Private m_blnPaste As Boolean
Public Property Let Paste(ByVal vData As Boolean)
    m_blnPaste = vData
End Property
Public Property Get Paste() As Boolean
    Paste = m_blnPaste
End Property
Public Property Let Copy(ByVal vData As Boolean)
    m_blnCopy = vData
End Property
Public Property Get Copy() As Boolean
    Copy = m_blnCopy
End Property
Public Property Let Cut(ByVal vData As Boolean)
    m_blnCut = vData
End Property
Public Property Get Cut() As Boolean
    Cut = m_blnCut
End Property
```

The structure just created makes it easy to add extra menus to the MDIMenus class, each of which can be used in any of the child windows—just add another class and the code to the MDIMenus class to work with it.

The next batch of code goes in the child form and takes care of returning the form's menu settings when the MDI form requests them. The first line is another declaration that you need to add to the form.

```
Private m_objMenus As MDIMenus

Private Sub Form_Activate()
    m_mdiMain.Activate
End Sub

Private Sub Form_Deactivate()
    m_mdiMain.Deactivate
End Sub

Private Sub Form_Load()
    Set m_objMenus = New MDIMenus
    With m_objMenus.Edit
        .Copy = True
        .Cut = True
```

```
        .Paste = True
    End With
End Sub

Public Property Get MDIMenus() As MDIMenus
    Set MDIMenus = m_objMenus
End Property
```

The Form_Load event procedure takes care of storing the menu settings in the object. These flags in the object indicate whether the menu item should be made available when the form is active. By setting these three flags to True, we indicate that Cut, Copy, and Paste should be available when a form of this type is active.

Now add the following code to the MDI form. It takes care of updating the menus when a child form is activated. The MDI form doesn't know when a form is activated or deactivated, but the code we already added to the child form signals the MDI form when the child's Activate or Deactivate event is triggered.

```
Public Sub Activate()

    If TypeOf Me.ActiveForm Is frmFile Then
        With Me.ActiveForm.MDIMenus
            With .Edit
                mnuEditCut.Enabled = .Cut
                mnuEditCopy.Enabled = .Copy
                mnuEditPaste.Enabled = .Paste
            End With
        End With
    End If

End Sub

Public Sub Deactivate()

    If TypeOf Me.ActiveForm Is frmFile Then
        mnuEditCut.Enabled = False
        mnuEditCopy.Enabled = False
        mnuEditPaste.Enabled = False
    End If

End Sub
```

The last bit of code you need for Cut/Copy/Paste is shown here:

```
Private Sub mnuEditCopy_Click()
    Dim blnTestCtrl As Boolean
```

```
        blnTestCtrl = False
        If TypeOf Me.ActiveForm.ActiveControl Is TextBox Then
            blnTestCtrl = True
        End If
        If blnTestCtrl Then
            Clipboard.SetText Me.ActiveForm.ActiveControl.SelText
        End If
End Sub

Private Sub mnuEditCut_Click()
        Dim blnTestCtrl As Boolean
        blnTestCtrl = False
        If TypeOf Me.ActiveForm.ActiveControl Is TextBox Then
            blnTestCtrl = True
        End If
        If blnTestCtrl Then
            Clipboard.SetText Me.ActiveForm.ActiveControl.SelText
            Me.ActiveForm.ActiveControl.SelText = ""
        End If
End Sub

Private Sub mnuEditPaste_Click()
        Dim blnTestCtrl As Boolean
        blnTestCtrl = False
        If TypeOf Me.ActiveForm.ActiveControl Is TextBox Then
            blnTestCtrl = True
        End If
        If blnTestCtrl Then
            Me.ActiveForm.ActiveControl.SelText = Clipboard.GetText
        End If

End Sub
```

> **TIP**
> *The code first checks whether the control can be edited using standard*
> *Cut/Copy/Paste keys. If there are other controls that already support*
> *Cut/Copy/Paste, either add them to this code or create a function to determine*
> *whether the control can be edited.*

That's all there is to it! The edit options will be visible only when a child
form is visible. Otherwise, they remain disabled. You may wish to hide them
instead of disabling them, but the code is essentially the same for either choice.

Custom Menu Items

Sometimes a child form needs custom menu items—ones that shouldn't be available to every child form. Conveniently, we can implement these items within the framework we already set up. Each type of form determines the custom menu items it needs and stores them in the appropriate object (EditMenus class). Meanwhile, the MDI form has a sufficient number of menu items that stay hidden until needed. When the user selects one of the custom menu items, the child form receives the text of that menu item.

Initially, we're going to create five custom menu items on the Edit menu. They will be part of a control array so that we have the flexibility to add even more of them at run-time. Add the following choices to the MDI form's menu. All of them should be invisible:

CAPTION	NAME PROPERTY	INDEX VALUE
–	mnuEditDynamic	Index 0
Dynamic 1	mnuEditDynamic	Index 1
Dynamic 2	mnuEditDynamic	Index 2
Dynamic 3	mnuEditDynamic	Index 3
Dynamic 4	mnuEditDynamic	Index 4
Dynamic 5	mnuEditDynamic	Index 5

> *NOTE*
>
> *The first item will add a separator bar between the Cut/Copy/Paste choices and the custom ones at the end. The separator bar will be visible only when a custom item is visible.*

Next, we need to modify the Activate and Deactivate subroutines on the MDI form because these routines need to set and clear the custom items on the Edit menu. The new code for these two subroutines is shown here:

```
Public Sub Activate()
    Dim i As Integer

    If TypeOf Me.ActiveForm Is frmFile Then
        With Me.ActiveForm.MDIMenus
            With .Edit
                mnuEditCut.Enabled = .Cut
                mnuEditCopy.Enabled = .Copy
                mnuEditPaste.Enabled = .Paste
                If .MenuItemCount > 0 Then
                    For i = 1 To .MenuItemCount
```

```
                    mnuEditDynamic(i).Caption = .MenuItems(i)
                    mnuEditDynamic(i).Visible = True
                Next i
                mnuEditDynamic(0).Visible = True
            End If
        End With
    End With
End If

End Sub

Public Sub Deactivate()
    Dim i As Integer

    If TypeOf Me.ActiveForm Is frmFile Then
        mnuEditCut.Enabled = False
        mnuEditCopy.Enabled = False
        mnuEditPaste.Enabled = False
        For i = 0 To 5
            mnuEditDynamic(i).Visible = False
        Next i
    End If

End Sub
```

The final change to the MDI form is the addition of an event procedure for the custom Edit menu items. This procedure passes the menu item's caption to the requesting child form, as shown here:

```
Private Sub mnuEditDynamic_Click(Index As Integer)
    ActiveForm.EditMenu mnuEditDynamic(Index).Caption
End Sub
```

The event procedure calls the EditMenu method, which should be placed in the child form to process the selected menu item, as shown here:

```
Public Sub EditMenu(strCaption As String)
    MsgBox "Just received the " & strCaption & " from the MDI menu."
End Sub
```

> **NOTE**
> *The EditMenu routine above contains placeholder code. The idea is to handle the selected menu item. The details of the processing code are not presented because our focus is the communication technique.*

The child form needs another change in the Form_Load event procedure. We have to add the custom items to the object, as shown in the boldface code here:

```
Private Sub Form_Load()
    Set m_objMenus = New MDIMenus
    With m_objMenus.Edit
        .Copy = True
        .Cut = True
        .Paste = True
        .AddMenuItems "Test 1", "Test 2", "Test 3"
    End With
End Sub
```

Now add the following code to the EditMenus class:

```
Public Sub AddMenuItems(ParamArray strCaptions())
    Dim i As Integer
    Dim iNew As Integer

    ReDim m_arrMenuItems(UBound(strCaptions) - LBound(strCaptions) + 1)
    iNew = 1
    For i = LBound(strCaptions) To UBound(strCaptions)
        m_arrMenuItems(iNew) = strCaptions(i)
        iNew = iNew + 1
    Next i
End Sub

Public Function MenuItems(intIndex As Integer) As String
    MenuItems = m_arrMenuItems(intIndex)
End Function

Public Property Get MenuItemCount() As Integer
    MenuItemCount = UBound(m_arrMenuItems)
End Property
```

You should also add this declaration to the EditMenus code:

```
Private m_arrMenuItems() As String
```

The AddMenuItems routine accepts an array of parameters and configures itself appropriately to hold all the items. It doesn't add new items if it's called again—instead, it replaces them with the new parameter values. (Because the form only calls this routine once, that's fine.) This routine can also handle a virtually unlimited number of menu items. Because the MDI form only has five spaces, you may want to add code to this class to limit the number of items being added.

The MenuItems function enables the calling code to retrieve an element from the menu items array. This is used when the MDI form is populating the menu. The MenuItemCount routine returns the number of elements in the array. As the AddMenuItems routine shows, the elements are numbered 1 to N, which coincides with the MDI menu choices, as item 0 is the separator bar.

After you have made all the changes you can test the application. When you run the application and load a new window, you'll see the items Test 1, Test 2, and Test 3 added to the Edit menu, and the Cut/Copy/Paste choices will be enabled. Closing the window will cause those edit items to disappear and the Cut/Copy/Paste items to be disabled.

Chapter 14

Database Programming

It's a truism that major business applications, such as those performing system functions or principal business tasks, generally need a permanent data storage mechanism. However, even simple business utilities, such as a virus-scanning tool, need a database of sorts; for example, a file with all the virus definitions. So, what's the best way to code your application to interact with databases? Visual Basic provides a wealth of tools and controls designed just to answer this question.

Database Features in Visual Basic

Visual Basic 6.0 includes a variety of new features that simplify database programming. Many of the features enable you to work solely within the Visual Basic development environment, eliminating the need to keep Visual Basic and your database client open simultaneously. The following sections cover all the new database features and their purposes.

OLE DB Support

Object Linking and Embedding-Database (OLE DB) is a set of COM interfaces that provide applications with uniform access to data stored in diverse information sources, both relational and nonrelational. These interfaces support the amount of database management system (DBMS) functionality appropriate to the data source, enabling it to share its data. All the new data-bound controls, the Data Environment, and the Data Report designer are OLE DB-aware. This feature is available in all editions of VB. See Chapter 15 for more information about OLE DB.

Active Data Objects

Active Data Objects (ADO) is a new data access technology that features a simpler object model, better integration with other Microsoft and non-Microsoft technologies, a common interface for both local and remote data access, disconnected recordsets, a user-accessible data-binding interface, and hierarchical recordsets. Unlike open database connectivity (ODBC), ADO can handle nonrelational databases such as object-oriented databases. ADO is the way that programmers access OLE DB.

One of the best things about ADO is that it is available for use in several other platforms, including Active Server Pages (ASP) and the new Windows Scripting Host utility, which is available in the latest editions of Windows and Windows NT. ADO is available in all editions of Visual Basic. See Chapter 15 for a more in-depth discussion of ADO.

The Data Environment

The *Data Environment designer* provides an interactive, design-time environment for creating ADO objects. These can be used as a data source for data-aware objects on a form or report, or accessed programmatically as methods and properties exposed by the *Data Environment object,* which is essentially a container for all your data connections, queries, and other database-related objects in your application. The Data Environment designer supports all the functionality of Visual Basic's UserConnection designer, as well as additional features such as drag and drop, hierarchies, grouping, and aggregates. The Data Environment is available in the Professional and Enterprise Editions of Visual Basic. You learn more about this feature later in the "Using the Data Environment Designer" section.

The ADO Data Control

The ADO Data control is a new OLE DB-aware data source control that functions much like the Intrinsic Data and Remote Data controls. As with these older controls, the ADO Data control enables you to create a database application with minimum code, but it takes advantage of the new ADO libraries so that you can use a consistent set of objects throughout your application. This feature is available in all editions of VB.

Enhanced Data Binding

In previous versions of Visual Basic, it was only possible to bind controls together on a form. In Visual Basic 6.0, it is possible to bind *any* ADO/OLE DB data source to *any* ADO/OLE DB data consumer. You can set the DataSource property of controls at run-time to dynamically bind to data sources. You can create classes that are data sources and consumers, and bind them through the new BindingsCollection object. You can create user controls that are data sources, similar to the ADO Data control. You can create user controls that are complex-bound, similar to the DataGrid control. This feature is available in the Professional and Enterprise Editions of Visual Basic.

The Query and Database Designer

In the Enterprise Edition of VB, you can visually create and modify database schemas and queries. You can also create Structured Query Language (SQL) Server and Oracle database tables, drag and drop to create views, and automatically change column data types. These tools are similar to those included with Microsoft Access and SQL Server Enterprise Manager. Having all these tools included with Visual Basic enables you to keep all the development all in one tool instead of spread between many different tools. You can also use this tool to create Oracle- and SQL Server-stored procedures. This editor also enables you to write triggers for the databases.

The Data Report Designer

For many years, Crystal Reports provided the only reporting tools available within VB. This tool was separate from Visual Basic and used files that were not compiled into the application. Microsoft Data Report, while severely limited in function, is designed within the VB environment and is then compiled into the final executable. The Data Report designer enables you to use drag and drop to quickly create reports from any recordset, including hierarchical recordsets. This feature is available in the Professional and Enterprise Editions of Visual Basic.

Data Sources

Instead of being restricted to just the ADO Data control and the bound controls included with VB, you can now create user controls and classes that are data sources, to which other controls can be bound. You can use this design feature to build validation into your data sources to help separate the functional layers in your applications. This feature is available in the Professional and Enterprise Editions of Visual Basic.

The Data View Window

You can use the Data View window to browse all of the databases you are connected to and see their tables, views, stored procedures, and so on. You can see all your Data Environment objects as well as all the Data Links from a single view instead of having to switch back and forth. You can drag and drop fields from the window to a form or report to bind a control to the field. This feature is available in the Professional and Enterprise Editions of Visual Basic.

The DataRepeater Control

You can use the DataRepeater control to create a custom view of a database, similar to Access forms. The DataRepeater control can contain TextBox, CheckBox, DataGrid, or other controls bound to data fields. The DataRepeater control is similar to the one used for ASP development with Visual InterDev. This feature is available in the Professional and Enterprise Editions of Visual Basic.

Data Form Wizard Enhancements

The Data Form Wizard was available in previous versions of Visual Basic, but now gives you the ability to build code-only forms in which controls are not bound to a data control. It enables you to use ADO code. The Data Form Wizard is integrated with the Application, Chart, and FlexGrid wizards. You can use the Data Form Wizard to learn to use the ADO library in your code. This feature is available in the Professional and Enterprise Editions of Visual Basic.

The Data Object Wizard

The Data Object Wizard is a new wizard that automates creating a middle-tier object that is bound to the Data Environment or to a UserControl object. This tool is available in the Professional and Enterprise Editions of Visual Basic.

ADO-Aware Data Controls

All editions of Visual Basic include ADO-enabled controls that provide a grid, a list box, and a drop-down combo box that can be bound to databases. There is also an updated version of the FlexGrid control that, in addition to supporting all the functionality of the FlexGrid control, can display a hierarchy of ADO Recordsets. Each Recordset returned is displayed as a separate band within the grid and can be formatted independently. They are able to use both the ADO Data control and the features made available through the Data Environment. These controls are discussed in the next section after you've created your Data Environment.

Using the Data Environment Designer

The Data Environment makes it easier to manage your database connections in a single place. Instead of having to load settings for each data control you wish to use, you use the Data Environment as a data source for any bound control. This section teaches you to create a Data Environment and then bind it to a form. You also learn to access the actual objects, such as the connections and recordsets, represented by the Data Environment.

Creating the Data Environment

First, you need to add a Data Environment to your project. In a new Standard EXE project, you can select Project→More ActiveX Designers→Data Environment to add this designer to your application. Adding this designer automatically adds a code module to your project for the code that will be created by manipulating the Data Environment Designer. You can see the associated module by right-clicking in the designer and choosing View Code.

> **TIP**
>
> *When you select New Project, you can select a type of project called a Data Project. This type of project adds a bunch of other types of files that you probably won't need, such as a Data Report and all of the data-bound controls mentioned earlier. It's easier just to add modules, as you need them, when working with a Data Environment.*

After you've added the Data Environment, the Data Environment designer will appear (as shown in Figure 14-1), displaying a connection, named Connection1, already added to the Data Environment.

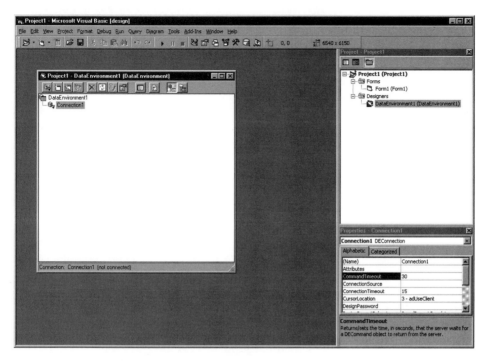

Figure 14-1: The Data Environment designer window

Next, rename the Data Environment to something other than DataEnvironment1. You can use any name that suits you, but be consistent in your naming convention. One common naming convention is to use **denv** as the prefix to indicate an object is a Data Environment and to use **dcn** as the prefix for a data connection. For this example, let's rename the Data Environment **denvData** in the Properties Window. Let's also rename the data connection from Connection1 to something more memorable and logical. This data connection will link to the Biblio database, so name the data connection **dcnBiblio**. Again, use whatever prefix you want, but be consistent.

> **TIP**
>
> *You have to rename the Data Environment in the Properties window; you can't do it by hovering over the item in the designer window. You can, however, rename the data connection by clicking and hovering over it in the Designer window.*

We now need to configure the data connection so that the Biblio database is found in the main VB directory. To do this, follow these steps:

1. Right-click the connection and select Properties.
2. In the first dialog that appears, select the type of driver to use to connect. Because this is an Access database, you should use the Microsoft Jet 3.51 OLE DB Provider. Click it and then click Next to continue.
3. Next, you need to specify the pathname of the database file. You can browse to the file or you can type in the pathname to it. There is also a place to enter a username and password. By default, the username is Admin and the password is empty. This is required, even for Access databases. Unless you've added security to your database, you shouldn't change these settings at this time.
4. Click Test Connection to make sure you did everything right. (If you don't get a success message box, press Cancel and repeat steps 1 to 4. There's not much that can go wrong with Access database connections, unless you are pointing to the wrong filename.) Click OK.

At this point, we can access the tables and views in the database by using the Data View window. Select View→Data View Window to open this window in your VB environment.

Adding a Query

Next, we want to add a command to the Data Environment. A command can be a number of things, including a stored procedure, a query, or an SQL query entered manually. Let's create a query that retrieves title, ISBN number, and book publisher by joining the Titles table to the Publishers table. Sound complicated? It's actually a piece of cake using the query designer described earlier. To begin, follow these steps:

1. Right-click the dcnBiblio connection in the Data Environment Designer and select Add Command from the pop-up menu. Command1 will be added beneath the data connection.
2. Rename Command1 in the Properties window to **cmdTitles**. This is the name of the query we'll bind to later.
3. Right-click cmdTitles and select Properties. The dialog box shown in Figure 14-2 will appear.
4. Because we're going to write the SQL query ourselves and our custom query doesn't already exist in the database, select the option button next to SQL statement and then click SQL Builder.
5. The window that appears enables you to design your query graphically. Instead of having to write the SQL query, the SQL Builder will create the SQL query for you. You just have to select the appropriate fields and options. This window is shown in Figure 14-3.

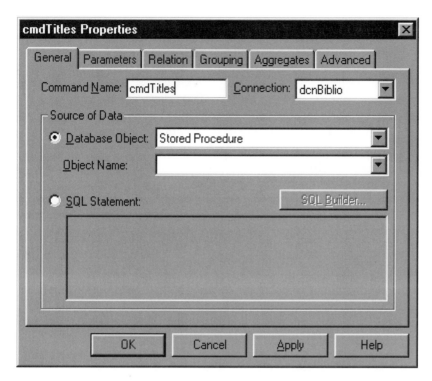

Figure 14-2: The Properties dialog box for the cmdTitles object

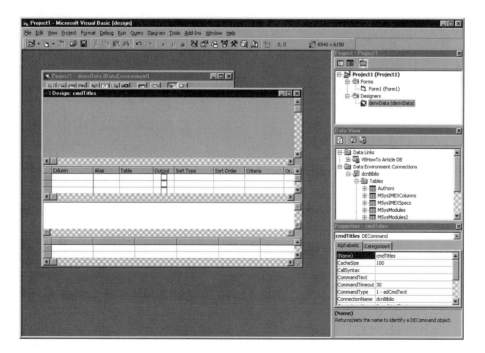

Figure 14-3: The SQL Builder window

6. Make sure you have the Data View window open with your list of tables visible, because you can drag the Titles and Publishers table to the top part of the SQL Builder window. These tables will appear there and will be linked graphically, based on the PubID field. The SQL Builder knows, because there is a relationship in the database between these two fields, that they will be used to link the two tables in a join. As you drag the tables over, the third pane will show the SQL needed so far.

7. With the two tables added, you can select the fields to show. In the Titles table, check the ISBN and Title fields. In the Publishers table, check the Company Name field. They will populate the second pane.

8. Let's sort the results by the title of the book. In the second pane, select an Ascending sort on the Title field in the Sort Type drop-down list box. VB will add a sort order value of 1 because that field is the first one by which you are sorting. If you had multiple fields included in the sort, you could specify which one comes first in the sort by changing these values. The first field in the sort is always given a 1.

9. After you've made all these changes, the SQL query showing in the third pane should look like this:

```
SELECT Titles.ISBN, Titles.Title,
    Publishers.`Company Name`
FROM Publishers, Titles
WHERE Publishers.PubID = Titles.PubID
ORDER BY Titles.Title
```

10. You may have been wondering what the bottom pane was for. If you right click in the pane and choose Run, you can run your query and see the results of the query. This enables you to test the query to make sure the results are correct. Run your query and then go to the next step.

11. To save the query, either select Save cmdTitles from the File menu or can just close the window and answer Yes to the dialog box that appears.

Now, choosing Properties from the context menu in the Data Environment Designer for cmdTitles displays the SQL query you designed in the box below the SQL Builder button. If you click the plus (+) sign next to the query name in the Data Environment designer window, the fields that are part of the query will display. If you see all this, your query was created successfully.

One thing to note is that this query only exists in the Data Environment, not in the database itself. Users accessing the database directly won't see this query. If you have a query that needs to be used by users not using your VB application, it should be added to the database directly. If you have a stored procedure or query in the database that you want to use for binding, add it to your Data Environment by selecting it in the Command properties instead of creating an SQL statement.

Binding a Data Grid to the Data Environment

Now that the query is added to the Data Environment, we can bind our form to it. For this type of query, the easiest way to display the data is in a data grid. Select Project'Components to add the Microsoft DataGrid Control 6.0 (OLE DB) control to your toolbox, and then draw the control on the form already loaded in your project. Name the data grid **dgrTitles**, and name the form **frmTitles**.

To bind the form to the cmdTitles query, set the following properties for the DataGrid control:

1. Select denvData as the DataSource.
2. Select cmdTitles as the DataMember.

If you want to, you can add this code to resize the grid to the size of the form:

```
Private Sub Form_Resize()
    dgrTitles.Height = Me.ScaleHeight - (dgrTitles.Top * 2)
    dgrTitles.Width = Me.ScaleWidth - (dgrTitles.Left * 2)
End Sub
```

When you run the application, you'll see the form shown in Figure 14-4:

ISBN	Title	Company Name
0-8802234-6-4	1-2-3 Database Technic	QUE CORP
1-5676127-1-7	1-2-3 For Windows Hyp	ALPHA BOOKS
0-8802280-4-0	1-2-3 Power MacRos/B	QUE CORP
0-5533496-6-X	1-2-3 Power Tools (Ban	BANTAM ELECTRONIC
0-8802262-5-0	1-2-3 Release 2.2 PC T	QUE CORP
1-8780587-3-8	1-2-3 Secrets/Book and	IDG BOOKS WORLDW
1-5676123-0-X	10 Minute Guide to Acc	ALPHA BOOKS
1-5676145-0-7	10 Minute Guide to Acc	ALPHA BOOKS
0-7897055-5-9	10 Minute Guide to Acc	QUE CORP
1-5676153-9-2	10 Minute Guide to Act!	ALPHA BOOKS
1-5676140-7-8	10 Minute Guide to Lotu	ALPHA BOOKS
1-5676117-6-1	10 Minute Guide to Lotu	ALPHA BOOKS
1-5676102-7-7	10 Minute Guide to Para	ALPHA BOOKS
1-5676149-4-9	10 Minute Guide to Para	ALPHA BOOKS
0-6722283-2-7	10 Minute Guide to Q &	Sams Publications
0-6723003-5-4	10 Minute Guide to Q &	Sams Publications

Figure 14-4: The DataGrid bound to the Data Environment

That's all there is to binding the data grid to the Data Environment. You don't have to add a Data control to the form when you're using the Data Environment. This helps save valuable system resources for more important things!

Binding a Record Viewer to the Data Environment

The next binding exercise creates a single record form, with navigation buttons, for viewing individual records. Data grids work for many cases, but they aren't easy to edit, especially with a large number of fields. This form will work fine for viewing the fields in the recordset.

To do this exercise, follow these steps:

1. Add a new form to your project and name it **frmRecordViewer**.
2. Just as we dragged tables from the Data View window to the SQL Builder, we can drag fields from the Data Environment to the new form. Drag each of the fields from the cmdTitles query to the form and watch what happens. (You may need to tile the windows from the Window menu to do this successfully.)
3. As you drag the fields to the form, VB automatically names the controls and draws both a text box and a label on the form for each field. In addition, it names the controls using common prefixes and not just as Text1. For instance, the controls that were added were named txtISBN, txtTitle, and txtCompanyName. The labels were put in a control array named lblFieldLabel. In addition, all of the controls are bound to the Data Environment's cmdTitles command already.
4. You can run this form now (for example by making it the Startup form) and have the first record appear. However, you don't yet have the capability to navigate among the records. To add this capability, add two buttons to your form and name them **cmdPrevious** and **cmdNext**. Give them appropriate captions for their functions.
5. Add this code to the form to handle the navigation:

```
Private Sub cmdNext_Click()
    If Not denvData.rscmdTitles.EOF Then
        denvData.rscmdTitles.MoveNext
    End If
End Sub

Private Sub cmdPrevious_Click()
    If Not denvData.rscmdTitles.BOF Then
        denvData.rscmdTitles.MovePrevious
    End If
End Sub
```

The rscmdTitles function is the recordset that holds the data retrieved from the command named cmdTitles. To perform any operation on the recordset, you have to use this property of the Data Environment and not the command itself. In this case, we use the MoveNext and MovePrevious methods to navigate within the recordset. We also check to make sure that we don't run past the beginning or the end of the recordset.

At this point, you can run your form and you will see something that looks like the form shown in Figure 14-5:

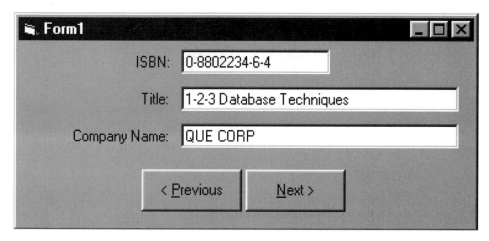

Figure 14-5: Binding a form to a database without a Data control

You can use the navigation buttons to move back and forth within the database. Once again, we don't need a data control because we are using the Data Environment for all our data binding.

> **TIP**
> *The recordsets created by commands in the Data Environment Designer always consist of the prefix rs followed by the name of the command.*

Binding a Data Report to the Data Environment

Our last exercise in binding will be to create a Data Report. The report, by default has five sections, as shown in Table 14-1:

Table 14-1: Sections of a Data Report

SECTION	HOW IT IS PRINTED
Report Header	Once at beginning of the report
Page Header	At top of each page of the report
Detail section	For each record in the recordset
Page Footer	At bottom of each page of the report
Report Footer	Once at the end of the report

The Data Report is also built into the VB environment as another designer file. Building a Data Report is just the same as building the form you just did. We're going to place content in the first three sections of the Data Report. To build the Data Report, do the following:

1. Add a Data Report to the project by selecting Project→Add Data Report. Name the Data Report **drptTitles**.
2. Draw a label in the Report Header using the RptLabel control on your Toolbox. Fill in the Caption property with a title, such as "All Titles in Database."
3. Drag each of the three fields to the Detail section from the Data Environment Designer. When you drop a field into the Detail section, both the field and a label will be drawn. Remove each of the labels that are drawn. Also, you'll need to close up the size of the detail section so that it is just large enough to hold the labels. Any extra space in this section will be repeated for every record being shown.
4. Add three labels to the Page Header section so that they are positioned over each of the columns. Look at Figure 14-6 for a sample layout.
5. The final step is to point the Data Report to the appropriate data source. Change the Data Source property of the Data Report form to denvData and the Data Member property to cmdTitles.

Now, run your Data Report. Change the StartupForm of the project to point to the report. Depending on the speed of your machine you may need to wait while the report loads, but when it does display, the report will look like Figure 14-7.

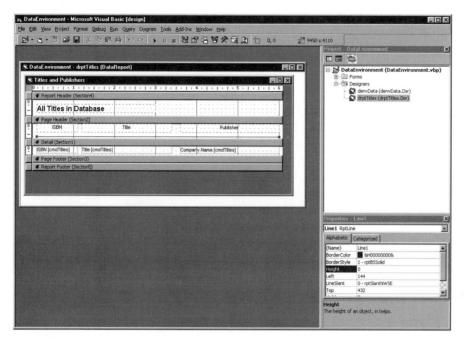

Figure 14-6: Sample column header layout for the report

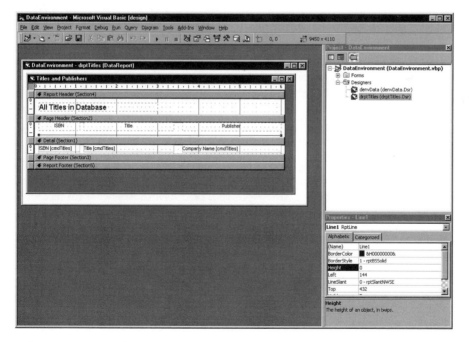

Figure 14-7: Sample report using the Biblio database

The Data Report provides several controls for viewing the report, including a page control and a zoom control. In addition, the report can be printed automatically without another line of code. The other good thing is that the Data Report is actually compiled into the application and no extra files are required to make the report show up.

Using the DataList and DataCombo Controls

The DataList and DataCombo control are two helpful controls that are also at your disposal. The DataList control is a standard ListBox that can be bound to a database recordset. A list box can be used for large lists of more than 50 to 100 items. The DataList control is part of the Microsoft DataList Controls 6.0 component, which you can add by selecting Project→Components.

Let's add another command to the Data Environment that you created in the last section to provide data for this control. Let's display a list of authors, sorted by last name. To do this exercise, follow these steps:

1. Go to the Data Environment Designer and add a new command named cmdAuthors, and add the following SQL code for the command in the Properties dialog box you get from the context menu:

```
SELECT Author FROM Authors ORDER BY Author
```

2. Add a new form to your project and name it frmLists. Draw a DataList control on the form and name it dlstAuthors.
3. Set the RowSource property of the DataList control to denvData, set the RowMember property to cmdAuthors, and set the ListField property to Author. This will instruct the control how to populate itself.
4. Set frmLists to be the Startup form.
5. Optionally, you can add these lines of code to resize the control to the form's dimensions:

```
Private Sub Form_Resize()
    dlstAuthors.Height = Me.ScaleHeight - (dlstAuthors.Top * 2)
    dlstAuthors.Width = Me.ScaleWidth - (dlstAuthors.Left * 2)
End Sub
```

When the form runs, it will look like Figure 14-8 with all the author names loaded in it.

> **TIP**
> *One good thing about bound controls is that they don't actually use memory to hold all the values from the database. Instead, the names are retrieved as needed.*

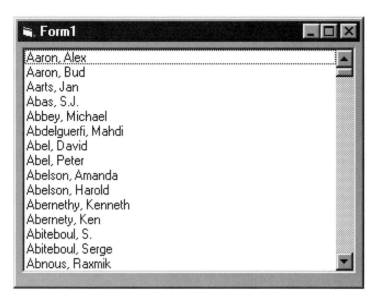

Figure 14-8: List box bound to the database

The DataCombo control works in a similar manner to the DataList control. The properties should be set in the same manner. In general, combo boxes should only be used for small numbers of items (less than 100 or so). It's up to you, but a combo box is a little harder to navigate than a list box. If you follow the same basic steps for a DataCombo control, you'll have a form that looks like Figure 14-9:

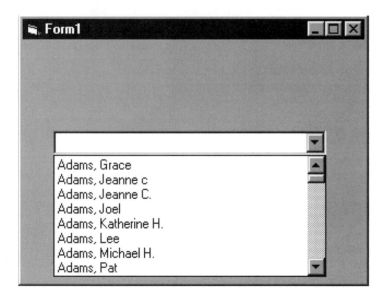

Figure 14-9: Combo box bound to the database

Building a Database Analyzer

One of the most important skills you can learn is how to look at the structure of your database through code. It's fine to hard-code stored procedure names and table names in your code, but there are often cases in which your code can be more generic, and hence more useful, if you can do this. In this section, you learn how to build a tool that lets you view a database's structure.

To do this, we use a part of the ADO 2.1 library that you probably haven't used before: the ActiveX Data Objects Extensions for DDL (Data Definition Language) and Security, or ADOX. This library comes with Office 2000 and is also available for download by going to this URL: www.microsoft.com/data/ado.

(The names in the References dialog box are: Microsoft ActiveX Data Objects 2.1 Library (the 2.0 library works also) and the Microsoft ADO Ext. 2.1 for DDL and Security.) The combination of these two libraries gives you access to the structure of any database that you can connect to using OLE DB. Our example will use the Jet 4.0 provider, which can open any Access database up through and including Access 2000. However, you can change the connection code to connect to any type of database.

After you've referenced both the Microsoft ActiveX Data Objects 2.1 Library and the Microsoft ADO Ext. 2.1 for DDL and Security libraries, add the Common Dialog and Windows Common Controls to your toolbox. We use these controls to build the user interface, which, when populated, looks like Figure 14-10:

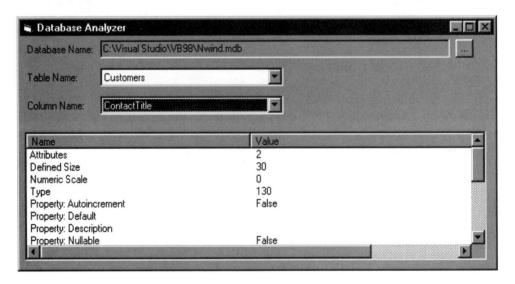

Figure 14-10: The Database Analyzer in use

The form is named frmDBAnalyzer and as its caption is "Database Analyzer." Table 14-2 describes the other controls and their names that are used in Figure 14-10.

CONTROL	NAME
ListView	lvwProperties
ComboBox (as drop down list box)	cboColumns
ComboBox (as drop down list box)	cboTables
TextBox	txtDBFilename
CommandButton	cmdDBFilename
CommonDialog	cdlDialog
Label	lblStatic (part of control array)

Table 14-2: Database Analyzer Controls

The first code you need is for configuring the column headers for the ListView control. We like to do this in code; however, you can also do this at design time. Here is the code for the Form_Load event:

```
Private Sub Form_Load()
    lvwProperties.ColumnHeaders.Add 1, "Name", "Name", 4000
    lvwProperties.ColumnHeaders.Add 2, "Value", "Value", 6000
End Sub
```

The next code handles the button next to the filename box and makes use of the Common Dialog control. The text box is locked and the background is set to the Button Face color, to make it obvious that you can't type in it. Here's the code for the button to select and open a database file:

```
Private Sub cmdDBFilename_Click()

    On Error GoTo EH

    With cdlDialog
        .DialogTitle = "Open Database"
        .CancelError = True
        .DefaultExt = ".mdb"
        .Filter = "Microsoft Access Databases (*.mdb);*.mdb"
        .FilterIndex = 1
        .ShowOpen
    End With

    On Error GoTo 0
    Set m_dcnDB = New ADODB.Connection
    m_dcnDB.Open "Provider=Microsoft.Jet.OLEDB.4.0;" _
        & "Persist Security Info=False;" _
```

```
            & "Data Source=" & cdlDialog.FileName
        txtDBFilename = cdlDialog.FileName

        Set m_catDB = New ADOX.Catalog
        Set m_catDB.ActiveConnection = m_dcnDB

        FillTableList

        Exit Sub

EH:
        If Err.Number = cdlCancel Then
            Exit Sub
        End If
End Sub

Private Sub FillTableList()
        Dim tabLoop As ADOX.Table

        cboTables.Clear
        For Each tabLoop In m_catDB.Tables
            If tabLoop.Type = "TABLE" Then
                cboTables.AddItem tabLoop.Name
            End If
        Next tabLoop
        cboTables.Enabled = True

End Sub
```

After opening the database, we then create an instance of an ADOX.Catalog object, which we named m_catDB. After we set the ActiveConnection property to the active database, the Catalog object instantly has access to the entire structure of the database.

A Catalog object has these major components:

- Groups
- Procedures
- Tables
- Users
- Views

Catalog objects have some additional methods that enable you to create databases and to get and set object ownership. Refer to the MSDN documentation you received with Visual Basic for more information on these methods.

The FillTableList iterates through the Tables collection to retrieve all the user tables. If you step through this code as it reads the table list, you will see a wide variety of things that aren't really tables. The code filters out the nonuser tables and adds the rest to the drop-down list. If you watch the Type property, all of these values will come up in the Northwind Traders database (located in your Visual Basic installation directory), for instance:

TABLE—Normal user-defined table

SYSTEM TABLE—Internal table used by Access

ACCESS TABLE—Internal table used by Access

VIEW—Query that returns a recordset; action queries (insert, delete, update) are stored in the Procedures collection

The next piece of code, shown below, loads the columns of the table when the user clicks a table name.

```
Private Sub cboTables_Click()

    Dim tabTemp As ADOX.Table
    Dim colTemp As ADOX.Column
    Set tabTemp = m_catDB.Tables(cboTables.Text)
    cboColumns.Clear
    For Each colTemp In tabTemp.Columns
        cboColumns.AddItem colTemp.Name
    Next colTemp
    cboColumns.Enabled = True

End Sub
```

Again, the Columns collection represents all the fields that are part of a table. We are simply adding all the columns to the cboColumns drop-down list box.

The last step is to display the information about a column when it is selected. That information will be shown in the ListView control, so there is a bit more work to do to display it. In addition, the Properties collection of a Column is iterated separately in this routine.

```
Private Sub cboColumns_Click()
    Dim colTemp As ADOX.Column
    Dim prpTemp As ADOX.Property
    Dim lstTemp As ListItem
    Set colTemp = _
        m_catDB.Tables(cboTables.Text).Columns(cboColumns.Text)

    With lvwProperties
        .ListItems.Clear
```

```
            Set lstTemp = .ListItems.Add(, "Attributes", "Attributes")
            lstTemp.SubItems(1) = colTemp.Attributes

            Set lstTemp = .ListItems.Add(, "DefinedSize", "Defined Size")
            lstTemp.SubItems(1) = colTemp.DefinedSize

            Set lstTemp = .ListItems.Add(, "NumericScale", "Numeric Scale")
            lstTemp.SubItems(1) = colTemp.NumericScale

            Set lstTemp = .ListItems.Add(, "Type", "Type")
            lstTemp.SubItems(1) = colTemp.Type

        For Each prpTemp In colTemp.Properties
            Set lstTemp = .ListItems.Add(, "Property:" & prpTemp.Name, _
                "Property: " & prpTemp.Name)
            lstTemp.SubItems(1) = prpTemp.Value
        Next prpTemp
    End With
End Sub
```

This code provides a handy tool for looking at all the otherwise hidden properties of your tables, queries, and stored procedures. If you'd like to expand this code, try adding in a drop-down list box that enables you to select which type of object to view, whether that be tables, stored procedures, or any of the other collections of the ADOX Catalog object.

Chapter 15

Active Data Objects

At one time, data access using Microsoft products was one of the worst alphabet soups in the industry. From DAO to RDO to ODBC, you were never sure what the favored data access strategy of the week was. Active Data Objects (ADO), which were introduced in the Chapter 14, is Microsoft's current attempt at a single, unified data access strategy. Because ADO is used for both client/server and Web programming, you need to learn only a single data-access method. This chapter goes much further with ADO then the brief introduction in the last chapter.

Microsoft's Universal Data Access Strategy

A major complaint of developers using Microsoft products has been the confusing array of choices for working with databases. Until recently, different data-access technologies—with different object models—were required for different types of databases. Something had to change to simplify the whole landscape, and that change was the introduction of Object Linking and Embedding-Database (OLE DB) and the Active Data Objects (ADO) method of working with OLE DB. The idea is to provide programmers with a single set of objects that can be used in any Microsoft environment on any platform. If you use Visual Basic with SQL Server, you can use ADO. If you use Visual Basic with Oracle, you can use ADO. Even if you use Windows CE or Active Server Pages, you can still use ADO because ADO can hook up using Open Database Connectivity (ODBC). You can even use ADO for remote database manipulation through Remote Data Service (RDS).

More on OLE DB

OLE DB is a technology designed by Microsoft to make it easier to access all types of data through a single set of interfaces. Most programmers know how to access some type of database, whether that is an Access, Oracle, SQL Server, or dBase database. However, each database has a slightly different query language. Some use languages very close to standard Structured Query Language (SQL), but dBase, for example, uses a language that is not like SQL at all.

Besides traditional databases, there are other sources of data that might be of interest to your users. If you're working on a Web server, you may wish to access data that Microsoft Index Server has produced from your Web site. Index Server is designed to make searchable indexes of your Web data. You may also want to access information in plain text files or in other known document types, such as Microsoft Word or Adobe Acrobat. You may also have a need to do some data mining using Online Analytical Processing (OLAP) tools.

All of these sources of data are now accessible through OLE DB. OLE DB uses a driver called a provider. A provider knows how a particular type of data is arranged, regardless of the data type. The provider translates the request given it into a request that it can process against the particular type of data. The programmer only has to worry about submitting a request that resembles standard SQL language; the provider takes care of the rest.

OLE DB emphasizes the break among the components involved in an application. The application submits a request to the provider, which then translates the request to the data source so that the data can be sent to the application. If the data source driver changes, it won't necessarily affect the application's functionality. Just as with object-oriented applications, encapsulation helps protect your applications from the whims of your product vendors who do tend to like to change their interfaces just as you've gotten used to one!

ODBC

Open Database Connectivity (ODBC) is a specification for a database application programming interface (API). The API is an independent standard that is supported by a variety of product vendors, including Oracle, Informix, Sybase, and Microsoft. Both the vendors and third-party companies, such as Intersolv, provide drivers for these databases.

While OLE DB is able to talk directly to several different types of databases, there are some databases that do not yet have OLE DB providers available. In these cases, you can use the ODBC driver for the database in combination with the OLE DB provider for ODBC. Using this method creates an extra layer of interface between your code and the database; that is, ADO talks to OLE DB, which talks to ODBC, which talks to the database. This method is recommended if you are planning to upgrade the application or the database at some point. Because more product vendors are releasing OLE DB providers, new applications should be built using ADO and OLE DB, even if that means using the extra layer of ODBC for the time being. This method requires the least amount of code to change to OLE DB/ADO when your database releases an OLE DB provider.

Remote Data Service

A part of Microsoft's strategy is to make data available everywhere on every platform. Besides traditional applications, the Web is gaining ground as a popular way to publish corporate data. The use of this method will only gain ground as the Internet grows and the use of corporate extranets becomes more popular. A feature introduced in Internet Explorer (IE) 3.0, and found in newer versions of IE, is the use of RDS. RDS enables applications to access OLE DB providers running on remote machines or in separate processes on the same machine.

This feature makes it easier to create dynamic Web pages. Instead of bringing down all the possible data a page could use, you get data as you need it. A good example of this might be a tree-based interface. You load the tree with the top-level data when the page loads. As the user clicks on a node, you request the data for the node. Microsoft makes use of this on its MSDN Online site and it makes the page operation quicker than it would be otherwise. The only downside to this technology is that the only browser that works with RDS is Microsoft Internet Explorer. If you can't guarantee that all your users are using IE, you will have to look at doing more server-side database operations or use another language, such as Java, to make your components work properly.

Active Data Objects

ADO provides a number of objects that are used to traverse all types of data. If you're familiar with Data Access Objects (DAO) or Remote Data Objects (RDO), using ADO should be a pretty easy transition. There are a few differences, which are discussed in the next section of this chapter. ADO defines seven objects:

- Connection
- Recordset
- Field
- Command
- Parameter
- Property
- Error

In addition, there are four collections used in ADO:

- Fields
- Parameters
- Properties
- Errors

To use any of these objects, you need to reference the Microsoft Active Data Objects library in the References window in Visual Basic. Be sure to get the at least the 2.0 version and not version 1.5. (The current version is 2.5.)

> **NOTE**
> *This chapter doesn't discuss the Property object because all the dynamic properties are specific to the given OLE DB provider.*

The Connection Object

A Connection object represents a single session with a data source. ADO enables you to have multiple Connection objects with each object pointing to a different data source. This can be helpful if you are accessing multiple data sources and combining the results on a Web page of some sort. In the case of a client/server database system, it may be equivalent to an actual network connection to the server.

> **TIP**
> *Depending on the functionality supported by the OLE DB provider, some collections, methods, or properties of a Connection object may not be available.*

MAKING A CONNECTION

To get started with any other ADO object, you first have to have a Connection object. A Connection object must first be given information about which OLE DB data provider to use to connect to the data source. Then you give it any specific connection information. You can do this in two ways: either by setting the Provider property of the Connection object or through the connection string that you supply. If you don't assign a provider, the default is to use the Microsoft OLE DB provider for ODBC. The code that follows is an example of how to connect to an Access 97 database using a connection string. In this case, we would connect to the BIBLIO database included with Visual Basic using the default location for it.

```
Dim dcnDB As New ADODB.Connection
dcnDB.ConnectionString = _
    & "Provider=Microsoft.Jet.OLEDB.3.51;" _
    & "Data Source=C:\Program Files\Visual Studio\VB98\Biblio.mdb"
dcnDB.Open
```

What we did in the above code is to first create a new Connection object using the New keyword in a Dim statement. However, at this point the data connection is still not open. The next line specifies how to connect to the database. The Provider parameter specifies the OLE DB Provider to use; in this case, we are using the Jet 3.51 Provider, which corresponds to the engine used by an Access 97 database. We also have to specify the pathname to the database in the Data Source parameter. As was mentioned, you can also directly set the Provider property as follows:

```
dcnDB.Provider="Microsoft.Jet.OLEDB.3.51"
```

Finally, the Open method activates the connection to the database.

The ConnectionString property varies from data source to data source, but in all cases the form is Option=Value. The following code is a sample that can be used to connect to an SQL Server 6.5 database. Notice the extra parameters in the ConnectionString property.

```
Dim dcnDB As New ADODB.Connection
dcnDB.ConnectionString = _
    & "Provider=SQLOLEDB.1;" _
```

```
        & "User ID=myuser;Password=mypassword;" _
        & "Initial Catalog=Northwind;" _
        & "Data Source=db.northcomp.com"
dcnDB.Open
```

Notice that the Provider property is different for SQL Server. Next, SQL Server requires a user ID and password, so both of these parameters are provided in the ConnectionString property. We then need to specify both the database server and the database name we want to use. The Data Source can be either a Local Area Network (LAN) server name, an Internet-style address as shown in the example, or a numerical IP address such as 252.100.100.0.

USING A DATA LINK FILE

Although the previous examples show how to hard-code the database information into your application, putting the user ID and password directly in a Web page can be dangerous. While most Web servers are secure, it is best to assume that anything on the Web server is vulnerable. Luckily, Microsoft provides another way to specify the database connection information: the Data Link file. Data Link files can be used to specify all the same information about a database connection that we did in the previous two examples *but* that information is kept outside of the application. This makes it both more secure and easier to manage. If you have any part of Visual Studio 6.0 installed on your machine, you can follow these steps to create a Data Link file:

1. Start Windows Explorer.
2. Navigate to the directory in which you wish to create the Data Link file.
3. Select File→New→Microsoft Data Link. Enter in a name for the Data Link file and then press Enter.
4. Right-click the file and select Open from the pop-up menu. You will see the Data Link Connection Dialog appear.
5. By default, the Data Link is created using the ODBC OLE DB provider. For this example, we use an Access database on your machine. To select the Jet provider, click the Provider tab at the top. Click the Jet OLE DB Provider and then click Next.
6. Select a database to use and then click the Test Connection button to verify that the Data Link is set up correctly. If the connection test succeeds, click OK to save the Data Link file.

At this point, you can use the code shown below to select and open the database. You need to supply the full pathname for the Data Link file for it to work properly, so be sure the pathname is correct before using the code.

```
Dim dcnDB As New ADODB.Connection
dcnDB.ConnectionString = "File Name=C:\Windows\Sample.udl"
dcnDB.Open
```

The advantage of this method is that if the database location or connection method changes, you can make a single change to the Data Link file (which could be shared between many applications) and all of the connections will be changed. Data Link files can be used for any and all types of connections.

CLOSING A CONNECTION

When you are at the end of your application, you should always close any open data connections. This enables the data source server to release the system resources associated with that connection. Too many connections left open will, over time, cause the system to run out of resources and grind to a halt. Closing a connection is quite easy. Simply use the Close method as shown here:

```
dcnDB.Close
```

Before closing the connection, make sure that any other objects using the connection have been closed.

The Recordset and Field Objects

A *Recordset* is just what its name says—a set of records. A record is a row from the result of a query. If the query accesses a single table, a record is one row out of the table. If the query joins more than one table, a record is a row from the result. The ADO Recordset object is fairly intelligent and knows how to manage the results to minimize the amount of delay. For example, if you run a query that returns a large number of rows, the Recordset object knows to only bring back a small batch at a time. Although this can cause problems when you are trying to determine the number of records you have, in most cases, this helps the performance of your application.

EXECUTING A QUERY

The easiest way to create a Recordset is to execute a query against your database. The results are returned in a Recordset object. The code shown below determines the number of customers in the Customers table in the Northwind Traders database (located in the VB installation directory on your computer), and returns that value as a single row in a Recordset. The code assumes that a data connection, stored in the dcnDB variable, has already been defined and opened.

```
Dim rsCount    As ADODB.Recordset
Set rsCount = dcnDB.Execute("SELECT COUNT(*) FROM Customers")
MsgBox "There are " & rsCount(0) & " customers."
```

Note that the New keyword is not used to instantiate the Recordset object before using it; rather, we let the Execute method do its thing and return a Recordset for us. When we are printing the number of records, using a zero subscript in the rsCount variable returns the first field of the first record; in this case, the count of records will be there.

While the Execute method can be used to run SQL commands entered directly in your VB code, it can also execute stored procedures (as they are known in Oracle and SQL Server) and predefined queries (as they are known in Access). In the following code example, we want to run a stored procedure named spCountRecords. As you can see, the code is even shorter.

```
Dim rsCount As ADODB.Recordset
Set rsCount = dcnDB.Execute("spCountRecords")
MsgBox "There are " & rsCount(0) & " customers."
```

> **TIP**
> *The method by which you create a stored procedure or query varies with the database that you are using. Refer to your database documentation for help on creating queries and stored procedures.*

Execute is the method that uses the least code to retrieve a read-only Recordset, and it can also be used to execute all the other types of queries, such as deletes. Because these queries don't return Recordsets, you can call the Execute method as follows:

```
dcnDB.Execute "DELETE FROM Customers WHERE CustomerID = 'ALFKI'"
```

Although you could also build an update query in SQL, it's a lot less complicated to edit records in a Recordset. For more information, see the "Editing Records in a Recordset" section later in the chapter.

OPENING A RECORDSET

The Open method is much more flexible and provides many more options for getting to data than the Execute method. Open does, however, require that you define and instantiate your Recordset variable before using it. The following code, which assumes that you've already opened a connection with the dcnDB variable, opens a Recordset object using the same query as was used in the Execute example:

```
Dim rsQuery As New ADODB.Recordset
rsQuery.Open "SELECT * FROM Customers", dcnDB
```

This will open a read-only, forward-only Recordset of the Customers table. *Forward-only* means that you can only move forward through the Recordset and not use any of the positioning methods (other than MoveNext). It is used for cases in which you are dumping data to a page, such as in a report or as part of a data entry form. This type of Recordset is more efficient because it doesn't need to store as much navigation information, and because after you've passed a record, it can get rid of the record, thereby saving your system resources.

The previous code takes advantage of the default parameter values used in the Open method. The following code lists all of the arguments with their proper values. The constants are part of the ADO library.

```
Dim rsQuery As New ADODB.Recordset
rsQuery.Open "SELECT * FROM Customers", dcnDB, adOpenForwardOnly, _
    adLockReadOnly
```

The adOpenForwardOnly constant, which is the default value, specifies the cursor type. In this context, a cursor is a pointer to a Recordset and not the icon that marks where you type. The valid values for this parameter are listed in Table 15-1:

Table 15-1: CursorType Parameter Values

CONSTANT	VALUE	DESCRIPTION
adOpenForwardOnly	0	Creates a read-only Recordset that can only scroll forward.
adOpenKeyset	1	Cursor enables you to add, modify, and delete records, but you won't see changes made by other users while your Recordset is open.
adOpenDynamic	2	Cursor enables you to add, modify, and delete records, and you will see any changes made by other users.
adOpenStatic	3	Creates a read-only Recordset that has all the capabilities for positioning; that is, forward and backward, as well as bookmarking.

The adLockReadOnly constant, which is also the default value, specifies the method by which the records should be locked. In this case, we don't want to change the records, so the read-only constant is the appropriate choice. The other available values are listed in Table 15-2:

Table 15-2: LockType Parameter Values

CONSTANT	VALUE	DESCRIPTION
adLockReadOnly	1	Records are read-only and cannot be changed.
adLockPessimistic	2	Records are locked when you start editing them.
adLockOptimistic	3	Records are locked when you call the Update method to commit your changes.
adLockBatchOptimistic	4	Required if you are performing batch updates to a set of records.

As you probably guessed, some of the constant combinations you could make don't really make sense. For instance, using any type of lock with a static Recordset is silly because you can't edit the records anyway. When you are editing records, however, having these options available makes your programming easier to predict. If you are in a high-traffic environment, pessimistic locking of records will prevent two users from changing the same record simultaneously. In a lighter traffic environment, optimistic locking may be more appropriate because it only locks the records for the occasional update you may need to make.

NAVIGATING THROUGH A RECORDSET

After the Recordset is open, you need to be able to navigate through the records. You can display them or process them as you loop. The following code can be used for any type of Recordset to loop through the records:

```
Dim rsQuery As New ADODB.Recordset
rsQuery.Open "SELECT * FROM Customers", dcnDB
Do While Not rsQuery.EOF
    Debug.Print rsQuery("CustomerName")
    rsQuery.MoveNext
Loop
rsQuery.Close
```

This code assumes that the Customers table has a field called CustomerName. After opening the Recordset as a read-only, forward-only Recordset, a Do loop continues until the end-of-file (EOF) flag is true. The EOF flag is true after the last record has been passed by the cursor. This means that you can look at the last record, do another MoveNext, and then the EOF flag will be True. After the loop exits, the Recordset is closed using the Close method. Like the Connection object, you should close all your Recordsets when you are done with them.

Table 15-3 lists all the methods available for navigating in a Recordset. However, if you are in a forward-only Recordset, only MoveNext is available.

Table 15-3: Methods of Navigating a Recordset

METHOD	DESCRIPTION
MoveFirst	Moves to the first record in the Recordset.
MoveLast	Moves to the last record in the Recordset.
MoveNext	Moves to the next record in the Recordset. Check for EOF before calling.
MovePrevious	Moves to the previous record in the Recordset. Check for beginning-of-file (BOF) tag before calling.

EDITING RECORDS IN A RECORDSET

After the Recordset is opened, you can edit the records in that Recordset. As an example, the code below updates the name of a customer (stored in the ContactName field) in the Customers table of the Northwind Traders database.

```
Dim dcnDB As New ADODB.Connection
Dim rsQuery As New ADODB.Recordset
dcnDB.ConnectionString = "Provider=Microsoft.Jet.OLEDB.3.51;" _
    & "Data Source=c:\db\nwind.mdb"
dcnDB.Open
rsQuery.Open "SELECT * FROM Customers WHERE CustomerID = 'ALFKI'", _
    dcnDB, adOpenKeyset, adLockOptimistic
rsQuery("ContactName") = "The New Name Goes Here"
rsQuery.Update
rsQuery.Close
dcnDB.Close
```

In this example, the record to edit is selected by using a simple SELECT query. The Recordset is created as a keyset with optimistic updates. The assumption is that we don't need to see other people's changes to this one record in this Recordset, which will be closed after the update has been made. Optimistic locking doesn't make the record lock until the Update method has been called.

> *NOTE*
> *Unlike with DAO, you don't have to call an Edit method explicitly. As soon as you make a change to a field, as we did to the ContactName field, the record is considered "edited." The Update method is still necessary to commit the changes at the end, however.*

One bonus with this method is that you don't have to worry whether the values you are storing into the fields have single quotes. Single quotes, if placed in an SQL Update statement, cause the statement to have errors unless each single quote is replaced with two single quotes.

ADDING NEW RECORDS TO A TABLE

Adding records is similar to editing, except for a few small details. The code shown below adds a new record to the Shippers table in the Northwind Traders database.

```
Dim dcnDB As New ADODB.Connection
Dim rsQuery As New ADODB.Recordset
dcnDB.ConnectionString = "Provider=Microsoft.Jet.OLEDB.3.51;" _
    & "Data Source=c:\nwind.mdb"
```

```
dcnDB.Open
rsQuery.Open "SELECT * FROM Shippers", dcnDB, adOpenKeyset, adLockOptimistic
rsQuery.AddNew
rsQuery("CompanyName") = "Airborne Express"
rsQuery("Phone") = "800-AIRBORNE"
rsQuery.Update
rsQuery.Close
dcnDB.Close
```

The addition of the new record is started with the AddNew method. After that, each of the required fields is supplied with a value, and the Update method finishes the job. You can check the Shippers table in the database to see the new record.

Also, look at the table design for this table. There are actually three fields in the table. The one not specified here is an AutoNumber field that automatically supplies a unique ID for the shippers you add. Because the table has a default value, we don't need to even specify it when we add the record.

The Command and Parameter Objects

The Command object is at the heart of ADO. It is the primary mechanism for instructing the database about the results you want. It contains all the information needed to use a connection, process a query, and return a Recordset. This section discusses the most common uses of the Command object.

CREATING A RECORDSET WITH A COMMAND OBJECT

The simplest task to do is to create a Recordset using the Command object. The code to do this is as follows:

```
Dim dcnDB As New ADODB.Connection
Dim cmdQuery As New ADODB.Command
Dim rsQuery As ADODB.Recordset
dcnDB.ConnectionString = "Provider=Microsoft.Jet.OLEDB.3.51;" _
    & "Data Source=c:\nwind.mdb"
dcnDB.Open
cmdQuery.CommandText = "SELECT * FROM Shippers"
Set cmdQuery.ActiveConnection = dcnDB
Set rsQuery = cmdQuery.Execute
Do While Not rsQuery.EOF
    Debug.Print rsQuery("CompanyName")
    rsQuery.MoveNext
Loop
rsQuery.Close
dcnDB.Close
```

In this example, we're using a selection query similar to the previous one, but we are using the Command object to do it. We first set the CommandText parameter, which holds the text of the query we wish to run. The active database connection, which is an object, is stored in the ActiveConnection parameter. You have to use the Set statement because you are dealing with objects. Finally, the Execute method runs the query and actually creates the desired Recordset object.

You shouldn't use this technique for simple queries; use the Execute method of the Connection object instead. This technique is more appropriate when you need to perform advanced operations with your query. Some of the instances in which a Command object is more appropriate are:

- Creating queries that use parameters
- Allowing the query to be prepared on the fly to make later executions quicker
- Change the timeout of your query

RUNNING A QUERY WITH PARAMETERS

A benefit of stored procedures or queries stored with the database is that the database has already determined the quickest way to execute the query. Because this precompilation is done when the developer created the query, the user doesn't have to wait while plain SQL is interpreted by the database. However, many queries will require input data to function properly. Each piece of data given to a stored procedure or query is called, aptly, a *parameter*.

Parameters each have a name, a data type, a direction, and a size. If a parameter is text-based, the size, or length, of the parameter will need to be supplied as part of the Parameter object. The direction refers to whether the parameter is passing data to the stored procedure, getting data from the stored procedure, or both.

For this example, let's create a simple lookup query. The query accepts one parameter named paramShipperID, which corresponds to a particular shipper's ID number. The query selects all the rows from the Shippers table where that ID is found. In Access, the query is set up as shown in Figure 15-1:

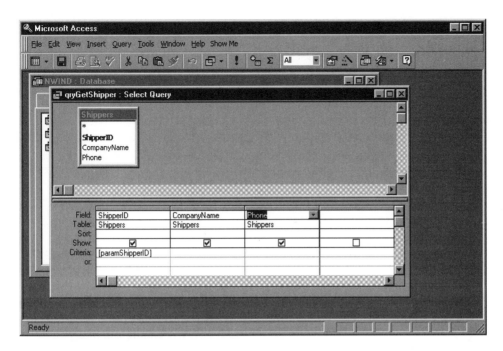

Figure 15-1: The select query in Microsoft Access

The query has been saved as qryGetShipper, but feel free to use your own names. In SQL Server and Oracle, common practice is to prefix stored procedures with sp.

You might think the code required to use this query looks a little messy, but it's really straightforward once you understand how parameters are created for Command objects. The code is shown here:

```
Dim dcnDB As New ADODB.Connection
Dim cmdQuery As New ADODB.Command
Dim rsQuery As ADODB.Recordset
Dim parID As ADODB.Parameter
dcnDB.ConnectionString = "Provider=Microsoft.Jet.OLEDB.3.51;" _
```

```
             & "Data Source=c:\nwind.mdb"
dcnDB.Open
cmdQuery.CommandText = "qryGetShipper"
Set cmdQuery.ActiveConnection = dcnDB

Set parID = cmdQuery.CreateParameter("paramShipperID", _
    adInteger, adParamInput, ,2)
cmdQuery.Parameters.Append parID
Set rsQuery = cmdQuery.Execute

Do While Not rsQuery.EOF
    Debug.Print rsQuery("CompanyName")
    rsQuery.MoveNext
Loop

rsQuery.Close
dcnDB.Close
```

The result of this query is the name of shipper #2, United Package, printed in the immediate window. You can print any or all of the fields in the Recordset after the query is executed.

The interesting lines follow immediately after the active connection is stored in the Command object. The first line calls the CreateParameter method of the Command object. This method takes a number of arguments, which are described in Table 15-4, each of which corresponds to a property of the Parameter object.

Table 15-4: Parameter Object arguments

ARGUMENT	DESCRIPTION
paramShipperID	Represents the name of the parameter as created in Access.
adInteger	Represents the data type of the parameter. The integer data type in ADO can be used for any integer up to four bytes; that is, a Long in Visual Basic. (All the valid data types are listed following this example.)
adParamInput	Represents the direction of the parameter; in this case, an input parameter. (The possible values for this parameter are listed after this example.)
missing parameter	Represents the size of the parameter, which only applies if you are using strings. The value that we want to give to this parameter is 2 so that shipper #2 is retrieved from the database.

The resulting Parameter object is stored in the parID variable and then appended to the Parameters collection of the Command object. The query is then executed as before, but only the matching record is returned.

> *NOTE*
> You can add as many parameters to your Command object as are necessary. Of
> course, the limit also depends on your database and on how many parameters it
> allows to be part of a query or stored procedure.

The available data-type constants that you can use in your parameters are
listed in Table 15-5:

Table 15-5: Data-type Constants Usable in a Parameter

CONSTANT	VALUE	MEANING
adBigInt	20	An eight-byte signed integer
adBoolean	11	A Boolean value
adChar	129	A String value
adCurrency	6	A Currency value
adDate	7	A Date value
adDouble	5	A double-precision floating point value
adInteger	3	A four-byte signed integer
adSingle	4	A single-precision floating point value
adSmallInt	2	A two-byte signed integer (Integer type)
adTinyInt	16	A one-byte signed integer (Byte type)
adVarChar	200	A String value

The available constants for determining the direction of a parameter are
listed in Table 15-6:

Table 15-6: Constants for Determining Parameter Direction

CONSTANT	VALUE	MEANING
adParamInput	1	Input parameter
adParamOutput	2	Output parameter
adParamInputOutput	3	Input/output parameter
adParamReturnValue	4	Return value

The Errors Collection

The Errors collection, which is a property of the Connection object, holds all the
database errors that occur as you run your application. Each error is contained
in an Error object stored in the Errors collection. Forcing errors is the easiest
way to learn about this collection, as shown in the following code:

```
Dim dcnDB As New ADODB.Connection
Dim cmdQuery As New ADODB.Command
Dim rsQuery As ADODB.Recordset
Dim parID As ADODB.Parameter
Dim intLoop As Integer
On Error Resume Next
dcnDB.ConnectionString = "Provider=Microsoft.Jet.OLEDB.3.51;" _
    & "Data Source=c:\nwind.mdb"
dcnDB.Open
cmdQuery.CommandText = "SELECT * FROM Shipppers"
Set cmdQuery.ActiveConnection = dcnDB

If dcnDB.Errors.Count > 0 then
    For intLoop = 0 to dcnDB.Errors.Count - 1
        Response.Write dcnDB.Errors(intLoop).Description
    Next intLoop
Else
    Set rsQuery = cmdQuery.Execute
    Do While Not rsQuery.EOF
        Debug.Print rsQuery("CompanyName")
        rsQuery.MoveNext
    Loop
    rsQuery.Close
End If

dcnDB.Close
```

In case you didn't notice, the table name is spelled wrong in the query placed in the CommandText property. The key to making this work is the adding of the On Error Resume Next code at the top of the routine. In this example, we're just allowing errors to occur. We handle them after the line of code where they might occur. You may want to replace this with a more comprehensive error handler later. We first open the database connection and then we set up the Command object. We then check whether any errors occurred to that point by checking the number of items in the Errors collection. If it isn't zero, something went wrong and we print out the error description and bail out. If no errors occurred, we execute the query and display the data.

Advanced ADO Techniques

Now that you've got the basics of ADO down, you're probably wondering about some more complex and useful examples. How do you pass a recordset from a COM object back to a caller without having to worry about the connection? How do you use output parameters from an SQL Server query? The tips in this section teach you how to handle these and similar situations in your application.

Passing Recordsets

One of the handiest features of the ADO Recordset, unlike previous iterations of Microsoft's database layers, is its capability to disconnect from the database. After the ActiveConnection property of the Recordset is set to Nothing, the Recordset is a free agent and is a pretty convenient way to move data around within your application. For example, you can now pass a Recordset back from a function without having the database still connected.

In this section, we build a generic query tool that enables the caller to request any query and get back a disconnected Recordset. There are two benefits to putting this in a component. First, the application doesn't have to know where the database is or what the required settings are to connect. This makes it easier to change database settings without having to update all the client machines. Second, if you are using Microsoft Transaction Server (MTS), you can take advantage of object and connection pooling. The object doesn't have to drop the connection to the database each time you need data. This makes your requests process much faster because you don't have to wait for the connection to be opened. In this section, we don't implement the object on MTS; however, making the changes is quite simple if you know MTS.

The object, named Query, will have one function: Execute. This function will accept an SQL string as input and will return a disconnected Recordset. The input string can be a stored procedure or a plain SQL statement, so we will add a second argument to indicate whether the SQL refers to a stored procedure or not.

To build this example, the first thing we need to do is to create an ActiveX DLL project and add the ADO 2.0 Library to it. Add a code module to the ActiveX DLL project with a blank Sub Main, as shown here:

```
Option Explicit

Sub Main()
'
' No code needed here, since this is an
' ActiveX DLL
End Sub
```

Give the project a name of **DataAccess** and be sure to provide the Project Name in the Project Properties dialog, as well. Next, add a class module to the project and name it Query. The code for this class is fairly short and is shown here:

```
Option Explicit
Private m_dcnDB As ADODB.Connection

Public Function Execute(strSQL As String, _
    Optional blnIsSP As Boolean = False) As ADODB.Recordset

    Dim rsData As ADODB.Recordset
    Set rsData = New ADODB.Recordset
```

```
            With rsData
                Set .ActiveConnection = m_dcnDB
                .CursorLocation = adUseClient
                .CursorType = adOpenStatic
                .LockType = adLockReadOnly
                .Source = strSQL
                .Open
            End With
            Set rsData.ActiveConnection = Nothing
            Set Execute = rsData

End Function

Private Sub Class_Initialize()

            Set m_dcnDB = New ADODB.Connection
            m_dcnDB.ConnectionString = "Provider=SQLOLEDB.1;" _
                & "User ID=user;Password=password;" _
                & "Initial Catalog=Northwind;" _
                & "Data Source=ENTERPRISE"
            m_dcnDB.Open

End Sub

Private Sub Class_Terminate()
            m_dcnDB.Close
            Set m_dcnDB = Nothing
End Sub
```

This code uses the SQL Server OLE DB provider and is set up to connect to the default Northwind database provided with SQL Server 6.5 and 7.0. The important code is in the Execute method. The key to making the Recordset "disconnectable" is to set the CursorLocation property to adUseClient. Otherwise, you'll get an error when you set the ActiveConnection property to Nothing.

To test your code, add a second project to the VB environment. Go to the References dialog and add the DataAccess reference so that you can use the object you just built. Here's a sample Sub Main routine you can use to test your object:

```
Option Explicit

Sub Main()
    Dim objQuery As New DataAccess.Query
```

```
Dim rsReturn As ADODB.Recordset

Set rsReturn = objQuery.Execute("SELECT COUNT(*) FROM Customers")
Debug.Print rsReturn(0)
Set objQuery = Nothing

End Sub
```

You can replace the SQL string here with any stored procedure or SQL statement and the object will return a disconnected Recordset. The database connection stays within the DataAccess object and the client doesn't even know where the database is. This helps isolate the layers of your application from each other. In the DataAccess object, you would typically need to read settings from the System Registry to determine where the database is and how to connect to it, but that's not the point of this example. The point is that the Recordset that the client gets back is a fully functional set of records that can be manipulated without having a live database connection.

Using Output Parameters

Another feature is the capability to receive output parameter values from your queries. This is especially helpful for stored procedures that return counts, IDs, or other data that doesn't need the overhead of a full Recordset object. This section teaches you to create an SQL Server stored procedure that provides return values through its parameters. You also learn to access those stored procedures through the use of the Command and Parameter objects.

The first step is to build the SQL query. Using the Query Analyzer or another tool, use the following code to create the sp_GetProductCount query:

```
Create Procedure sp_GetProductCount
@lngCount integer OUTPUT
As
SELECT @lngCount = COUNT(*)
FROM Products
RETURN
```

This creates a stored procedure with one output parameter (specified by the OUTPUT keyword) that is a long integer named lngCount. The SQL statement stores the count of records in this parameter, and the RETURN keyword sends back a zero on successful completion of the stored procedure. Any errors would return a nonzero value to the caller.

The next step is to write the VB code to execute this stored procedure. Because we already have the Query class with the data connection being created, we'll use it and add a new public function to execute this stored procedure. Feel free to slice and dice the code as you see fit; just remember to make the connection or create a connection string first.

```
Public Function GetProductCount() As Long

    Dim cmdQuery As ADODB.Command
    Set cmdQuery = New ADODB.Command
    With cmdQuery
        Set .ActiveConnection = m_dcnDB
        .CommandText = "sp_GetProductCount"
        .CommandType = adCmdStoredProc
        .Parameters.Append .CreateParameter("ReturnValue", _
            adInteger, adParamReturnValue)
        .Parameters.Append .CreateParameter("@lngCount", _
            adInteger, adParamOutput)
        .Execute

        If .Parameters("ReturnValue") = 0 Then
            GetProductCount = .Parameters("@lngCount")
        End If
    End With
    Set cmdQuery = Nothing

End Function
```

After creating the Command object and setting the name and type of the stored procedure we're using, we create two parameters. The first will hold the return value from the stored procedure and has a special return type signified by the adParamReturnValue constant. The second parameter is the lngCount parameter we created. This will hold the data we requested.

After the command is executed, the parameters are filled with their return values. If the query completes successfully, the ReturnValue parameter will have a zero in it. We then pull out the value of the @lngCount parameter and return it to the calling code.

This technique eliminates lots of unnecessary recordsets from needing system resources allocated to them. Use this technique in cases in which you have many return values, such as for a customer record or a lookup table, but don't need multiple records returned.

Chapter 16

Objects, Objects, and More Objects

Object-oriented programming has been around a long time and has been part of Visual Basic, at least to some degree, since VB was introduced. As you know, everything from a form control to a database is treated as an object. What's more, recent versions of Visual Basic continue to provide more features that facilitate creating your own object systems—of which some new, unique uses are presented here.

Creating Service Objects

Most Visual Basic programmers spend so much time wrapping objects around databases that they forget that objects can be used for other tasks. Objects can form the core of your reusable code library, which is important considering that a major goal of most programmers is to not write the same code twice. This chapter gets you started by presenting objects that can be used for two purposes: network services and Registry services.

Creating a Network Services Object

If you work with networks, you probably find yourself writing the same code over and over to handle certain network services. Wouldn't it be nice if you could build an object that encapsulates all that functionality in a reusable component that is easily updated and distributed to your team members or users?

Retrieving the Username

The first feature we'll add to our class object is the capability to retrieve the current username. The code for this function is shown here (remember to place the declaration at the top of the class module):

```
Private Declare Function WNetGetUser Lib "mpr.dll" Alias _
"WNetGetUserA" (ByVal lpName As String, ByVal lpUserName As String, _
```

```
lpnLength As Long) As Long
Public Function UserName(Optional strLocalPath As String = "")

    Dim strBuffer As String * 255
    Dim lngReturn As Long

    lngReturn = WNetGetUser(strLocalPath, strBuffer, 255)
    UserName = Trim(strBuffer)

    If lngReturn <> 0 Then
        Err.Raise vbObjectError, "NetworkServices.UserName", _
            "Error #" & lngReturn & " occurred during request."
    End If

End Function
```

This function has an extra feature that isn't immediately obvious. The WNetGetUser WinAPI function returns the current user's login name by default. However, if you supply a pathname in the first argument, the function returns the username for the selected resource. This is helpful if you need to retrieve the username for a network drive you might have on the system.

Connecting a Network Drive

We are often asked how to connect a network drive through code. This is a useful trick if you are trying to reach a network share where some application information is being stored. If you can't tell whether the drive is already mapped, this code will let you map it.

```
Public Sub AddConnection(strLocalPath As String, _
    strNetworkPath As String, _
    Optional strUserName As String, _
    Optional strPassword As String)

    Dim typNet As NETRESOURCE
    Dim lngReturn As Long

    With typNet
        .dwType = RESOURCETYPE_DISK
        .lpLocalName = strLocalPath
        .lpRemoteName = strNetworkPath
        .lpProvider = ""
    End With

    lngReturn = WNetAddConnection2(typNet, strPassword, strUserName, 0)

    If lngReturn <> 0 Then
```

```
        Err.Raise vbObjectError, "NetworkServices.AddConnection", _
            "Error #" & lngReturn & " occurred during connection."
    End If
End Sub
```

The WinAPI functions used above require that a number of constants and data types be defined, as shown here:

```
Private Type NETRESOURCE
            dwScope As Long
            dwType As Long
            dwDisplayType As Long
            dwUsage As Long
            lpLocalName As String
            lpRemoteName As String
            lpComment As String
            lpProvider As String
End Type

Private Const RESOURCE_GLOBALNET As Long = &H2&
Private Const RESOURCE_REMEMBERED As Long = &H3&
Private Const RESOURCE_CONNECTED As Long = &H1&
Private Const RESOURCETYPE_ANY As Long = &H0&
Private Const RESOURCETYPE_DISK As Long = &H1&
Private Const RESOURCETYPE_PRINT As Long = &H2&
Private Const RESOURCEDISPLAYTYPE_DOMAIN As Long = &H1&
Private Const RESOURCEDISPLAYTYPE_GENERIC As Long = &H0&
Private Const RESOURCEDISPLAYTYPE_SERVER As Long = &H2&
Private Const RESOURCEDISPLAYTYPE_SHARE As Long = &H3&
Private Const RESOURCEUSAGE_CONNECTABLE As Long = &H1&
Private Const RESOURCEUSAGE_CONTAINER As Long = &H2&
Private Declare Function WNetAddConnection2 Lib "mpr.dll" Alias
"WNetAddConnection2A" (lpNetResource As NETRESOURCE, ByVal lpPassword As
String, ByVal lpUserName As String, ByVal dwFlags As Long) As Long
```

The LocalPath parameter to the AddConnection method should contain the drive to which you want to map the remote resource, for example, R:. The strNetworkPath parameter is the full network pathname that you wish to map, for example, \\server\remotedirectory. The strUserName and strPassword fields should contain the username and password to use for the connection. If you call the function without either of these parameters, the connection is attempted using the current username. If you set both of these parameters to the empty string "", the connection is attempted with no user specified. There is a difference between empty parameters (which contain NULL values) and passing "" for parameters (which is a valid string that contains no characters). And the WNetAddConnection2 function responds differently to NULL values and empty strings.

Disconnecting a Network Drive

The last function in this object takes care of disconnecting a network drive:

```
Declare Function WNetCancelConnection2 Lib "mpr.dll" Alias _
"WNetCancelConnection2A" (ByVal lpName As String, _
ByVal dwFlags As Long, ByVal fForce As Long) As Long

Public Sub DropConnection(strLocalPath As String, _
    Optional blnForce As Boolean = False)

    Dim lngReturn As Long

    lngReturn = WNetCancelConnection2(strLocalPath, 0, blnForce)

    If lngReturn <> 0 Then
        Err.Raise vbObjectError, "NetworkServices.DropConnection", _
            "Error #" & lngReturn & " occurred during connection drop."
    End If

End Sub
```

Putting It All Together

Using the new object is a piece of cake using this code:

```
Dim objNet As New NetworkServices
objNet.AddConnection "F:", "\\Server\C$"
MsgBox "Current user is " & objNet.UserName
objNet.DropConnection "F:"
```

Any errors that occur are raised and can be trapped using standard error handling techniques.

Creating a Registry Services Object

Chapter 7 taught you that communicating with Windows Registry via Visual Basic's GetSetting and SaveSetting functions is extremely limited. These functions cannot access information outside the VB and VBA Program Settings section. Because most of the good stuff is outside that small area, you learned to use WinAPI functions to obtain complete access to the Registry. In this section, we encapsulate some of those functions in a reusable service object.

Understanding the Windows Registry

The Registry is Windows' permanent memory. Any application that stores personalization settings is probably keeping them in the Registry. Other important information, such as database locations and network settings, are also kept here. The Registry is also a fount of information for a VB developer who wants to integrate an application with a user's environment. For example, if you need to display a Web browser, the proper behavior is to show the user's default browser. This information, along with other related information, is stored in the Registry.

The Registry is fairly simple in its organization. There are three levels of organization in the Registry:

- Hive
- Key
- Value

The Registry Editor is installed in every Windows 32-bit environment (95, 98, NT). If you're in Windows 95 or 98, you can start it by typing Regedit at the command prompt. NT users need to type Regedt32 to start the editor. Figure 16–1 shows the Windows 98 version of the Registry Editor.

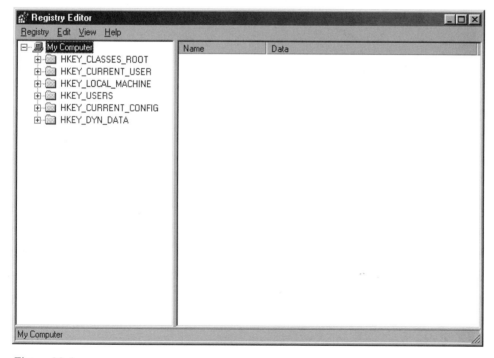

Figure 16-1

Each of the names beneath "My Computer" represents a hive. Each hive contains information about a particular piece of the operating system. Table 16-1 describes the hives and the information they contain:

Table 16-1: Registry's Hives

HIVE	TYPE OF INFORMATION
HKEY_CLASSES_ROOT	Stores information about all the registered file types on your system.
HKEY_CURRENT_USER	Stores information about the current user of the machine. This hive's data is actually stored in the HKEY_USERS hive and this one is just an alias.
HKEY_LOCAL_MACHINE	These settings are used for all users on this machine, whereas some settings in HKEY_CURRENT_USER are specific to a user.
HKEY_USERS	Information about all users for this system.
HKEY_CURRENT_CONFIG	This hive stores internal Windows settings.
HKEY_DYN_DATA	Dynamic data about Windows, including performance information.

TIP

Most of the data in the HKEY_CURRENT_CONFIG and HKEY_DYN_DATA hives are indecipherable and shouldn't be edited by hand.

Most of the information you'll be using is in the first three hives, but the class you'll be building later includes access to all sections of the Registry.

The second level of the Registry is the key. A Registry key is similar to a section in an INI file, as you saw in Chapter 7. Figure 16-2 shows the first level of keys in the HKEY_CURRENT_USER hive.

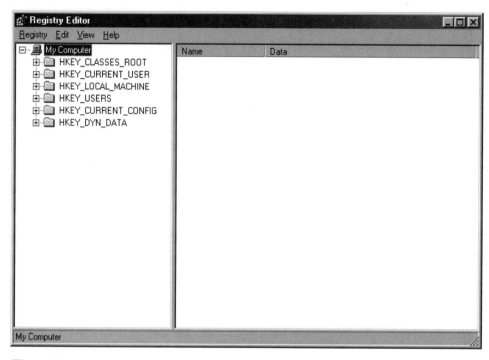

Figure 16-2

A plus (+) sign next to a key means that the key has subkeys. The key level in the Registry is where the complexity occurs, because each key can have an unlimited number of subkeys. If you're a developer and have a lot of complex information that needs to be stored in the Registry, this is extremely useful. The INI files that were used in Windows 3.1 only had a single key (or section) level. Because of this, INI files had many sections and there was no way to create a hierarchy for information.

The final level of the Registry is the value level. The information that we care about is located in the values, which are data entries stored in a particular key. Figure 16-3 shows six values in the InstallLocationsMRU key in the HKEY_CURRENT_USER hive.

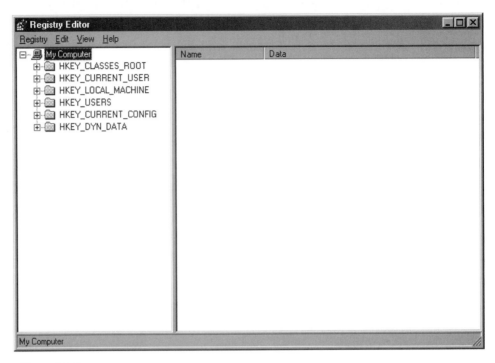

Figure 16-3

Adding the WinAPI Declarations to the Registry Service Object

The first step in building the class is to declare all the WinAPI functions involved. You can retrieve the definitions by using the API Viewer, which is an Add-in for the VB environment. The WinAPI functions, which you should declare as Private, are:

- FileTimeToSystemTime
- FileTimeToLocalFileTime
- RegCloseKey

- RegCreateKeyEx
- RegDeleteKey
- RegDeleteValue
- RegOpenKeyEx
- RegQueryInfoKey
- RegQueryValueEx
- RegSetValueEx

For this class, you should redefine RegQueryValueEx to retrieve a string data type, since it will make our class work more cleanly. The change is as follows:

```
Private Declare Function RegQueryValueExString Lib "advapi32.dll" _
    Alias "RegQueryValueExA" (ByVal hKey As Long, _
    ByVal lpValueName As String, ByVal lpReserved As Long, _
    lpType As Long, ByVal lpData As String, lpcbData As Long) As Long
```

You also need to declare the following constants, type declarations, and enumerated types:

```
Private Const ERROR_SUCCESS = 0&

Private Const HKEY_CLASSES_ROOT = &H80000000
Private Const HKEY_CURRENT_CONFIG = &H80000005
Private Const HKEY_CURRENT_USER = &H80000001
Private Const HKEY_DYN_DATA = &H80000006
Private Const HKEY_LOCAL_MACHINE = &H80000002
Private Const HKEY_PERFORMANCE_DATA = &H80000004
Private Const HKEY_USERS = &H80000003

Private Const KEY_CREATE_SUB_KEY = &H4
Private Const KEY_ENUMERATE_SUB_KEYS = &H8
Private Const KEY_QUERY_VALUE = &H1
Private Const KEY_SET_VALUE = &H2
Private Const KEY_NOTIFY = &H10
Private Const KEY_CREATE_LINK = &H20
Private Const REG_OPTION_NON_VOLATILE = 0
Private Const REG_SZ = 1
Private Const STANDARD_RIGHTS_ALL = &H1F0000
Private Const SYNCHRONIZE = &H100000
Private Const REG_CREATED_NEW_KEY = &H1
Private Const REG_OPENED_EXISTING_KEY = &H2

Private Const KEY_ALL_ACCESS = ((STANDARD_RIGHTS_ALL Or _
    KEY_QUERY_VALUE Or _
    KEY_SET_VALUE Or _
    KEY_CREATE_SUB_KEY Or _
    KEY_ENUMERATE_SUB_KEYS Or _
```

```
            KEY_NOTIFY Or _
            KEY_CREATE_LINK) And (Not SYNCHRONIZE))


Private Type FILETIME
        dwLowDateTime As Long
        dwHighDateTime As Long
End Type

Private Type SYSTEMTIME
        wYear As Integer
        wMonth As Integer
        wDayOfWeek As Integer
        wDay As Integer
        wHour As Integer
        wMinute As Integer
        wSecond As Integer
        wMilliseconds As Integer
End Type

Private m_blnSelected As Boolean
Private m_hCurrentKey As Long
Private m_lngCurrentSection As RegistrySection
Private m_strCurrentKey As String

Private m_strKeyClass As String
Private m_lngSubKeyCount As Long
Private m_lngMaxSubKeyLen As Long
Private m_lngMaxClassLen As Long
Private m_lngNumOfValues As Long
Private m_lngMaxValueNameLen As Long
Private m_lngMaxValueLen As Long
Private m_lngSecurityDescriptor As Long
Private m_typLastWriteTime As FILETIME

Public Enum RegistrySection
    ClassesRoot = HKEY_CLASSES_ROOT
    CurrentConfig = HKEY_CURRENT_CONFIG
    CurrentUser = HKEY_CURRENT_USER
    DynamicData = HKEY_DYN_DATA
    LocalMachine = HKEY_LOCAL_MACHINE
    PerformaceData = HKEY_PERFORMANCE_DATA
    Users = HKEY_USERS
End Enum
```

The RegistrySection enumerated type provides a pop-up list of options for the user who is using various methods of this class. It also helps prevent users from providing bad values, because the only acceptable values are the constant values within this enumerated type.

Adding the Class Properties

All the properties we're adding to the class are read-only; that is, they only have Get properties and not Let or Set properties. This is because the methods we will be adding to the class have parameters that specify all the required information to retrieve a key, open a key, and so on. This method is easier to manage because the user is forced to provide all the parameters in the function call. The alternative method would be to use a series of properties on the object, all of which would need to be populated before calling the method. This leads to the possibility for more errors and requires more validation than our selected method does. You would end up with a lot more error handling and, in our opinion, a more difficult class to use.

Most of the properties correspond to a WinAPI function or a value returned by one of the WinAPI functions included in the class. Most of the relevant WinAPI functions were introduced in Chapter 7. Here is the code for the properties:

```
Public Property Get CurrentKey() As String
    CurrentKey = m_strCurrentKey
End Property

Public Property Get KeyClass() As String
    RefreshKeyInfo
    KeyClass = m_strKeyClass
End Property

Public Property Get NumOfSubKeys() As Long
    RefreshKeyInfo
    NumOfSubKeys = m_lngSubKeyCount
End Property

Public Property Get MaxSubkeyNameLength() As Long
    RefreshKeyInfo
    MaxSubkeyNameLength = m_lngMaxSubKeyLen
End Property

Public Property Get MaxClassNameLength() As Long
    RefreshKeyInfo
```

```
        MaxClassNameLength = m_lngMaxClassLen
End Property

Public Property Get NumOfValues() As Long
    RefreshKeyInfo
    NumOfValues = m_lngNumOfValues
End Property

Public Property Get MaxValueNameLength() As Long
    RefreshKeyInfo
    MaxValueNameLength = m_lngMaxValueNameLen
End Property

Public Property Get MaxValueLength() As Long
    RefreshKeyInfo
    MaxValueLength = m_lngMaxValueLen
End Property

Public Property Get SecurityDescriptor() As Long
    RefreshKeyInfo
    SecurityDescriptor = m_lngSecurityDescriptor
End Property
Public Property Get LastWriteTime() As Date
    Dim typSystemTime As SYSTEMTIME
    Dim typLocalTime As FILETIME
    Dim lngReturn As Long

    On Error Resume Next ' This is in case something bad
                         ' is passed to the CDate function

    RefreshKeyInfo

    '
    ' Convert number to GMT time format
    '
    lngReturn = FileTimeToLocalFileTime(m_typLastWriteTime, typLocalTime)

    '
    ' Convert GMT time to local time
    '
    lngReturn = FileTimeToSystemTime(typLocalTime, typSystemTime)

    '
    ' Convert time structure to VB date format
    '
```

```
        With typSystemTime
            LastWriteTime = CDate(.wMonth & "/" & .wDay & "/" & .wYear _
                & " " _
                & .wHour & ":" & .wMinute & ":" & .wSecond)
        End With
    End Property

Private Sub RefreshKeyInfo()
    Dim lngReturn As Long
    Dim lngKeyClassSize As Long
    Dim strLongBinary As String

    lngKeyClassSize = 255
    m_strKeyClass = Space(lngKeyClassSize)

    lngReturn = RegQueryInfoKey(m_hCurrentKey, m_strKeyClass, _
        lngKeyClassSize, 0&, _
        m_lngSubKeyCount, m_lngMaxSubKeyLen, m_lngMaxClassLen, _
        m_lngNumOfValues, m_lngMaxValueNameLen, m_lngMaxValueLen, _
        m_lngSecurityDescriptor, m_typLastWriteTime)

    If lngReturn <> ERROR_SUCCESS Then
        Err.Raise vbObjectError + 2, "CRegistry:RefreshKeyInfo", _
            "Failed to retrieve key information."
        Exit Sub
    End If

    If lngKeyClassSize > 0 Then
        m_strKeyClass = Left(m_strKeyClass, lngKeyClassSize - 1)
    End If
End Sub
```

Most of the properties simply return the private variable holding the value in question. The LastWriteTime property has a bit of conversion code in it to convert the FILETIME and SYSTEMTIME structures. This saves time because no conversion is done unless the user actually requests the timestamp from the Registry. The RefreshKeyInfo subroutine retrieves information about a particular key and caches it in the class's private variables.

> *NOTE*
> *You might not need to use all the properties; however, they're all included for completeness.*

Adding the Class Methods

The first method we'll add is OpenKey, which is the first method that you need to call after instantiating the object. This method enables you to pick the hive you wish to use, the key name, and, optionally, whether you want to create a new key if one doesn't exist already. (In cases where you are just reading, you don't need to specify this because the method has a default value.) The code is shown here:

```
Public Sub OpenKey(Section As RegistrySection, _
    strKey As String, _
    Optional blnCreateNew As Boolean = False)

    Dim lngReturn As Long
    Dim lngAction As Long

    If m_blnSelected = True Then
        CloseKey
    End If


    '
    ' Remove any leading backslashes, because they
    ' cause the function to fail
    '
    If Left(strKey, 1) = "\" Then
        strKey = Mid(strKey, 2)
    End If


    '
    ' Allow forward slashes, as they are a logical
    ' way to separate the keys
    '
    strKey = Replace(strKey, "/", "\")

    lngReturn = RegOpenKeyEx(Section, strKey, 0, _
        KEY_ALL_ACCESS, m_hCurrentKey)

    If lngReturn = ERROR_SUCCESS Then
        m_blnSelected = True
        m_strCurrentKey = strKey
        m_lngCurrentSection = Section
    Else
        If blnCreateNew Then
            lngReturn = RegCreateKeyEx(Section, strKey, 0&, vbNullString, _
                REG_OPTION_NON_VOLATILE, KEY_ALL_ACCESS, _
```

```
                ByVal (0&), m_hCurrentKey, lngAction)
        If lngReturn = ERROR_SUCCESS Then
            m_blnSelected = True
            m_strCurrentKey = strKey
            m_lngCurrentSection = Section
        Else
            Err.Raise vbObjectError + 2, "Registry:OpenKey", _
            "Failed to create key " & strKey & "."
        End If
    Else
        Err.Raise vbObjectError + 2, "Registry:OpenKey", _
            "Failed to open key " & strKey & "."
        Exit Sub
    End If
End If

End Sub
```

The Registry expects a key to be formatted like this:

```
Software\Microsoft\Data Access\Version
```

To be user friendlier, OpenKey has some code at the beginning to translate forward slashes to backslashes. In addition, leading slashes are removed from the key. The method then opens the key, stores the returned data, and handles any errors that occur. Errors are sent back to the caller via the built-in Error objects. As the key is being opened, the OpenKey method calls the RefreshKeyInfo method to query the key and retrieve information into all the property values.

> **TIP**
>
> *To test OpenKey's error-handling capabilities, be sure your error handling options (under Tools→Options) are set to Break on Unhandled Errors.*

> **NOTE**
>
> *Rather than calling RefreshKeyInfo, you could call RegQueryKeyInfo each time a property is requested. However, if you're using a lot of the information stored in the key, it's better to make a single WinAPI call to RefreshKeyInfo than multiple WinAPI calls to RegQueryKeyInfo.*

The ReadValue method shown below enables you to retrieve a single value from an open key:

```
Public Function ReadValue(Optional strValueName As String = "") As String

    Dim strBuffer As String
    Dim lngLength As Long
    Dim lngReturn As Long

    If Not m_blnSelected Then
        Err.Raise vbObjectError + 2, "Registry:ReadValue", _
            "No key is currently open."
        Exit Function
    End If

    strBuffer = Space(255)
    lngLength = 255
    lngReturn = RegQueryValueExString(m_hCurrentKey, strValueName, _
        0, 0, strBuffer, lngLength)
    If lngReturn = ERROR_SUCCESS Then
        ReadValue = Left(strBuffer, lngLength - 1)
    Else
        Err.Raise vbObjectError + 2, "Registry:ReadValue", _
            "Failed to read value " & strValueName & " from Registry."
        Exit Function
    End If

End Function
```

ReadValue verifies that the key is actually open and returns an error if it isn't open. If you don't specify the value's name, the method assumes you want the default value of the key. The method also takes care of cleaning up the string by removing the extra spaces and null characters that normally come back with WinAPI function results.

The WriteValue method shown below enables you to restore a value in a key:

```
Public Sub WriteValue(strValueName As String, strNewValue As String)
    Dim lngReturn As Long

    If Not m_blnSelected Then
        Err.Raise vbObjectError + 2, "Registry:WriteValue", _
            "No key is currently open."
        Exit Sub
    End If

    lngReturn = RegSetValueEx(m_hCurrentKey, strValueName, 0&, _
        REG_SZ, ByVal (strNewValue), Len(strNewValue))
    If lngReturn <> ERROR_SUCCESS Then
        Err.Raise vbObjectError + 2, "Registry:WriteValue", _
```

```
                    "Failed to write new value to " & strValueName & " from
Registry."
        Exit Sub
     End If

End Sub
```

WriteValue uses strings only because they are the easiest types of data to deal with. We prefer to use strings, even if we are storing numbers. However, it's easy to write additional methods if you want to be able to write other types of data into the Registry. If you do write other methods, be sure to add corresponding read methods. Like ReadValue, WriteValue allows you to omit the value name in order to write to the default value of the key.

If you need to delete a value or a key, the DeleteValue and DeleteKey methods is handy. The DeleteValue method removes a value from the key that is currently open and the DeleteKey method removes the currently selected key. The code for these two methods is shown here:

```
Public Sub DeleteValue(strValueName As String)

    Dim lngReturn As Long

    If Not m_blnSelected Then
        Err.Raise vbObjectError + 2, "Registry:DeleteValue", _
            "No key is currently open."
        Exit Sub
    End If

    lngReturn = RegDeleteValue(m_hCurrentKey, strValueName)
    If lngReturn <> ERROR_SUCCESS Then
        Err.Raise vbObjectError + 2, "Registry:DeleteValue", _
            "Failed to delete value " & strValueName & " from Registry."
        Exit Sub
    End If

End Sub
Public Sub DeleteKey()
    Dim lngReturn As Long
    Dim strKey As String

    strKey = m_strCurrentKey
    CloseKey
    lngReturn = RegDeleteKey(CLng(m_lngCurrentSection), strKey)
    If lngReturn <> ERROR_SUCCESS Then
        Err.Raise vbObjectError + 2, "Registry:DeleteKey", _
            "Failed to delete key " & strKey & "."
```

```
        Exit Sub
    End If

End Sub
```

DeleteKey closes the open key before removing it. Both methods also include error handling.

The CloseKey method shown below cleans up the open references to the Registry, clears some of the data in the object, and changes the internal flag to closed:

```
Public Sub CloseKey()
    If m_hCurrentKey <> 0 Then
        RegCloseKey m_hCurrentKey
        m_hCurrentKey = 0
        m_blnSelected = False
        m_strCurrentKey = ""
    End If
End Sub
```

There's really nothing of importance that can happen if you attempt to close a key that isn't open, but CloseKey includes a trap to skip the code if the object isn't currently viewing a key. CloseKey is also called during the Class_Terminate event to make sure that an open key is closed when an object is released.

```
Private Sub Class_Terminate()
    CloseKey
End Sub
```

Putting It All Together

You have learned how to create a reusable Registry Service object. This class is especially helpful for applications that are services or Microsoft Transaction Server components. The components can access their sections in the Registry to determine how they should be initialized, as well as obtain information, such as the database parameters, that you might need to make a database connection.

Included on the CD-ROM is a test project, named RegistryClassTester.vbp, that lets you exercise the class. Here's the code from the Sub Main so that you can see how the class can be used:

```
Sub Main()
    Dim objReg As Registry
    Set objReg = New Registry

    objReg.OpenKey LocalMachine, "Software\Microsoft\SchedulingAgent"
    Debug.Print objReg.ReadValue("LogPath")
    objReg.CloseKey

    objReg.OpenKey CurrentUser, "Software\APress\Registry Class Test", True
    objReg.WriteValue "", _
        "This is a test to see if the default value filled properly."
    objReg.CloseKey

    objReg.OpenKey CurrentUser, "Software\APress\Registry Class Test"
    objReg.DeleteKey
    objReg.OpenKey CurrentUser, "Software\APress"
    objReg.DeleteKey

End Sub
```

Chapter 17

WebClasses: A New Way to Program for the Web

Until now, a Web page consisted of a static HTML page or, for Microsoft Internet Information Server (IIS) users, an interpreted Active Server Page (ASP) page. Your Web server wasn't able to easily run compiled code generated from a familiar product such as Visual Basic—until WebClasses.

Introduction to WebClasses

Visual Basic 6 introduces the concept of a WebClass in a new type of project: the IIS Application. With WebClasses, your Web-based applications will run faster and your code will be more reliable because you're creating compiled Visual Basic code from the Visual Basic environment. You'll also be able to easily debug your Web-based application—a capability unheard of until now. No more plunking down lots of Print statements everywhere that you need to remove later. You can fully test your Web page before it even touches your Web server.

WebClass applications also have the capability to access the built-in ASP objects you may have already used in ASP applications. You can access all the built-in objects, including Request, Response, and so on. And just like ASP applications, you don't have to worry about someone stealing your source code because the code is never sent across the Internet and because the code is compiled into a library and resides entirely on your server.

> *NOTE*
>
> *To build the samples in this chapter, you must use the Professional or Enterprise Edition of Visual Basic 6. You also need Windows NT Server 4 (or newer) with IIS 3 or newer, Windows NT Workstation 4 (or newer) with Peer Web Services installed, or Windows 95/98 with Personal Web Server installed. Internet Explorer 4.01 is installed with Visual Basic 6 and it, or a newer version, is recommended for use with the WebClass samples in this chapter. Output can be viewed in most Web browsers, including Internet Explorer 5.*

Building a WebClass Application

To introduce WebClass applications, let's build a simple program. This program will be known as the "Hello, World!" WebClass. This application will take you through the creation and deployment of a WebClass and generate some output to your Web browser. The steps you'll go through in this section are basically the same steps that you would follow for any WebClass you build.

To get started, create a new application. Start Visual Basic, select New from the File menu, and select IIS Application from the dialog shown. After Visual Basic is done creating the new project, you might expect to see a class module in your project. That's not quite the case. A WebClass isn't quite the same as a regular class module. It has many of the same events and properties of a class, but it is designed to do much more. When you created your new IIS application, Visual Basic automatically added a designer file to your project and named it WebClass1. Each WebClass will have its own designer file added to the project.

To continue, double-click the WebClass1 item in the Project Explorer window. The WebClass Designer will appear. The standard VB Properties window displays the WebClass' key properties. If you wish, you can rename the WebClass to FirstProject or another valid name (no spaces allowed). The other property values should remain as is for now. You learn more about them later in the chapter.

Most of the work involved in building a WebClass involves the WebClass Designer. This window displays two categories of items:

- HTML Template WebItem—an HTML document used by a WebClass. This document consists of just plain HTML text and is edited in either Notepad or your default HTML editor. This template uses special tags that enable VB to manipulate the HTML in the template, eliminating the need for you to write all the pages' HTML through code. The HTML template is not compiled into the WebClass, so you can make changes to the template without having to rebuild the WebClass itself.
- Custom WebItem—a name that you define as part of the WebClass module. A custom WebItem (also known simply as a WebItem) can have custom events, giving you essentially a two-level hierarchy. Custom WebItems are often used for dynamic data that does not lend itself to simple substitution in a template.

Both types of WebItems are the heart of your code when you start building IIS applications.

Besides what you see in the Designer window, you can also look at the underlying code by selecting View→Code. When you create a new WebClass, Visual Basic automatically adds the code that follows.

NOTE
In the code that follows, some of the longer lines are broken for clarity.

```
Private Sub WebClass_Start()
    'Write a reply to the user
    With Response
        .Write "<HTML>"
        .Write "<body>"
        .Write "<h1><font face=""Arial"">" _
            & "WebClass1's Starting Page</font></h1>"
        .Write "<p>This response was created " _
            & "in the Start event of WebClass1.</p>"
        .Write "</body>"
        .Write "</html>"
    End With
End Sub
```

This code, which is alterable, will generate a simple Web page if you use the WebClass by itself without creating any WebItems. To see this in action, select Run→Start. A dialog box that lets you specify how the application should be run appears. In this case, VB assumes that we want to run WebClass1 (or whatever name you gave the WebClass), and will show its output in the browser that exists on your system. The HTML code will work with any Web browser, including non-Microsoft models.

In the Project Properties dialog, click OK to continue. Visual Basic will prompt you to create a temporary virtual directory for testing these applications. The directory you defined as your temporary Windows directory (typically C:\Windows\Temp) will become a shared directory known as Temp. This shared directory is used to enable VB to load the page in your browser. If you've already saved your files and project, VB will create a share name for the folder in which your project resides. For this reason, you should create a new directory for each IIS application you build; it will be easier to manage the shared directories that are created. Visual Basic will also prompt you to save the project.

The results of all this work will be displayed in your default browser. The Start event of the WebClass will have triggered and you'll see the welcome message you created.

The HTML code is pretty simple to view using the View Page Source option in your browser, and is shown here:

```
<html><body><h1><font face="Arial">WebClass1's Starting
Page</font><></h1><p>This response was created in the Start event of
WebClass1.</p></body></html>
```

In your source viewer, the HTML will show up all as one big long line. Why is it all on one line? Because the WebClass didn't add any line breaks to the HTML put in the page. Even though your code is generating HTML that the browser can read in any format or layout, it is good to add line breaks so that *you* can tell whether the HTML is correct. Having one long line of HTML tends to hamper readability. To break up the HTML, use the vbCrLf constant within the WebClass procedure. vbCrLf adds a line break in the output HTML, which makes it much easier to read. The revised code for the WebClass_Start event procedure is as follows:

```
Private Sub WebClass_Start()
    Dim sQuote As String
    sQuote = Chr(34)
    ' Write a reply to the user
    With Response
        .Write "<HTML>" & vbCrLf
        .Write "<body>" & vbCrLf
        .Write "<h1><font face=" _
            & sQuote & "Arial" & sQuote _
            & ">WebClass1's Starting Page</font></h1>" _
            & vbCrLf
        .Write "<p>This response was created " _
            & "in the Start event of WebClass1.</p>" & vbCrLf
        .Write "</body>" & vbCrLf
        .Write "</html>" & vbCrLf
    End With
End Sub
```

The resulting HTML is much easier to read with the line breaks in place, as shown here:

```
<HTML>
<body>
<h1><font face="Arial">WebClass1's Starting Page</font></h1>
<p>This response was created in the Start event of WebClass1.</p>
</body>
</html>
```

You may happen to notice that the URL in the address line of your browser is referencing a file ending with the extension .ASP. You didn't have to create the ASP page—Visual Basic did it for you. If you haven't stopped your VB program yet, use Explorer to look in your temporary directory where you'll find the ASP page. When you stop your program, the ASP page will disappear. If you're quick, you can open up the ASP page to see what it contains. The contents of the ASP file are as follows:

> NOTE
> *The line breaks in the code that follows might not appear in the ASP file.*

```
<%
Server.ScriptTimeout=600
Response.Buffer=True
Response.Expires=0

If (VarType(Application("~WC~WebClassManager")) = 0) Then
    Application.Lock
    If (VarType(Application("~WC~WebClassManager")) = 0) Then
        Set Application("~WC~WebClassManager") = _
            Server.CreateObject("WebClassRuntime.WebClassManager")
    End If
    Application.UnLock
End If

Application("~WC~WebClassManager").ProcessNoStateWebClass _
    "Project1.WebClass1", _
    Server, _
    Application, _
    Session, _
    Request, _
    Response
%>
```

Visual Basic automatically created this ASP page for you. The script in this
ASP page creates an instance of your WebClass1 and executes it. When you
compile and deploy your application, VB will build a copy of this file for you and
put it with your compiled library. Both the ASP page and the library need to be
placed on your Web server. You can't run the library by itself; it has to be started
in exactly the manner shown in the ASP page. The ASP page is simply a wrapper
around your class; any HTML that you want to build yourself should be made
part of your WebClass.

> **TIP**
> *You should avoid editing the ASP page because VB will simply overwrite*
> *your changes later.*

The final step in creating a WebClass application is the same as for creating
other Dynamic Link Libraries (DLLs): to compile and deploy it using the
Packaging and Deployment Wizard. This involves compiling the application into
a DLL, packaging it with all of the required files needed for it to run, and then
installing the package on your Web server.

Using an HTML Template

Building a WebClass by manually generating HTML is one way to do the job; however, it has several disadvantages. First, even minor changes to the HTML code require you to recompile the entire WebClass. Second, only programmers can work on the WebClasses, unless you can convince your graphic artists to learn VB to write their HTML! Last, you'll find after a while that having to deal with all the double quote characters gets quite tedious. A better solution is to create an HTML template file that can be used in conjunction with your WebClass to produce easier-to-maintain Web sites.

An HTML template is simply an HTML file with some special tags added. These special tags look like HTML tags, but are interpreted by your WebClass before they make it to the user's browser. Because you're writing plain HTML, you can use any text editor or HTML editor that gives you access to the actual HTML. I recommend and use Allaire's HomeSite 4.0 product, because it makes it easy to create the necessary custom tags and rarely rearranges them against your will. FrontPage enables you to insert custom HTML or edit using the HTML view, but sometimes moves tags to the incorrect locations—especially when placing them in forms or input controls. You can also use Visual InterDev, but it is a more costly solution than HomeSite is. If you can't get any of these tools, just fire up Notepad or WordPad. You can even use Microsoft Word, but be sure to save your text as Text Only.

To get started, we're going to create a relatively simple HTML page that has two special tags in it. The code for this page is shown here:

```
<HTML>
<HEAD>
<TITLE><WC@Title>Title</WC@Title></TITLE>
</HEAD>
<BODY BGCOLOR="<WC@BGC>BGColor</WC@BGC>">
<H1><WC@TITLE>Title</WC@TITLE></H1>
The title and background color of this page were substituted
through code.
</BODY>
</HTML>
```

The special tags are within double quotes in the BODY tag. This is designed to isolate them from the parsing that Visual Basic does. After you've saved this file, do the following:

1. If you're not already in a new IIS application (the one from the previous section is fine to use), create a new project.
2. Open the Designer window and right-click on HTML Template WebItems.
3. On the menu that appears, select Add HTML Template. If you created a new project, you may be prompted to save your project before VB will allow you to add a new template.

4. From the dialog box that appears, select your HTML file and click Open to let VB load it.

5. The name will be highlighted and you can edit it.

At this point, the WebClass Designer has parsed your HTML template and added it to the WebClass. Right-click on the template in the WebClass Designer and select Edit Template to view the template. You'll see the following HTML:

```
<HTML>
<HEAD>
<TITLE>Title</TITLE>
</HEAD>
<BODY BGCOLOR="#00b000">
<H1><WC@TITLE>Title</WC@TITLE></H1>
The title and background color of this page were substituted
through code.
</BODY>
</HTML>
```

What happened to the WC@BGC tags? According to Microsoft document #Q189539, this is apparently a "feature" of Visual Basic. The Microsoft design does not allow you to put replacement tags in HTML tags, which seems like an important capability to include—especially because you can do a similar thing in ASP when you print a variable's value in HTML. Microsoft doesn't provide a workaround, but we do. To make the change, perform these steps:

1. Right-click the template in the WebClass Designer and select Edit Template.

2. Change the HTML code to look like the following:

```
<HTML>
<HEAD>
<TITLE><WC@Title>Title</WC@Title></TITLE>
</HEAD>
<WC@BGC>BGColor</WC@BGC>
<H1><WC@TITLE>Title</WC@TITLE></H1>
The title and background color of this page were substituted
through code.
</BODY>
</HTML>
```

3. Save the template file and close your editor.

4. Reload the template when prompted by the WebClass designer.

5. Again, you'll notice that the display is not correct. The WebClass designer has added a BODY tag in the right-hand pane even though there isn't one in the template. This time VB didn't actually change the

template. You can verify this by editing the template again to make sure it's still working. Don't worry about the missing Body tag—we'll re-add it in code.

The next step in using the template is to write the code to handle the substitutions. VB will provide you the tags through an event procedure, but you have to do the work to figure out what to substitute for what. Add the code in the following listing to your WebClass:

> *NOTE*
> *The code here assumes that the name of the template is TemplateTest. If you named your template something else, there will be an item for it in the object drop-down list in the code window.*

```
Option Explicit
Private Sub TemplateTest_ProcessTag( _
    ByVal TagName As String, _
    TagContents As String, _
    SendTags As Boolean)

    TagName = Mid(TagName, Len(TemplateTest.TagPrefix) + 1)
    Select Case UCase(TagName)
    Case "TITLE"
            TagContents = "The Test Worked!"
    Case "BGC"
        TagContents = "<BODY BGCOLOR=""#F0F0F0"">"
    End Select

    SendTags = False

End Sub


Private Sub WebClass_Start()
    TemplateTest.WriteTemplate
End Sub
```

Each time the WebClass engine finds a substitution tag, it calls the ProcessTag event procedure and passes the name of the tag to it. You then have to figure out what tag was sent and what you want to replace the sent tag with.

You might have noticed that all the tags in the page were prefixed with WC@. This is the default prefix for substitution tags, and is stored in the Webclass's TagPrefix property. First, let's remove the prefix so that we can deal with the meat of the tag. Depending on the value of the tag, whether it is TITLE or BGC, we put the replacement text in the TagContents parameter, which is sent back to the WebClass engine. Because Microsoft does not allow us to place tags within tags, we have to send the entire BODY tag.

The WebClass_Start event procedure contains an important line of code. The WriteTemplate command causes the template to be processed. In the previous example, we had code to print the HTML that we wanted to show. The template approach is much easier to maintain, because you can edit the HTML templates outside of Visual Basic and simply reload them.

Creating WebItems and Custom Events

Although the WebClass provides a few default events, they are too generic to distinguish among very specific actions—such as a user clicking a customer entry on a page that displays 100 customers. Without another approach, you'd have to place the code for all the customers in a single event procedure, which would be difficult to maintain. Instead, Visual Basic provides the capability to add WebItems to a WebClass.

You can think of a *WebItem* (also known as a *custom WebItem*) as a set of functions or a class. Although each WebItem contains a default Respond event, you have the option of defining a number of *custom events* that are specific to the WebItem. These custom events represent the tasks that are performable by the WebItem. WebItems and custom events belonging to a WebClass module can be triggered from the same ASP page simply through different arguments supplied to the page. You can then use these arguments in your code to produce URLs in the HTML output that the user can click, or you can call the URLs from other HTML pages on your site.

Using WebItems

To learn the basics of employing WebItems, you'll create three that each contain a Respond event procedure. The first thing to do is to add the three WebItems to your WebClass. To do this, follow these steps:

1. Open the Designer window.
2. Change the name of the HTML Template to tmpColorTest.
3. Right-click on Custom WebItems and select Add Custom WebItem from the pop-up menu.
4. VB will add a new WebItem to the tree and prompt you to rename it. Add three WebItems with these names: DisplayRed, DisplayYellow, DisplayBlue.

Next, add some code behind the scenes. As was mentioned before, the WebClass can have variables just like any other class. In the Declarations section of the WebClass, add the following variable declaration:

```
Dim strColorCode As String
```

Add the following event procedures for the three WebItems:

```
Private Sub DisplayBlue_Respond()
    strColorCode = "#0000FF"
```

```
        tmpColorTest.WriteTemplate
End Sub

Private Sub DisplayRed_Respond()
        strColorCode = "#FF0000"
        tmpColorTest.WriteTemplate
End Sub

Private Sub DisplayYellow_Respond()
        strColorCode = "#FFFF00"
        tmpColorTest.WriteTemplate
End Sub
```

Next, change the WebClass_Start event procedure. Because we need to give
the user a few choices to choose from, WebClass_Start has to generate some
HTML dynamically, as shown here:

```
Private Sub WebClass_Start()
        strColorCode = "#FFFFFF"
        With Response
                .Write "<HTML><HEAD><TITLE>"
                .Write "Pick Your Color"
                .Write "</TITLE></HEAD>" & vbCr
                .Write "<BODY BGCOLOR=#FFFFFF>" & vbCr
                .Write "Pick the color you'd like to see:<P>" & vbCr
                .Write "<A HREF=""" _
                    & URLFor(DisplayRed) _
                    & """>Red</A><BR>" & vbCr
                .Write "<A HREF=""" _
                    & URLFor(DisplayYellow) _
                    & """>Yellow</A><BR>" & vbCr
                .Write "<A HREF=""" _
                    & URLFor(DisplayBlue) _
                    & """>Blue</A><BR>" & vbCr
                .Write "</HTML>"
        End With
End Sub
```

The important feature of this code is the URLFor function. This function
generates the proper URL to access a WebItem belonging to this WebClass. The
first time it is used in the above code, it generates the URL to access the
DisplayRed WebItem. The advantage of using URLFor is that it generates the
internal identifier that the Web server uses to access the WebItem. This identifier
retrieves the location of the WebItem from within the WebClass object. If you're
generating code, use the URLFor function for WebItems that are in your
WebClass so that you don't have to keep track of the actual filenames involved
in your application – let VB do the work for you.

Now delete the previous TemplateTest_ProcessTag procedure and replace it with the slightly modified tmpColorTest_ProcessTag procedure, shown here:

```
Private Sub tmpColorTest_ProcessTag _
    (ByVal TagName As String, _
    TagContents As String, _
    SendTags As Boolean)

    TagName = Mid(TagName, _
        Len(tmpColorTest.TagPrefix) + 1)
    Select Case UCase(TagName)
    Case "TITLE"
        TagContents = "The Test Worked!"
    Case "BGC"
        TagContents = "<BODY BGCOLOR=""" & strColorCode & """" & ">" End
    Select
        SendTags = False
End Sub
```

Instead of always using a particular color, this procedure will use the color stored in the strColorCode variable, which was assigned earlier by the WebItem triggered by the user.

Look at the HTML source for the color selection page sent by the Webclass_Start procedure. The WCI= reference following the question mark is known as a parameter. This is one technique by which one page can reference another page. The identifier refers to the WebItem you built. The rest of the URL is the same as before—the project name followed by the WebClass name.

> **TIP**
> *The URLFor function automatically creates the identifiers as you run the page, so you don't have to worry about the exact URL information.*

If you click one of these URLs, you will see the same HTML template as before except that there is a different background color for each. While this may seem like a trivial example, the basic idea really expands the scope of how you can use WebClasses and HTML templates.

Using Custom Events

By adding custom events to your WebItems, you can provide additional functionality to your users. Creating a WebItem with custom events is similar to creating the WebItems you just built. The main difference is that each WebItem will contain several custom event procedures rather than a single Respond event procedure. The example you'll build modifies the previous example, which used three different WebItems, to use a single WebItem containing three custom events.

To begin, open your Designer window and perform these steps:

1. Add a Custom WebItem named ChangeColor.
2. Right-click on ChangeColor in the list, and select Add Custom Event from the pop-up menu.
3. Add three Custom Events named Red, Yellow, and Blue.

You now have to write event procedures for the custom events that you just added. That code is shown below:

```
Private Sub ChangeColor_Blue()
    strColorCode = "#0000FF"
    tmpColorTest.WriteTemplate
End Sub

Private Sub ChangeColor_Red()
    strColorCode = "#FF0000"
    tmpColorTest.WriteTemplate
End Sub

Private Sub ChangeColor_Yellow()
    strColorCode = "#FFFF00"
    tmpColorTest.WriteTemplate
End Sub
```

As you can see, the custom event procedures use the same instructions as the Respond event procedures built earlier, although the procedures' names are different to account for the new events.

The last change you need to make is in the WebClass_Start event handler. The changes are to the three calls to URLFor, as shown in boldface in this listing:

```
Private Sub WebClass_Start()
    strColorCode = "#FFFFFF"
    With Response
        .Write "<HTML><HEAD><TITLE>"
        .Write "Pick Your Color"
        .Write "</TITLE></HEAD>" & vbCr
        .Write "<BODY BGCOLOR=#FFFFFF>" & vbCr
        .Write "Pick the color you'd like to see:<P>" & vbCr
        .Write "<A HREF=""" _
            & URLFor(ChangeColor, "Red") _
            & """>Red</A><BR>" & vbCr
        .Write "<A HREF=""" _
            & URLFor(ChangeColor, "Yellow") _
            & """>Yellow</A><BR>" & vbCr
        .Write "<A HREF=""" _
            & URLFor(ChangeColor, "Blue") _
```

```
        & """>Blue</A><BR>" & vbCr
    .Write "</HTML>"

  End With

End Sub
```

While the name of the WebItem passed to URLFor method (ChangeColor, in this case) represents an object defined to Visual Basic, the name of the event has to be passed as a string in quotes. It is not defined to Visual Basic and thus has to be "protected" from Visual Basic's syntax checker. When you run your program, the string will be passed to the URLFor function that understands how to interpret it.

If you prefer to write this HTML page manually, you can reference custom WebItems easily by referring to the ASP page for the WebClass, followed by the name of the WebItem as the WCI parameter, and the name of the custom event (if any) as the WCE parameter. For example: the ChangeColor "Red" custom event can be referenced as follows:

```
<A HREF="WebClass1.ASP?WCI=ChangeColor&WCE=Red"
```

This syntax enables you to create plain HTML pages that can start WebClass applications. When you use this syntax, make sure you have a default response in case parameters are accidentally omitted from the name of the ASP page. This may happen if plain HTML pages are referring to ASP pages that require certain information to run properly. Typically, you want a URL entered by hand to be as simple as possible. In most cases, you'll be calling the main Respond event handler in a class first, after which references to all other URLs will be generated by the WebClass itself.

Combining WebClasses with Active Data Objects

Now you're ready to start using databases with your templates, which will show you more of the real power behind this new technology. If you've created ASP pages by hand, this may convince you not to do them by hand any longer.

The main purpose of the ASP technology was to make it easier to publish dynamic pages. These pages were typically based on database tables and queries. WebClasses are no different and make it even easier to build these types of applications. In this section, you build an HTML template with substitution tags. These tags will be replaced by data from a database that you access by way of ADO. You also build a UserEvent to make it easier to show detailed information about records in a table of data.

The database you'll use is the Northwind Traders database because it already has a nice structure with quite a bit of sample data. You'll build a list of the customers in the database and provide the user the ability to click on a customer name to see more information about that customer. The functionality here is very similar to that which you built using VB forms, except that the output is directed through the Web to any browser supporting a minimal set of HTML.

Let's start by building an HTML template that will be used for the customer list. The only things you need to put in this page are general tags, such as TITLE and BODY. All of the customer entries will be generated dynamically with the WebClass. The HTML template should look similar to the one here:

```
<HTML>
<HEAD>
<TITLE>Northwind Traders - Customer List</TITLE>
</HEAD>
<BODY>
<H1>Northwind Traders Customer List<BR>
<H3>As Of <WC@DATE></WC@DATE> </H3></H1>
<HR>
<WC@CUSTOMER></WC@CUSTOMER>
</BODY></HTML>
```

After you've saved this template in another directory, add it to your IIS application as a new HTML Template WebItem and name it tmpCustomerList. Next, add a Custom WebItem to show the customer list because your WebClass will probably have a wide variety of other features that will be shown first on a menu or other interface. Name the WebItem ListCustomer. The Respond event for this will trigger an event that handles displaying the list of customers. Create a Custom Event called ListAll as part of the ListCustomer WebItem.

After the WebItem and custom event are defined, you can start writing code. We'll begin with the WebClass_Start event procedure. You probably want to have a menu to show the customer list from, but these instructions will serve as test code so that the list of customers will come up automatically when the WebClass is started.

```
Private Sub WebClass_Start()
    Set NextItem = ListCustomer
End Sub
```

The NextItem property tells Visual Basic which WebItem to process next. This enables you to process a sequence of Web items in a single response to the user.

The ListCustomer_Respond event procedure is next and is very simple.

```
Private Sub ListCustomer_Respond()
    tmpCustomerList.WriteTemplate
End Sub
```

This triggers the CustomerList template to load and be processed. Because we have substitution tags to deal with, the tmpCustomerList_ProcessTags event procedure is next. The code for it is shown here:

```
Private Sub tmpCustomerList_ProcessTag _
    (ByVal TagName As String, _
    TagContents As String, _
    SendTags As Boolean)

    Dim strTag As String

    strTag = UCase(Mid(TagName, _
        Len(tmpCustomerList.TagPrefix) + 1))
    Select Case strTag
        Case "DATE"
            TagContents = Format(Date, "mmmm d, yyyy")
        Case "CUSTOMER"
            TagContents = CustList()
    End Select
    SendTags = False

End Sub
```

The CustList function reads the database and creates a table with the customers in it, as shown here:

TIP

Remember to use the path to your Northwind Traders database in the ADO connection. Also, remember to add a reference to the Microsoft Active Data Objects library using the VB Project-References menu command.

```
Private Function CustList() As String
    Dim dcnDB As ADODB.Connection
    Dim rsData As ADODB.Recordset
    Dim strResult As String

    Set dcnDB = New ADODB.Connection
    dcnDB.CursorLocation = adUseClient
    dcnDB.Open "PROVIDER=Microsoft.Jet.OLEDB.4.0;" _
        & "Data Source=C:\Visual Studio\VB98\NWind.MDB;"

    Set rsData = New ADODB.Recordset
    rsData.Open "SELECT * FROM Customers " _
```

```
                & "ORDER BY CompanyName", _
                dcnDB, adOpenForwardOnly, adLockReadOnly

        If rsData.RecordCount = 0 Then
            strResult = _
                "<H1>No records are in the database.</H1>"
        Else
            strResult = "<TABLE CELLPADDING=3 BORDER=1>" & vbCr _
                & "<TR><TH>Customer Name</TH>" & vbCr _
                & "<TH>City</TH>" & vbCr _
                & "<TH>Country</TH>" & vbCr _
                & "</TR>" & vbCr

            Do While Not rsData.EOF
                strResult = strResult & "<TR>" & vbCr _
                & "<TD>" _
                & rsData("CompanyName") & "</TD>" & vbCr _
                & "<TD>" _
                & rsData("City") & "</TD>" & vbCr _
                & "<TD>" _
                & rsData("Country") & "</TD>" & vbCr _
                & "</TR>" & vbCr
            rsData.MoveNext
        Loop
        strResult = strResult & "</TABLE>" & vbCr
        strResult = strResult & "<HR><H3><I>" _
            & rsData.RecordCount _
            & " customers listed.</I></H3>" & vbCr

        End If
        CustList = strResult

        '
        ' Clean up objects
        '
        rsData.Close
        Set rsData = Nothing
        dcnDB.Close
        Set dcnDB = Nothing
End Function
```

TIP

If you have not yet upgraded to Microsoft Office 2000, you may need to specify the provider as Microsoft.Jet.OLEDB.3.51.

After making a connection to the Northwind Traders database, a recordset is created of all the customers, sorted by company name. The TABLE header tags are generated next, including column headers. The entire HTML is appended to the strResult string variable because it all needs to be returned to the ProcessTags event procedure at the end. For each record that was retrieved, a new table row is added. When it is generated, the HTML looks like this for a single row:

```
<TR>
<TD>Ernst Handel</TD>
<TD>Graz</TD>
<TD>Austria</TD>
</TR>
```

Creating Dynamic WebClass Event Procedures

Now that you've got the basics to combining ADO with WebClasses, you can move on to a more advanced technique for building useful applications: creating dynamic events associated with a WebClass. These events enable you to respond with different results, based on the event that is triggered. To see how this works, you will modify the example from the previous section to enable users to click a customer name to see more information about that customer. In addition, you'll learn a few tricks to help simplify your code when dealing with WebClasses.

First, you need to build a new HTML template. This template will be used to show a customer's information. An example HTML template is shown here:

```
<HTML>
<HEAD>
<TITLE>Northwind Traders - View Customer</TITLE>
</HEAD>
<BODY>
<H1><WC@#FLD#COMPANYNAME></WC@#FLD#COMPANYNAME></H1>
<HR>
<TABLE border=1 cellPadding=3>
<TBODY>
<TR>
<TD>
<H3>Customer ID:</H3>
</TD>
<TD>
<H3><WC@#FLD#CUSTOMERID></WC@#FLD#CUSTOMERID></H3>
</TD></TR>

<TR>
<TD>
<H3>Contact Name:</H3></TD>
```

```
<TD>
<H3><WC@#FLD#CONTACTNAME></WC@#FLD#CONTACTNAME></H3>
</TD></TR>

<TR>
<TD>
<H3>Contact Title:</H3></TD>
<TD>
<H3><WC@#FLD#CONTACTTITLE></WC@#FLD#CONTACTTITLE></H3>
</TD></TR>

<TR>
<TD>
<H3>Address:</H3>
</TD>
<TD>
<H3><WC@#FLD#ADDRESS></WC@#FLD#ADDRESS></H3>
</TD></TR>

<TR>
<TD>
<H3>City:</H3></TD>
<TD>
<H3><WC@#FLD#CITY></WC@#FLD#CITY></H3>
</TD></TR>

<TR>
<TD>
<H3>Region:</H3>
</TD>
<TD>
<H3><WC@#FLD#REGION></WC@#FLD#REGION></H3>
</TD></TR>

<TR>
<TD>
<H3>Postal Code:</H3>
</TD>
<TD>
<H3><WC@#FLD#POSTALCODE></WC@#FLD#POSTALCODE></H3>
</TD></TR>

<TR>
<TD>
<H3>Country:</H3>
</TD>
```

```
<TD>
<H3><WC@#FLD#COUNTRY></WC@#FLD#COUNTRY></H3>
</TD></TR>

<TR>
<TD>
<H3>Phone:</H3>
</TD>
<TD>
<H3><WC@#FLD#PHONE></WC@#FLD#PHONE></H3>
</TD></TR>

<TR>
<TD>
<H3>Fax:</H3>
</TD>
<TD>
<H3><WC@#FLD#FAX></WC@#FLD#FAX></H3>
</TD></TR>
</TBODY>
</TABLE>
</BODY>
</HTML>
```

Create an HTML template using this template and name it tmpViewCustomer. In this particular template, all of the tags to be filled with data from the database are prefixed with the code #FLD#. You'll see why shortly.

Next, add the following declarations, which enable event procedures to communicate with each other and to save some database activity that would be required otherwise, to the general declarations section of the WebClass:

```
Dim dcnDB As ADODB.Connection
Dim rsData As ADODB.Recordset
```

The next changes are to the CustList function, shown here:

```
Private Function CustList() As String
    Dim strResult As String

    Set dcnDB = New ADODB.Connection
    dcnDB.CursorLocation = adUseClient
    dcnDB.Open "PROVIDER=Microsoft.Jet.OLEDB.4.0;" _
        & "Data Source=C:\Visual Studio\VB98\NWind.MDB;"

    Set rsData = New ADODB.Recordset
    rsData.Open "SELECT * FROM Customers " _
```

```
            & "ORDER BY CompanyName", _
            dcnDB, adOpenForwardOnly, adLockReadOnly

        If rsData.RecordCount = 0 Then
            strResult = _
                "<H1>No records are in the database.</H1>"
        Else
            strResult = "<TABLE CELLPADDING=3 BORDER=1>" & vbCr _
                & "<TR><TH>Customer Name</TH>" & vbCr _
                & "<TH>City</TH>" & vbCr _
                & "<TH>Country</TH>" & vbCr _
                & "</TR>" & vbCr

            Do While Not rsData.EOF
                strResult = strResult & "<TR>" & vbCr _
                    & "<TD><A HREF=""" _
                    & URLFor(tmpViewCustomer, _
                        CStr(rsData("CustomerID"))) _
                    & """>" & rsData("CompanyName") _
                    & "</A></TD>" & vbCr _
                    & "<TD>" & rsData("City") _
                    & "</TD>" & vbCr _
                    & "<TD>" & rsData("Country") _
                    & "</TD>" & vbCr _
                    & "</TR>" & vbCr
                rsData.MoveNext
            Loop
            strResult = strResult & "</TABLE>" & vbCr
            strResult = strResult & "<HR><H3><I>" _
                & rsData.RecordCount _
                & " customers listed.</I></H3>" & vbCr

        End If
        CustList = strResult

        '
        ' Clean up objects
        '
        rsData.Close
        Set rsData = Nothing
        dcnDB.Close
        Set dcnDB = Nothing
    End Function
```

The first change to the CustList function is the removal of the declarations
for dcnDB and rsData because they are now defined at the WebClass level. The

other change is that instead of just printing the company name, the name is wrapped with a URL by the URLFor function. Omitting all of the host and directory information, this URL looks like this when it is complete:

```
ADOWebClass_NWind.ASP?WC=tmpViewCustomer&WCE=ERNSH
```

The customer ID has been appended to the URL by way of the URLFor method and is called a *user-defined event*. Obviously, we're not going to create a separate event for each possible customer ID. Instead, we will have the tmpViewCustomer WebItem respond to the UserEvent event procedure and show the customer's information when it is requested. This task is significantly easier than the same task using ordinary ASP without VB. In the ASP environment, you would have to break up the URL yourself (using the Request object) and then fill the page yourself. In addition, you don't get the benefit of being able to change the template for the page without changing the code because the HTML and VBScript code are linked in ASP programming.

The next piece of code you need is shown in the next listing. When a user clicks on a customer name, this code is triggered because we are providing an unknown event name (the customer ID). The customer ID is placed in the EventName parameter to the tmpViewCustomer_UserEvent subroutine. It is then used in the SQL query to retrieve the correct piece of data.

```
Private Sub tmpViewCustomer_UserEvent(ByVal EventName As String)
    Set dcnDB = New ADODB.Connection
    dcnDB.CursorLocation = adUseClient
    dcnDB.Open "PROVIDER=Microsoft.Jet.OLEDB.4.0;" _
        & "Data Source=C:\Visual Studio\VB98\NWind.MDB;"
    Set rsData = New ADODB.Recordset
    rsData.Open "SELECT * FROM Customers " _
        & "WHERE CustomerID = '" & EventName & "'", _
        dcnDB, adOpenForwardOnly, adLockReadOnly

    tmpViewCustomer.WriteTemplate
End Sub
```

The purpose of this code is to find the customer record and place it in the module-level recordset. This action is done here because we don't want the ProcessTags event procedure to create a new recordset for every tag that it processes.

The next code is the ProcessTags event handler for the tmpViewCustomer template and it is shown here:

```
Private Sub tmpViewCustomer_ProcessTag _
    (ByVal TagName As String, _
```

```
        TagContents As String, _
        SendTags As Boolean)

        '

        ' At this point, we only care about tags
        ' that have the word "Field" in them.
        ' You may wish to expand this over time
        ' to handle other tags.
        '

        Dim iLoc As Integer
        iLoc = InStr(TagName, "#FLD#")
        If iLoc > 0 Then
            TagContents = rsData(Mid(TagName, iLoc + 5)) & ""
        End If
        SendTags = False
End Sub
```

This event procedure looks for all tags beginning with the word #FLD#, and substitutes the data from the field in the database whose name appears to the right of #FLD# in the HTML template. This enables you to change the database and the template without having to change the code in the WebClass. Simply reference the field in the template and this handler will find the corresponding database field.

The last change is to the WebClass_Terminate event procedure. This cleans up the open recordsets and connections that may have been left open by the UserEvent procedure. This code is shown below:

```
Private Sub WebClass_Terminate()
    On Error Resume Next

    rsData.Close
    Set rsData = Nothing
    dcnDB.Close
    Set dcnDB = Nothing

End Sub
```

Because the WebClass has ceased execution anyway, the Resume Next error handler will skip any errors in which the recordset or connection is not open.

With these changes in place, you can run your WebClass. The customer list will now have a link for each customer that shows the customer's information when you click on it.

The Upside and Downside of WebClasses

WebClasses are one of the most exciting parts of this release of Visual Basic. For anyone who dreads having to write and debug Web applications that use ASP pages and VBScript code, WebClasses will save you many headaches and a lot of time. In addition, the performance and reliability increases make it worth your while to learn this new technology.

Not only can you build simple pages, you can also build dynamic pages using the user-defined events you learned about. VB also provides the entire ASP object model to further expand your developer's palette. WebClasses are a great combination of the Visual Basic environment with the new Web programming model.

However, WebClasses present a number of problems. First, WebClasses are built in Visual Basic, and most Web designers don't know VB. This can limit the number of resources available to you on a project because only the VB programmers will be able to build the WebClasses for your site.

A second problem is in the final stages of development. Whenever you load and use a DLL with IIS, it's impossible to remove the DLL from memory unless you stop and restart the Internet Service Manager service in the Control Panel. This means that before you rebuild the DLL while you're testing, you have to bounce your Web server. If you have multiple Web sites running on the development machine, all of those sites will be down temporarily while you stop the IIS. This can be a major hindrance, especially if IIS takes a long time to shutdown.

A third problem is that debugging and revisions take much longer with WebClasses than they do with plain ASP or HTML pages. You can't just fire up Notepad, fix the page, and save it to the server. You have to recompile the DLL, bounce the Web server, and check whether it works. For these and other similar reasons, WebClass applications are not typically used for simple drill-down data viewers. ASP works quite nicely for these and is efficient about how it deals with the database.

Fortunately, the fact that you can test and debug your WebClasses using the Visual Basic environment tends to minimize the problems you'll have when actually deploying your WebClasses to your server—most problems can be diagnosed on the development system itself.

Be aware of the limitations to using WebClasses before you replace your entire HTML with WebClasses. As long as you can deal with these limitations, WebClasses can increase the options that are available to you to build Web sites.

Index

apress™

License Agreement (Single-User Products)

THIS IS A LEGAL AGREEMENT BETWEEN YOU, THE END USER, AND APRESS. BY OPENING THE SEALED DISK PACKAGE, YOU ARE AGREEING TO BE BOUND BY THE TERMS OF THIS AGREEMENT. IF YOU DO NOT AGREE TO THE TERMS OF THIS AGREEMENT, PROMPTLY RETURN THE UNOPENED DISK PACKAGE AND THE ACCOMPANYING ITEMS (INCLUDING WRITTEN MATERIALS AND BINDERS AND OTHER CONTAINERS) TO THE PLACE YOU OBTAINED THEM FOR A FULL REFUND.

APRESS SOFTWARE LICENSE

1. GRANT OF LICENSE. Apress grants you the right to use one copy of this enclosed Apress software program (the "SOFTWARE") on a single terminal connected to a single computer (e.g., with a single CPU). You may not network the SOFTWARE or otherwise use it on more than one computer or computer terminal at the same time.

2. COPYRIGHT. The SOFTWARE copyright is owned by Apress and BetaV Corporation and is protected by United States copyright laws and international treaty provisions. Therefore, you must treat the SOFTWARE like any other copyrighted material (e.g., a book or musical recording) except that you may either (a) make one copy of the SOFTWARE solely for backup or archival purposes, or (b) transfer the SOFTWARE to a single hard disk, provided you keep the original solely for backup or archival purposes. You may not copy the written material accompanying the SOFTWARE.

3. OTHER RESTRICTIONS. You may not rent or lease the SOFTWARE, but you may transfer the SOFTWARE and accompanying written materials on a permanent basis provided you retain no copies and the recipient agrees to the terms of this Agreement. You may not reverse engineer, decompile, or disassemble the SOFTWARE. If SOFTWARE is an update, any transfer must include the update and all prior versions.

DISCLAIMER OF WARRANTY
NO WARRANTIES. Apress disclaims all warranties, either express or implied, including, but not limited to, implied warranties of merchantability and fitness for a particular purpose, with respect to the SOFTWARE and the accompanying written materials. The software and any related documentation is provided "as is." You may have other rights, which vary from state to state.

NO LIABILITIES FOR CONSEQUENTIAL DAMAGES. In no event shall Apress or BetaV Corporation be liable for any damages whatsoever (including, without limitation, damages from loss of business profits, business interruption, loss of business information, or other pecuniary loss) arising out of the use or inability to use this Apress product, even if Apress has been advised of the possibility of such damages. Because some states do not allow the exclusion or limitation of liability for consequential or incidental damages, the above limitation may not apply to you.

U.S. GOVERNMENT RESTRICTED RIGHTS
The SOFTWARE and documentation are provided with RESTRICTED RIGHTS. Use, duplication, or disclosure by the Government is subject to restriction as set forth in subparagraph (c) (1) (ii) of The Rights in Technical Data and Computer Software clause at 52.227-7013. Contractor/manufacturer is Apress, 901 Grayson Street, Suite 204, Berkeley, California, 94710.
This Agreement is governed by the laws of the State of California.
Should you have any questions concerning this Agreement, or if you wish to contact Apress for any reason, please write to Apress, Apress, 901 Grayson Street, Suite 204, Berkeley, California, 94710.